ABOUT
THE AUTHOR

Todd Wassel is the Country Representative for The Asia Foundation in Lao PDR, a traveler, and author. An international aid and development professional, Todd has spent the last 20 years traveling the world, writing about far-off places, getting lost, and trying to make the world a better place in his search for a meaningful life.

Fluent in Japanese, Todd has a B.A. in Asian Studies and Comparative Religion from Colgate University and an M.A. in Law and Diplomacy from The Fletcher School at Tufts University. Todd won the People's Choice Award in the Southeast Asia Travel Writing Competition and has been featured in Lonely Planet, The Diplomat, as well as on ABC Australia.

Todd has worked in and traveled to more than 45 countries. He taught English in Japan for half a decade, was a conflict advisor in Timor-Leste, a human rights advocate in Sri Lanka, and a hiking consultant in Kosovo, a job he still doesn't know why he left.

He has seen the sun rise over Machu Picchu and from the top of Mount Fuji, dived the reefs of the Maldives, Indonesia, and Thailand, honeymooned in Bosnia and Herzegovina, danced for days at weddings in India, and walked the 750-mile, 88 temple Shikoku Henro pilgrimage in Japan, twice.

Todd, his wife, Kaoru, and their two young children live in Lao PDR along the banks of the Mekong. They divide their time between Lao PDR, Japan, the United States, and the rest of the world.

WALKING IN CIRCLES

FINDING HAPPINESS IN LOST JAPAN

TODD WASSEL

JIZO
PRESS

First edition paperback: July 2020

Edited by Jennifer Skutelsky

Proofread by Anna Mehta

Book design and map by Michael Wachs

Stamp image created based on the "Henro Michi" signs hung by the *Henro Michi Hozon Kyōryoku Kai* (Cooperative Society to Preserve the *Henro* Trail)

ISBN: 978-1-7353116-0-9 (paperback)

ISBN: 978-1-7353116-1-6 (eBook edition)

For orders and permissions contact: sales@toddwassel.com

For more adventures visit: www.toddwassel.com

For Kaoru, Kaito, and Sana.

CONTENTS

KAGAWA PREFECTURE
NIRVANA

EHIME PREFECTURE
ENLIGHTENMENT

TOKUSHIMA PREFECTURE
AWAKENING

KŌCHI PREFECTURE
ASCETIC TRAINING

SHIKOKU
AND THE EIGHTY-EIGHT TEMPLES

RETURN TO SHIKOKU

You would think walking 750 miles once would be enough. But here I was, my backpack pressing me onward once again. This time would be different. This time I'd finally break free from Japan and figure out what I wanted to do with my life. Fate, of course, doesn't entertain stupid questions and has a sick sense of humor.

The train slowed as it approached Bando station, on the outskirts of the small port city of Tokushima on the eastern coast of the island of Shikoku, during what passed as the morning rush hour in the sleepy suburb. The rickety one-car train was the same one I had taken in 1998 the first time I walked the pilgrimage around the rural island.

I stood waiting for the train doors to open. I slung my backpack over my right shoulder and clutched my walking stick and conical straw hat together in my left hand. Japanese boys surrounded me in the small car, dressed in sharp black military-style high school uniforms with brass buttons that ran in a straight line from the waist to the neck—a fashion throwback to the French army uniform from the early 1900s. They ignored me, just like the groups of high school girls, dressed in short plaid skirts and sailor uniform tops, with long white, baggy socks that swallowed their calves and bunched close to the knees. I was the only person getting off as I pushed through a small wave of new students getting on.

I walked out of the little station where human beings had long ago been replaced with electric ticketing and collection machines. The sun was an afterthought when faced with the humidity of the Japanese summer. You were always hot, always uncomfortable, and always sweating—not ideal walking conditions for a month straight. Ryōzen-ji, Temple One on the Shikoku *Hachijūhakkasho* (Pilgrimage to the 88 Temples of Shikoku), waited just a mile away, through a maze of backstreets and a mix of houses ranging from traditional wooden frames to molded prefabricated clones. It wasn't yet clear which was winning the battle.

Shikoku, which means "four countries," is the smallest of Japan's four main islands. The rest of Japan rarely gives it a second thought, except on weather reports as typhoons batter its coasts. Hiding some of Japan's most inaccessible areas, a rugged mountain range cuts the island in half, while its coast faces the might of the Pacific in the south and the tranquil Inland Sea to the north.

Despite its remoteness, or possibly because of it, Shikoku has inspired countless journeys for over 1,200 years. The pilgrim's path traverses the island's jagged peaks, coastal fishing villages, small cities, and farming hamlets.

Each year about 150,000 mostly Japanese *henro* (pilgrims) circle Shikoku, passing through its four prefectures. For over a thousand years, *henro* have followed a circuit of 88 Buddhist temples laid out in a ring around the perimeter of the island. They walk in the footsteps of Kūkai, founder of the Japanese esoteric Shingon Buddhist sect, which is a close relative of Tibetan Buddhism. Possibly the most important figure in Japanese religious history, he was born on Shikoku in 774 CE.

Kūkai wandered the island in his formative years, seeking enlightenment alone in the sacred mountains through secret rituals and meditating in caves for months at a time. He also left a steady stream of miracles in his wake, such as destroying resident water serpents, tapping wells with only his walking stick, and sealing a fiery dragon in a cave. According to pilgrim lore he still accompanies all *henro* on their journeys, appearing and offering help when needed.

Today, most *henro* fill bus tours, drive in cars, ride bicycles, the train, or use a combination. About 1,000 pilgrims each year still take the time to walk the 750-mile circuit connecting the 88 temples, on a journey that can take up to two months. The path is a loose set of old trails, modern roads, and a dizzying array of options based on which mountain you want to climb, go around, or tunnel through.

Pilgrims hike ancient footpaths that plunge deep into isolated mountains, along the rocky coastline, and through villages dominated by evergreens and rice paddies. Dressed in road-worn white that represents death and marks them as separated from society, pilgrims peer out from under conical straw hats that protect from sun and rain. Their staffs, representing Kūkai's constant presence, help to steady their weary bodies and spirits. Like a human prayer wheel, they circle Shikoku through all seasons and at all times of the day. They also choke on bus exhaust, dodge trucks in narrow tunnels, and are exposed to people, in both good and bad ways, as they weave their way through society in search of enlightenment. I was about to join their ranks.

I approached Temple One's giant wooden gate. Two fierce wooden *nio* statues, carved muscles bulging, stood guard on either side to ward off demons and thieves. I bowed before entering, just as millions of *henro* had done before me, and I found my way to the life-sized golden statue of the Buddha in the main temple hall. I was alone except for an old temple attendant going about his early morning duties. My throat burned from coarse tendrils of smoke that escaped the three thin green incense sticks I offered before approaching the main temple hall. Japanese Buddhist incense is a peculiar mix of sweet and acrid, not something you'd choose to burn in your own home.

I entered my name in the temple's registry for walking pilgrims. As proof I had visited, I received my first calligraphy and a vermillion stamp on my *kakejiku* (hanging scroll), and a paper slip depicting the temple's main Buddha. At 500 yen (about $5) apiece, receiving all 88 made for an expensive souvenir. With little indication of how important it would be, the attendant silently slipped me a photocopied paper with a handwritten list of possible places to stay for free while I walked. It was all in Japanese, of course, but was sure to be a life saver at some point, if I could read it.

No one spoke to me nor paid me any attention as I left. I guess big adventures often start silently, with little fanfare. I looked down the slightly used country road I would follow for most of the day and wondered if I would find the answers I sought.

I FIRST CAME to Shikoku at the age of 21. It was my first time traveling abroad, my first time on a plane, even. I spoke horrific Japanese, barely read a lick, and had no idea what I was getting myself into. It was the most difficult and the most rewarding time of my life. I thought I was looking for a good story, something that would turn a shy small-town kid from Rhode Island into someone more interesting, more capable.

I was searching for an adventure, a challenge to overcome and prove that I was an adult. What I found was a kid unwilling to give up, who latched onto an idea and wouldn't let it go, and in doing so found a profound sense of freedom. I could do anything I wanted as long as I tried and kept going. Not a day had passed since my first pilgrimage that my mind didn't wander back to Shikoku and the freedom I found living outside what everyone else considered a conventional life.

After college I moved to Japan within a month of graduation, planning to stay just a year or two. I was worried that if I didn't travel right away, I'd get stuck. All around me I saw a pattern of: get a job, get married, buy a house, work until retirement, and hope you have enough money and life left to travel then.

I wanted to love my job. I wanted to have adventures. But there was no one around me that seemed to think the same way. In Japan, undisturbed by the conformity at home, I was determined to figure out what I wanted to do with the rest of my life and have an adventure at the same time.

One year became two. Two became three. I continued teaching English because it was a job and kept me out in the world. Three jumped alarmingly to six, and I still had no idea what I wanted to do. Every time I visited home it felt like the gap was getting wider and more insurmountable. If I didn't get a job back in the US soon, I'd be left behind. All of my friends were moving up the career ladder, getting raises, getting married, and buying houses.

It didn't matter that I didn't want to be like them—it stung anyway. I was supposed to be the one that was living my passion, traveling the world. But I was failing at that. I wasn't satisfied with my teaching jobs, and life in Japan had begun to weigh on me. It was no longer fun, and I couldn't picture myself as an English teacher for the rest of my life. I needed more, but I had no idea what that was.

As my internal struggle grew, I decided it was time to find a career that I loved. I quit my job, broke up with my girlfriend, moved back to the United States, and enrolled in graduate school, determined never to return to Japan.

I still didn't know what I wanted to do career-wise, and a

year back in the US seemed to show me how isolated I had become while teaching in Japan for six years. Everyone around me seemed smarter, funnier, more accomplished. I had a chip on my shoulder, as if I needed to prove to everyone that I was worthy of being there. But inside I was struggling against the pressures to enter into the workforce and take a job just to get by.

The impending weight of new student loan debt, added to my previous school debts, made it feel like the choice would be made for me. Everything I had tried to escape initially was pulling me back.

The summer before my last year of graduate school, I saw a chance to have one last adventure before real life set in. I was already in Bangkok, Thailand, for a summer internship, so I skipped out on the last month and scraped together $1,500 to walk the Shikoku pilgrimage again. It was the only place I had found a sense of purpose in life, and it was my last-ditch effort to figure myself out.

A year after fleeing Japan for a new life in graduate school, I returned, trying to understand what it meant to me, why it kept drawing me back.

Like my first trip, I walked in the summer as that was when I had the time. It is the worst time of year due to humidity and the rainy season, and I only had enough money to camp outside each night. But I was determined to finally figure out what I wanted to be when I grew up. And once I knew, everything would be okay.

It never occurred to me that I was asking the wrong question.

2

THE
HENRO MICHI

The first part of the *henro michi* (pilgrim's path) hugs the northern edge of the Yoshino River valley in a somewhat straight line from Temple One through to Temple Ten, my goal for the day. Most walking pilgrims end their first day around Temples Five or Six. Mine was an ambitious and pretty stupid goal. Armed with my memories and a map book printed only in Japanese, I turned right out of Temple One, ready to start a new life.

Temples Two and Three came and went in quick succession as I pushed to reach Temple Ten before 5:00 p.m., when the stamp office would close. In order to get my calligraphy and temple slips for each of the temples, my timing had to be strategic. Arrive too early and I'd have to wait for the temple to open at 7:00 a.m.; arrive too late and I'd have to spend the night, waiting for the temple to open again in the morning. Enlightenment, it seems, has strict operating hours.

As I walked through the backstreets, I looked out for small stickers with an illustration of a stylized red pilgrim to reassure me that I was on the right track. Found on telephone poles, guardrails, traffic signs, and just about anywhere else one might not expect, they are placed by a variety of groups attempting to preserve the pilgrimage. The signs keep pilgrims on the path that winds its way around Shikoku along mostly asphalt streets.

"Beeeeep! BEEEEEP!!"

The horn pulled me out of my head. I turned to find an old man in a wide-brimmed hat, his arm and head leaning out of the window of a tiny white farming truck that was reminiscent of a toy.

I looked around the narrow road between rice fields, not sure if he was waving frantically at me or not. I took a tentative step the way I was headed, away from the truck. I wanted to keep moving.

"BEEEEEEEEEEEEEEEEP!"

The rice truck slammed into reverse and accelerated towards me. The truck screeched to a halt next to me, and a large glass bottle, with "*Sake* One Cup" printed in large letters along its side, came out of the truck's window first. It was followed by a red-faced, intoxicated man in a dirty gray jumpsuit.

"You're walking the wrong way," he rasped between swigs of *sake*. *Sake* drinking culture is intimately intertwined with Japan's history; the cup *sake* version is a more recent invention. Launched in 1964 with the first Tokyo Olympics, single-sized servings of the national beverage helped stave off declining sales and also the rise of beer and whiskey. It comes conveniently out of a vending machine hot or cold and is the iconic tipple of boozing older men.

"The *henro* path goes that way." He pointed to a narrow dirt path that broke away from the road between two small rice paddies.

There I saw an old, waist-high stone marker with a carved hand pointing down the path. The letters had been worn away by the unforgiving elements over hundreds of years. In front of the stone marker was a more recent white wooden sign. It confirmed the path and the next temple, Dainichi-ji, Temple Four, spelled out in red *kanji* characters.

I was barely into the walk and I was already lost. "*Arigatō, Ojiisan. Tasukarimashita,*" (Thank you, Grandfather. You saved me,) I said, bowing to him.

The old farmer smiled a toothless grin and offered me a swig of his *sake*. It was 10:00 a.m. I declined and he took a quick pull, slamming on the gas before his head was even back in the truck.

Glad to be off the paved road, I stepped onto the dirt path that led to Temple Four. Tiny green rice shoots poked their heads out of the water-filled paddies that straddled the path. Beyond the paddy on the right, straight rows of graves climbed up a steep slope in neat lines, followed by rows of cedar trees that are the torment of millions of Japanese hay fever sufferers. The smell of water, mud, and decomposing leaves from the forest hung in the heavy air.

I rounded a bend to find two 15-foot giant straw sandals flanking an old, faded temple gate. They were a harsh reminder that my own feet were starting to hurt way too early in my journey. The tiny temple is not officially part of the 88-temple route, but I stopped in anyway. Painted red, the Buddha hall was flanked by immaculately pruned trees, and I used the small bell and coin box to offer up prayers for my feet. There are plenty of temples, both attended and unattended, along the *henro* path. No one really knows why certain temples made it onto the official 88 list, but it is most likely a combination of historical records and local politicking.

Temple Four, Temple of the Great Sun, is unassuming and quaint, despite its grandiose name. Set back in a wooded valley, the temple greets you warmly and unpretentiously. It had none of the fanfare of larger temples, like gift shops or crowded parking lots. The temple staff were friendly and quick to offer advice and words of encouragement.

All 88 temples have the same basic features. Far removed from the grand temples of Nara, Kyoto, or Kamakura, the temples of Shikoku are beautiful in their simplicity and lived-in feeling. Unlike their more popular cousins on the mainland, they weren't created to serve the needs of the aristocracy. Most of the Shikoku temples cater to ordinary people and their troubles: fishermen in need of bountiful catches; their wives, anxious for their husbands to return home; farmers concerned about rain and harvests; students eager for a good test score; beggars desperate for survival; and families anxious for new births.

Each temple has an entrance gate where you bow as you enter and an intricately designed water fountain, usually in the shape of a dragon, for purifying your hands and mouth. A bell tower, or *shōrō*, houses the temple's large bronze bells that *henro* use to announce their arrival by swinging a large wooden beam suspended by ropes.

Inside there is a *hondō* (main hall housing the principal Buddha of the temple) and a *daishidō* (hall dedicated to Kūkai). There is always an office to get the temple's stamp and calligraphy, and buy whatever other talismans they're peddling. No temple design is the same, and their varied characters reflect the landscape in which they sit. Many contain pagodas, some flowing rivers, others mystical caves. Some have attached inns that cater to pilgrims. Each has a unique legend, usually related to a miracle performed by Kūkai.

I tried to follow most of the standard rituals *henro* perform at each temple. I was neither Buddhist nor Japanese, but I felt the need to do the pilgrimage the way it was intended. At both the *hondō* and the *daishidō*, I burned three incense sticks. I dropped a name slip, called *osamefuda*, in a metal box. In olden times, pilgrims would glue their name slips to temples as proof they had visited. The modern version didn't destroy the temple with unwanted graffiti and also contained ready-made prayers for health and happiness.

Next, I recited, in Japanese, the Heart Sutra, a condensed teaching of a branch of Buddhism called Mahayana, in which emptiness is the characteristic of everything. I skipped burning a candle due to the added weight and expense, which cut out at least 100 yen ($1) per temple and a couple of ounces per step. I was a broke student, after all, and had to be practical. I finished each visit by having my hanging scroll signed and collecting the temple's paper Buddha slip.

With one final prayer to stave off the inevitable blisters that accompany long walks, I headed back down the road I had arrived on. On my way out I met my first walking pilgrims, and we stopped for a short chat. A middle-aged couple from Aichi Prefecture in central Japan, they hoped to reach Temple Twelve by the end of the week, when they had to return to their jobs. They planned to cover in seven days what I hoped to cover in two.

"*Gambatte. Ki o tsukete kudasai,*" (Good luck. Please be careful,) we recited to each other as we passed in different directions. I never saw them again.

BY TEMPLE SIX I felt pressed for time. At 2:00 p.m. I had over seven miles to go before I reached Temple Ten. I had forgotten how long it takes to visit each temple and perform all the rituals. A soft-spoken man with a round face and a middle-aged woman with wavy brown hair worked at the stamp counter located inside the *hondō*. My anxiety levels rose as the man decided I needed help drying my hanging scroll.

Many pilgrims use books, called *nōkyōchō* in Japanese, to record their visit to each temple. I used one during my previous pilgrimage and decided on a hanging scroll this time. The only real difference was that temples charged 200 yen more to sign a scroll rather than a book. Some economist must have worked out that it's exactly $2 more difficult to write smaller characters. Both, however, are supposedly powerful talismans. Once completed they ensure not only long life, but happiness.

Who wouldn't want a bit of happiness guaranteed, especially if you are going to live a long life? An additional benefit is an automatic ticket to the Pure Land, a state of enlightenment free from rebirth. I somewhat doubted the automatic pass into enlightenment, but it couldn't hurt, and the scroll would at least be a source of constant inspiration for impressing dinner guests.

The man directed me to use two rectangular wooden blocks on a nearby table to keep the scroll from closing. A plugged-in hairdryer sat nearby, and as I picked it up, he offered to show me how to use it to dry the wet calligraphy ink in a fraction of the time. "Don't look into the dryer while it's on," he cautioned.

The rest of the day passed in a blur of emerging foot pain and dehydration-induced dizziness as I refused to stop for water or lunch. I had forgotten how hard the pilgrimage was and cursed myself for not getting into proper shape. Late nights in the library—okay, the bar—had added a few extra pounds to my waistline since I'd walked seven years ago.

As I stumbled down the road from Temple Eight at around 3:30 p.m., the road ended at a stone *torii* gate, before turning to the right. Two pillars supported two crossbars, standing alone before a sea of sprouting rice paddies. *Torii* gates mark the entrance to sacred spaces in Shintoism, Japan's native religion centered on *kami* (gods or spirits), supernatural entities believed to inhabit all things in nature.

With no actual Shinto shrine anywhere in sight, there was no way to tell which side was the sacred and which was the profane. I assumed the side opposite from me was the sacred, as my side had a beer vending machine and a sweaty foreigner desperate to drink the range of liquid salvation options, from 350 milliliters up to three liters.

The gate was a great reflection of Japan. Both the sacred and the profane exist together, defined at least in part by what the other is not. In Japan there is a very thin line between the two (if a line exists at all).

The Shikoku pilgrimage is a good example of this. It is much more than just a collection of roads and paths. It is a gateway to a life cut off from everyday society but grounded in a physical landscape. Pilgrims occupy a unique space. We travel over and through a world stained by all the excesses and pettiness of human existence, but also through a world filled with spiritual value and meaning. This little gate sitting between the tides of salvation and depravity was a reminder that you can't have one without the other.

Sometimes it seemed that the Japanese don't even try to make a distinction. Perhaps one can find enlightenment at the bottom of a beer bottle as well as at the top of a sacred mountain. Certainly, there were plenty of Japanese monks throughout history who thought sex and booze were integral parts of expressing their enlightenment. It would be crazy not to hedge my bets and experience both extremes.

Beyond the *torii* gate, I could see the southern edge of the Yoshino River valley. The overbearing mountain range was my destination for the next day. The land beyond offered the promise of real hiking, off the asphalt roads, away from the crowded neighborhoods and

exhaust-spewing trucks that filled Tokushima.

I blew through Temple Nine and reached the base of Temple Ten, Kirihata-ji (Cut Cloth Temple) at 4:30 p.m. In front of me, the steep road stretched straight up through a tunnel of inns and shops selling all the essential pilgrim gear. All but one or two were closed for the summer season. The road ended at an entrance to a shadowy forest and a set of stone steps that threatened to keep me from reaching the stamp office before closing time. Worried I'd arrive late, I launched my protesting body up the hill, dragging each of my whining legs up the 333 steps. I reached the top with a few minutes to spare and raced to have my scroll signed before allowing myself to relax.

I was not ready for this. My breath was gone, my heart beating so fast that I thought I was about to have a heart attack. My feet, swollen and red from the day's walking, pulsated with pain as I eased my shoes off. The first week is always the worst as the body adjusts to walking all day.

I sucked down three bottles of water from one of the five sacred vending machines next to the stamp office. I caught my breath and willed my heart to slow down.

My body demanded I take my time. Rather than stand on the wooden steps leading up to the *hondō* and the *daishidō*, I sat and recited the sutras. It was all rather painful and awkward, and I was thankful that I was the only person there.

Finished with my duties, I sat alone at the mountain temple as dusk settled in. I opened my map book for the first time to see where I was going to sleep, something I should have done before the day even started. No, it was something I should have done days before.

During my first pilgrimage, I'd started out with a tent but soon dropped it due to its weight. Luckily, I'd met another pilgrim who taught me how to read my Japanese map book and what to look for in a place to sleep. The map shows where pilgrims can camp out, including where there is water, toilets, and/or a roof available. Now, as I studied my map, these were the three necessities I looked for. Despite being more prepared mentally than I was the first time, money was still a major concern, and I was not even sure I had enough to complete the route. I definitely didn't have enough to sleep in hotels and inns over the next month. I had a list of free places to sleep, but they were not always available in the areas I'd find myself, like now.

I carried the bare minimum, made possible because it was summer: a T-shirt and pants to walk in, and a T-shirt and a bathing suit to sleep in. I also had five pairs of socks, four pairs of underwear, a rain suit, and a sleeping pad. My cotton sleeping bag was no more than a sheet stitched together, and I carried a small mosquito net to protect me at night. First aid supplies (98 percent dedicated to foot care), flip-flops, a knife, a headlamp, a camera, and an alarm clock rounded out my pack. No telephone, no computer—just me, my mind, and a mission to figure out my life.

I searched the map book for any nearby place where I could sleep. Most temples didn't let pilgrims camp out on their grounds, while some offered paid-for accommodation. When no free options were available, I tried to find a gazebo or rest area in a park. These usually had roofs, water, and toilets. After that I'd settle for bus stops, park benches, or anywhere else that had a bit of privacy in a public area. There were roof awnings along the street leading to the temple, but no water to wash my sweaty body and clothes. Nor was there any food nearby. The map did show a strange mark that I couldn't read, a long one mile away, down the road leading to the next temple. I had no idea what it was, but I decided to take a chance and check it out. I didn't really have a choice.

I limped to a stop at the intersection marked on the map, only to find a power station, locked and gated to keep wandering Americans out. On the bright side, I learned the *kanji* symbol for "Electrical Substation." Awesome.

Places to camp out or sleep outside are tough to come by in a town. Pilgrims need to be careful to avoid burdening communities. After all, who would want strange wanderers camping out night after night in their area? Towns also pose a mental challenge, as seeing the warm lights of homes while being stuck out in the darkness all alone can be demoralizing.

At least it wasn't raining.

As darkness took hold, people rushed down the busy road in their cars, eager to get home to dinners and families. I slumped to the ground and evaluated my options. The map indicated a small Shinto shrine, slightly off the path but on the way to the next temple. It was in the middle of a suburban neighborhood, and there were no markings that showed it was a place to sleep. However, another symbol indicated a grocery store near the shrine, where I could at least get dinner and ask where the caretaker for the shrine lived.

Ten minutes later I found the small grocery store. It had seen better days. Like so many shops in Shikoku, it was the front room of a family house. I searched for dinner under the dust; no fresh sushi or beer-massaged beef here. The main offerings were canned food with expiration dates sorted in years rather than days or even months. I settled on two liters of water, two rolls of nut bread (one for the morning), and an apple. Hardly enough nutrition after a full day of walking.

The young store clerk asked me to sit and offered tea. Wavy hair brushed his shoulders as he drew an overturned milk crate up for me to rest on. I thanked him and hurried to relieve the pressure on my feet.

"Excuse me, but do you know where the *jinja* [shrine] is?" I asked, praying that it was close.

"Yeah, it's just down the street on the left. Where are you from?" he asked through a mouthful of half-chewed dried squid, which many Japanese eat as a snack. He leaned in close, less than a foot from my face. Dried squid definitely smells worse than fresh.

"Is it possible to spend the night there?" I asked. "I'm from America," I added, almost as an afterthought. I leaned away. I once went on a date in Japan with someone who ordered dried squid with our first beer of the night. We didn't have a second drink, or a second date.

I hoped at least to find an overhang to protect against

possible rain. Rarely lived in, a neighborhood shrine usually has someone from the surrounding area who is responsible for its maintenance and, hopefully, to watch over a wandering American.

"I'm not sure. Ask the shopkeeper next to the shrine for permission. What's America like? Do you have apples there?" he asked. He had probably never left his town. He scooted closer, now leaving just a few inches between us.

I pushed myself up into the squid-free fresh air, offering my thanks and assurances that apples do indeed exist in America.

I reached the shrine after just a five-minute walk. To the left sat a two-story traditional Japanese house, perched, like most homes, just inches from the road. Shiny kiln-baked tiles swept the roof of the house into a perfect curve, where tin gutters ended in decorated linked chains that dropped to the ground. Two wooden sliding *shōji* doors ran across the front. An old, rusted sign, that at one point must have lit up the street, hung burnt out above one door, identifying it as a "Home Supplies Shop" in Japanese. I felt nervous about bothering a family, suddenly, in the middle of the evening. It was not something I would normally do, but I needed a place to sleep. I tried the shop first, knocking on the door to the right. I called out when no one answered. I tried the door, but it was locked. The door on the left led to the family home. Desperate, I rang the bell. When no one appeared, I slid it open tentatively, and stepped in.

"*Sumimasen. Sumimasen!*" (Excuse me!) I haltingly called into the dark entranceway, a step down from what is considered the inside of Japanese homes and thus still a public space, at least in the countryside. I could hear conversation in the back, behind another sliding door. No one heard my timid calls. It was awkward, yelling into a complete stranger's house at night, but I called out again, stronger, louder, still nervous. Silence hung across the dark entryway for what seemed like an eternity.

Finally, a plump middle-aged woman in a dull blue apron opened the sliding door at the back, and light flooded into the entranceway. "Yes?" she asked, startled to see a foreign *henro* in her house. I'm sure the smell wafting off me didn't help with first impressions.

"I'm sorry, but I am a *henro* and I was hoping that it would be okay if, perhaps, maybe, I might be able to stay the night at the shrine next door," I said in my best Japanese, which is usually tentative, never straightforward, and slightly apologetic. She stared silently at me, like a deer caught in headlights.

Maybe she didn't expect to understand me the first time. I repeated myself, this time slower, and even more vaguely.

"*Chotto matte kudasai.*" She disappeared back the way she had come, backing out the whole way and never taking her eyes off me until the sliding door was shut.

Success! Or she was calling the police? It could have gone either way.

As instructed, I waited.

A few minutes later the door opened again, and a short, skinny old man shuffled out. Wrinkled skin fell from his neck in even lines; his face was framed by wispy white hair. "Yes?" he said.

I assumed his daughter had told him why I was there, but I repeated my request anyway. He didn't seem surprised at all that I spoke Japanese.

"Sorry, but it's impossible to sleep there," he said.

Desperate, I asked again as he tried to leave. He turned and examined me more closely. I smiled and looked back, fluttering my eyelashes.

"There are no walls, no toilet, no *tatami* or futon to sleep on," he advised. But this time he didn't try to leave.

Sensing an opening, I rushed to fill the silence. "That's okay.

I have a sleeping pad and sleeping bag. I have dinner with me. I'm sleeping outside each night, and all I really need is a roof." I hoped to ease his fears about having to take care of me. In fact, all I wanted was to be left alone.

"Follow me," he said, shuffling into the store next door. "I'm Sumitomo," he called out from ahead.

I grabbed my gear and followed him into the old shop next door. We sat inches from each other, backs straight, on small rusted foldout chairs in the only clear area that I could see. A mass of heaped housing supplies threatened to bury us alive. Dusty brooms, light bulbs, and cleaning products filled every inch of the dark shop. It was a neglected mess, as if a truck just showed up one day, tilted the house on its side, and dumped everything in.

Sumitomo-san took out a pad of paper and looked at me through goo-encrusted eyes. Was that one day's worth, or had he not washed up in a long time? I could only assume, and hope, that his son supported the family with another job, as it looked like nothing had been sold in quite a while.

The interview began in a rush. "What's your name? Where are you from? Are you married? What's your job? Why are you walking the pilgrimage?"

This last one gave me some trouble, as I was still trying to figure that out myself. He wrote all my answers down. One cannot be too careful of out-of-towners, after all, and I was from as out of town as you could get.

The interrogation continued, but now at a faster pace. "What are your parents' names? What are their jobs? How much do they make? How many siblings? What are their names? Where did they go to college? What are their jobs? Where did *you* go to college? How much do *you* make?"

This was getting weird.

Ten minutes later Sumitomo-san had squeezed out my

whole personal history. The only thing I managed to hide from him was my crush on my second grade teacher.

He stood up and left. I assumed I should follow. Exhausted from the questioning, as much as from my long day of walking, and not knowing what was going to happen, I gathered my stuff and looked both ways before stepping out onto the street.

The large shrine next door was constructed from age-darkened wooden beams. A stylized sweeping roof covered the main shrine room with a long porch worn smooth by centuries of bare feet coming to pray. A coarse rope ran from a hanging bell for visitors to shake, announcing their presence to the *kami* (gods). A large wooden boat hung from the ceiling at one end of the porch. At the other end, two demons with long wooden noses and spiny black clumps of hair peered down with pig-like features, their heads nailed to the support beams.

I chose the side with the two demons to set up camp— better to sleep under the uncomfortable gaze of demons than become the first pilgrim ever to die in a boating accident while on dry land.

Sumitomo-san watched me put my gear down, without a word. Satisfied I was not going to need anything, or maybe steal anything, he turned to leave. It was just 6:30 in the evening but I was ready to sleep.

"We have a discussion group every last Wednesday of the month at 7:30 p.m. I'll stop by and get you," Sumitomo-san called out, not bothering to explain what he was getting me into, let alone why he wanted me to go.

I slumped in despair as he disappeared around the corner. Day One had been a much bigger day than I was ready for. I was lucky to have found a place to stay and I wanted to go to bed right away. But in Japan declining was not an option. The neighborhood was hosting me, and this was expected.

I washed my body under a shin-high faucet between the shrine and the road. To spare the community grandmothers any undue scandal, I kept my underwear on. Next, I set up my self-inflating sleeping pad, which only really worked if I blew it up. My mosquito net hung from my walking stick, which I then anchored in my backpack.

With my bed ready, I set about cleaning up my feet, a nightly ritual for the month to come. Blisters had formed on the heels and sides of each foot, sending lightning waves of pain with each step I took. I pulled out a needle and sterilized it with a cheap plastic lighter, then threaded a piece of iodine-soaked string and pierced each blister. I pushed and pulled the needle through each blister and cut the thread, to keep it from filling back up with liquid, speeding the recovery process.

Once I had finished torturing myself, I pulled out dinner and forced an apple and dry nut bread down with two liters of water. I finished everything by 7:00 p.m. and struggled to stay awake as I waited for Sumitomo-san to return. I was soaked with sweat, as Japanese summers offer little respite from the suffocating humidity, even at night. Just another reason most people avoid the pilgrimage in the summer.

Sumitomo-san shuffled up to my porch around 8:00 p.m., exactly 29 minutes after I hoped he'd decided to let me sleep for the night. He set a brisk pace for the community center, as if it were my fault we were late. I limped behind as best I could. I tried to ask where we were going and what we were doing. All I got in return were admonishments that we were late and a barrage of, "Faster, faster."

From the outside, the community center was a nondescript, two-story prefabricated building. On the inside, it was just as dull, with linoleum floors and yellowed wallpaper. I left my sandals at the entrance and squeezed into a pair of hard blue plastic slippers that were way too small and left half my feet hanging off the end. I cursed under my breath as I limped up a steep staircase to a set of sliding paper doors.

Sumitomo-san looked me over and gathered himself for a

moment. He took a deep breath, gave me a pointed look, and opened the door to what must have been his crowning achievement and would be his eventual legacy after he passed on. Twenty startled old men and one lone woman serving tea turned in unison as I stepped through the door.

"Hasegawa-san. I'm sure you don't mind letting our guest here speak this month instead, do you?" Sumitomo-san said with a commanding assuredness that hinted at a long-running political game played out amongst the community elders. The man standing before the group held a thick pile of papers. A mass of charts, graphs, and other oddities was pinned to a board behind him. They had something to do with irrigation and sewers in the area. No one uttered a word.

Moving into the silence, Sumitomo-san pushed me to the front of the room. I protested all the way, happy to return to my porch if he would just let me. I was maneuvered into place as the dejected Hasegawa-san moved back to his seat. I gave him an *I'm sorry, it's not my fault* face and mouthed, "I'm sorry." He just stared back with intense displeasure. It was not the best way to warm up a crowd.

It seemed I was Sumitomo-san's secret weapon in the neighborhood competition of who could put on the most interesting monthly topic. Fate had surely intervened by dropping a foreign pilgrim on his doorstep on the exact day of a monthly discussion group.

As I looked out, an ocean of white hair greeted me, broken by the occasional island of baldness. The reason for my previous interrogation became clear as Sumitomo-san took out his notebook and introduced me to the group. Somehow, in the two hours leading up to the meeting, my name had changed to "Tolu Wisalu," and my home state to New York (not Rhode Island). I had three siblings rather than two. And I attended some unknown university that garnered immense respect from the gathered crowd. Everyone was less impressed with my parents' salaries.

"You can start now," Sumitomo-san commanded, and stepped aside.

No one clarified where to start or what to talk about. I contemplated my options as a room full of strangers stared back at me. The rhythmic droning of cicadas filled the awkward silence. Should I talk about my family? Why I'm in Japan? Why I'm in Shikoku? Maybe I should raise the alarm about my interrogation and abduction. I decided to start from the beginning.

I recounted my whole life story—years 1 to 28—in Japanese, to a room of complete strangers. Their eyes began to close. One at a time white, gray, and bald heads hit chests as a growing chorus of snores accompanied my story. Sumitomo-san waved my concern away and promised me they were just trying to pay close attention. I ended their suffering a very long 10 minutes later.

With the group refreshed from their nap, I opened the room up for questions. No one seemed interested, except for Sumitomo-san. He stood, back straight, head held high, assured that he had pulled off the greatest coup the neighborhood had ever seen, despite painful evidence to the contrary. Slowly, the questions came, spurred on by the obligatory politeness I found so endearing in Japan.

At 8:30 p.m. I relinquished the stage to a moody Hasegawa-san. If he hurried, he might just have time to mention the title of his talk.

I left to a chorus of, "Thank you," "Good luck," and "Watch out for snakes." What?!

I thanked Sumitomo-san for the evening. He gave me two *manjū* cakes made from sweet red beans. I thanked him again, put on my own sandals, and limped back home. He turned back to his adoring crowd, done with me for the night.

I arrived back to the sound of frogs croaking in the rice paddy just one wooden railing from my sleeping pad. I stripped down and washed my whole body again, leaving just enough soap on my skin to ensure an itchy, restless night's sleep.

Conveniently, the light at the end of the porch not only attracted plenty of bugs but also showed them exactly where I was. This was particularly useful when my mosquito net came crashing down in the middle of the night—several times. It was impossible to get comfortable, as my feet hung off the two-thirds-size sleeping pad, leaving my blistered heels to rest on the hard wooden floor, and giving me a glimpse of how miserable sleeping would be for the next month or so. My only solace was the sweet sound of croaking frogs. A few hours later I learned that frogs don't get tired.

Sleep came around midnight. Day Two arrived five hours later.

3

PERILOUS PLACES

Shōsan-ji, Temple of the Burning Mountain, and I have something of a troubled past. Sitting 2,300 smug feet above the Yoshino River valley, Temple Twelve is the first of six *nansho* (perilous places) that pilgrims visit, meant to prevent the corrupt of heart from continuing.

With steep rises, exposed ridges, and no help along the way, the path up to this troublesome temple has caused countless failed pilgrimages. Modern times have made the path a safer place, especially with the advent of the cell phone for emergency calls and the various pilgrimage associations helping to keep it maintained on a regular basis. I had no cell phone.

The walking path leaves the city of Tokushima behind and plunges into the backcountry over three peaks, lined with the graves of fallen *henro*. Japan is home to 46 species of snakes, but it was not the long, green ones I was most wary of. The source of most pilgrims' worry was a one-foot, gray killer, the *mamushi*. A pit viper, it was a constant threat to my sanity as well as to the lives of thousands of farmers all over Shikoku. Usually found in early morning and at dusk, the venom is enough to kill if not treated immediately.

Heeding the warnings of the old men the night before, I came prepared and wore my snake guards—two pieces of coarse, thick, dirty cotton wrapped around my ankles—to protect me from the deadly, but dentally challenged, killer.

To get to Temple Twelve you must first pass through Temple Eleven, Fujii-dera, where I was now, sitting outside a public telephone booth working up the courage to call ahead. Learning my lesson from yesterday, I wanted to make a plan for the night. I took out the list of free accommodation I received at Temple One and found the phone number for Temple Twelve listed. I was hesitant to call, given the misunderstanding I had with the temple's monk seven years ago. It was a careless mistake I made, showing up at dusk and asking to camp in my tent on the temple grounds without any warning. I was a new pilgrim and didn't know all of the rules, but they weren't thrilled with me. Even so, they found a way to help me. I'm sure it was because I showed up without calling and caused them distress. The list clearly indicated to call first to arrange a place to sleep.

I spoke into a lime green public phone at Temple Eleven, conveniently located near the path into the mountains. "Excuse me," I said. "I'm a walking *henro*. May I please stay at your *tsuyadō* tonight?"

A *tsuyadō* is a free place to sleep along the *henro* path. It comes in many forms, such as a simple wooden gazebo, country barn, or a small prefabricated room, complete with electricity. What I was seeking for the night was the small, dirty tool shed in the middle of a plum orchard just past Temple Twelve to which I had previously been banished.

"That's not possible," the gruff voice on the other end said in Japanese.

"Ah, I see." I tried again. "I'm sorry, I must not have explained myself well enough. It's just that I have a long climb to reach your temple and no place to sleep tonight. I was hoping to sleep in the *tsuyadō*."

"There is no *tsuyadō* here."

Hmm. I switched tactics and began waving the list of free places as if the man could see it. "That's strange," I said, "because I'm looking at a list of *tsuyadō* I received at Ryōzen-ji and it lists your temple," I added, leaving him some room to backtrack. "It even says to call first to confirm."

"No! There is no *tsuyadō* here."

Maybe we were having a language problem. "I see. Well perhaps you don't call it a *tsuyadō*. I'd like to sleep in the tool shed in the orchard. I slept there when I walked the pilgrimage last time." I congratulated myself on remaining calm. Although, I did fantasize about jumping through the phone and beating some sense into him with the receiver.

"No, there's nothing like that here," he repeated with more than a touch of annoyance.

"Well, it's just that I have no place to sleep and . . ."

Loud beeps cut me off. He had hung up.

I replaced the phone in shock and with not a little bit of anger. The temple staff had been just as rude seven years ago. I had assumed their sourness was because I had not called first. It seemed that just made things worse.

I wasn't sure what else I could have done. Maybe I should have ignored the advice on the sheet, shown up at dusk, and brought a picture of the tool shed as proof. No doubt he still would have denied the existence of the *tsuyadō*.

Most likely it was my fault. I had assumed that reality and appearance were the same, and in Japan, they rarely ever are, and insisting they are is considered rude. He had a reason for saying no, for denying the existence of the *tsuyadō*. It didn't matter if it was there or not. The fact that there was a free place to stay for walking pilgrims ceased to exist the moment he denied it. Reasoning with him was not going to change things.

I should have stopped asking. I should have realized that, for whatever reason, this man did not want me to stay the night. Maybe he was new and did not know about the *tsuyadō*. Or he was worried a foreigner wouldn't know how to act in a Japanese tool shed. I might not take off my shoes or might fall asleep spooning the rice scythe. What a mess that would be to clean up in the morning.

I needed to learn to let things go. I did accept, although begrudgingly, that I wouldn't have a roof over my head that night. One of the rules I had decided to honor before walking the pilgrimage was that I would accept a refusal of help and move on without complaint. In this instance that meant cursing the temple and its staff in my mind, rather than calling back or trying to convince them in another way. Perhaps this is how people react internally in Japan. Behind stoic faces, deep bows, and profuse expressions of apology, they rant and rave and curse the other party to the lower levels of Buddhist hell. More likely, I was just being petty.

The repetitive beeping of the public telephone reminded me not to forget my phone card. The phone card, a present from the monk at Temple Eleven, in turn reminded me that there were still plenty of generous people out there. In fact, it was an example of *osettai*, or charitable offerings, the practice of which is unique to Shikoku, compared to the rest of Japan. *Osettai* is practiced all along the pilgrims' path where locals give *henro* presents. Anything works, including money, food and drinks, directions, a kind word, or free lodging.

Pilgrims have to receive all offerings with a thank you and a name slip given in return. The slips, filled in with your name, date, and hometown, are the same ones left at each temple, and residents believe they are talismans of good luck (*omamori*) for those who receive them. Before each *henro* sets out, they usually buy hundreds of them to have enough to last the journey. The more times a pilgrim completes the circuit, the greater the power of the slip. Most name slips left in temple bins and given out are white, indicating the *henro* has completed one to four pilgrimages. Green slips are used for those who have done

more than five circuits, and red for those who have completed
seven to twenty-four journeys. Silver or bronze slips indicate up
to 49 trips, while gold signifies 50 to 100. Finally, there are
multicolored slips called *nishiki*. Made from woven fabric, they
represent those who have managed to complete more than 100
pilgrimages.

Osettai is based on the belief that *henro* occupy a spiritual
realm and are closer to Kūkai than the average person. The
giver receives karma associated with helping someone
complete the pilgrimage, and the name slip, bearing my name
and prayers, becomes the vehicle for this spiritual boon.

For me, *osettai* was a constant reminder of people's good-
ness. On more than one occasion, the simplest of gestures lifted
me from the deepest of depressions. The telephone card
reminded me that temple staff really did care about pilgrims; I
was just being petty and should let Temple Twelve go.

I TOOK stock of my situation.

It was 9:30 in the morning already. I had walked the five
miles from Sumitomo-san's shrine, arriving at Temple Eleven
after picking up provisions for a few days' trek through the
mountains.

My map didn't show anywhere to sleep near Temple
Twelve, and there were no other listings of free places to stay
on my housing sheet. I checked back in with the head monk at
Temple Eleven, and he suggested my best bet was just to keep
walking and hope for the best. Sound advice for life in general
but pretty scary given the immediate circumstances. But there
was nothing I could do about it now, so I pulled on my pack
and said a final prayer at the friendly, sunlit temple.

I was about to leave when a middle-aged Japanese man
dressed in full white pilgrim regalia approached me.

"Excuse me," he said, "but I have never met a foreign *henro* before. Are you walking the whole way?" Large square glasses covered much of his face.

"*Hai.*" (Yes.)

"*Sugoi!*" (Wow!) he said with a long breath out.

He had just about every item a pilgrim can buy: a white *hakui* (vest), white pants, purple and gold vestment shawl, prayer beads on the left hand, walking stick in the right. He had two "official" bags for carrying more items, one a plastic box hanging down his chest made just for the pilgrimage, and the other more standard cloth bag sold to pilgrims, slung across his back, its main purpose seeming to be to hold whatever the first bag didn't. He was gleaming white while I was a mess after just two days. It was his hat, as much as his enthusiastic smile, that made me like him right away. He also wore the typical *sugegasa* (conical straw hat), but unlike mine, a plastic wrapper covered his. With about 150,000 traveling each year, the pilgrim regalia business was booming.

My *sugegasa* was an indispensable and beloved item. Besides pushing me to the height of island fashion, it protected from both the summer sun and rains. But the quality has diminished over the years, and as a result they are no longer waterproof. The cheap solution is to sell them with a plastic wrap that fits over the hat, which is attached when they are purchased. Most walking *henro* take the plastic covers off right away and keep them in their packs. They only come out when the rain starts falling. Most pilgrims these days perform the pilgrimage by car or bus. For some reason it never occurs to them to take the plastic off. The few I questioned about it thought the plastic was just a part of the hat and never gave it much thought.

The pilgrim's name was Moriyama-san and he was from Osaka, doing the pilgrimage by car. He had recently retired and was looking for something to do with his free time, which he seemed to have a lot of as this was his fifth time around the island in just two years.

"Shall we take pictures of each other?" he asked. He shook his camera, just in case I didn't understand. Why not? It might be the last picture anyone took of me if I ran into a *mamushi* on the way to the next temple.

I dug into my bag, found a white name slip, and filled it in. We exchanged them the way business cards are presented in Japan. Bowing down at 45 degrees, the right hand gives the card while the left hand receives. His was green, showing that he had been around at least five times.

We said goodbye and good luck. I hoisted my pack and he marveled at the size, which was actually small considering the distance I was hiking. I walked up the six concrete steps to the *hondō* at the back of the temple, turned left at a large statue of Kūkai, and plunged into a steep world of dark forests, graves, and imagined danger.

The added weight of food and water hit me immediately, as in no time the path began to climb. My heart pounded, and I wondered if it was possible to have a heart attack at age 28. I used my walking staff as a snake alert system. No leaf was safe as I prodded and banged the slight undergrowth in front of me, the staff's attached bell jingling away.

I passed a couple out for a morning stroll, as if they had no care in the world. I murmured a greeting, but it did not quite come out as I struggled for breath. About a mile up, the path reached a plateau, and the forest gave way to reveal a stunning vista of the Yoshino River valley. I took a grateful break and checked my feet. New blisters had formed already and the ones from yesterday were back. I cut extra moleskin, patched myself up as best I could, and limped on.

The path climbed steadily up again, descended cruelly, and then mocked me with yet another steep incline. It twisted and turned, clinging to the side of the mountain, as a 180-foot vertical drop reminded me to stay focused.

I ran out of water quickly and became dehydrated and dizzy, splitting my time between dry heaving and stumbling over exposed roots. While I wasn't overweight, neither had I done any type of preparation to hike 10-hour days, every day, for a month. I was having a great time.

The path cut through a clearing that housed a small Buddhist hermitage with no signs of life, or water. I pushed past the lonely clearing into the embrace of the forest and stumbled on.

Three and a half hours after leaving Temple Eleven, I picked my way down a steep stone stairway into a peaceful valley where Ryūsui-an, the Hermitage of the Flowing Water, and its attached inn nestled. Bright green moss glittered in the sunlight that filtered through green leaves high overhead. The hermitage—not part of the official 88 temples—was boarded up and closed for the season. Few pilgrims braved the stifling summer heat and humidity even on air-conditioned bus tours, let alone on foot. Without enough guests, most pilgrim-focused inns were closed this time of year.

Stripping down to my underwear, I filled up my water bottle and rinsed sweat-soaked clothes in the cold mountain stream that gave the temple its name. I eased my shoes and socks off and let them dry, allowing my feet to harden in the open air. I lay on a bench, and an extreme sense of satisfaction with my life washed over me. Sure, blisters covered my feet. Yes, I worried about chronic dehydration and a heartbeat that jumped like a banjo player on crack. True, I had no idea where I was going to sleep that night. But lying there, off my swollen feet, listening to birds chirp, the stream babble, cicadas buzz, and the wind ripple through bright green leaves, I could not have been any happier. Then I remembered lunch, and life got even better.

I unpacked vegetable sushi and fried chicken. I was just about to start drinking my fourth liter of the day when I heard a motor scooter amble up the dirt path to the inn. I rushed to get my clothes back on but had only succeeded in pulling my pants up when a bobbing white helmet came around the corner. Food in hand, my bare chest flashing white in the strong sun, I stared unblinking at a young man dressed in a starched and pressed tan jumpsuit.

"Mind if I join you for lunch?" he asked in Japanese. He didn't wait for an answer, or seem surprised I was half naked, and started unpacking his white, dirt-stained box attached to the back of his scooter.

"Not at all." I reached for my shirt and put it on. I was happy to have someone to talk with.

"You're walking, uh?" he asked. He pointed to my hat and staff to prove his point.

"Yup."

"*Demo gaikokujin janee no ka.*" (But you're a foreigner, right?) His heavy accent made understanding almost as challenging as the mountain paths.

"Yup," I replied.

He nodded and sat down to eat, apparently satisfied with my answers.

"It's hot, isn't it?" I said, trying to pick up the conversation.

"Yup," he mumbled, as small flecks of gooey white rice jumped from his mouth. He shoved more in.

"The valley is beautiful."

"*Un,*" he grunted, rice flying even further this time.

"It doesn't seem like anyone is living in the temple right now," I said, saving my best observation for last.

This one hooked him, and he shoved another load of rice in. "I know," he said, as he sat up straight and pulled out a map.

His name was Matsuzaka-san, he was 24 years old, and had lived in the area all his life. His job was to ride around on his

scooter checking if government maps properly listed all the
houses and their owners in the area, or if the houses became
abandoned. Eight million homes have been abandoned across
Japan as the population ages and younger people move to the
cities. Matsuzaka was on the front line of counting all the
rotting homes. He might have quite a career ahead, as by 2030 it
is estimated that 30 percent of Japan's 60 million homes will be
abandoned. For me it was less an abstract number than a fact
I'd come face-to-face with as I moved through Shikoku's depop-
ulating villages.

Once he had eaten, he said goodbye and climbed back onto
his scooter. After an hour's rest, I shoved my raw red feet back
into my shoes, refilled my water bottles, and pushed on, or up,
as it were. Marching out of the valley, the narrow path switched
back on itself, leading me upward in a dizzying maze. I tried to
forget the considerable distance left to the top, and the next
mountain waiting in the distance. I concentrated on placing
one foot in front of the other and fell into a steady, thoughtless
rhythm.

CLOTHES SOAKED THROUGH WITH SWEAT, I sloshed around a
corner and ran straight into a long cement staircase. I lifted my
eyes, afraid of how far they might travel. The stairs shot straight
up, lined on the right by a wall of green bamboo and on the left
by thin cedar trees. White and red tin *henro* signs fluttered in
the slight breeze, clinging to the rusted and bent handrails. At
the top of the staircase stood a giant 15-foot oxidized green
statue of Kūkai, waiting patiently for me to arrive.

At first glance, he seemed to be standing in front of a giant
wooden wall. But as I moved up the steps, I realized the
wooden wall was, in fact, a massive Japanese cedar tree. At
least 200 years of growth spread in every possible direction,

dwarfing the entire mountain top. My pain forgotten, I climbed the stairs, each step revealing a new section of the tree. I had found Ipponsugi-an, the Hermitage of the Lone Cypress.

All over Japan, natural monuments where Shinto gods are believed to reside are venerated. Two lone rocks standing in the sea become married through a twisted Shinto rope, lightning-patterned paper flipping in the wind to signify their power. Caves become the natural place to put small shrines and offer prayers. Large and small waterfalls tumble into coin-strewn rivers, churning the wishes of visitors. *Torii* gates and shrines top mountains across Japan to appease the local supernatural residents. It is without doubt one of the most fascinating aspects of Japanese culture, one that is so familiar to the average Japanese that it is often taken for granted.

Japanese tourists snap photos, two fingers raised in the peace sign. They drop coins at the base of small shrines, ring bells to announce their presence to the gods. They offer silent prayers for increased business, a happy family life, long health, or help on a particularly tricky exam. Yet, most Japanese I know do not identify as religious. Dropping coins, clapping hands, offering prayers are just things you do, they say. It is natural. It is a part of life. If there is a box, you drop a coin offering in. If there is a bell, you ring it and clap your hands to ask the gods for help.

If there is a large tree, you build a shrine around it. Of course, every big tree also needs a legend. Supposedly, Kūkai took a nap and used the roots of the tree at Ipponsugi as a pillow, and as he slept, he dreamt of the Buddha. I couldn't be happier. It brought me a shaded mountaintop, a magnificent Buddhist saint, and a bench to rest on.

I thought I was alone until I cleared the last set of steps. Two Japanese women, stooped with age, knelt at the feet of the statue. They weren't praying, but picking weeds from between the rocks. A huge pile of dead leaves, sticks, and grass rested on the path, testament to a hard day's work.

I stood, taking in the scene for a few minutes before they noticed me. The old woman on the right struggled to her feet. She wore a faded pink work smock, yellow work gloves, and a monstrous visor to protect her from the sun. From the shade of her oversized visor, a crinkled face greeted me with a large smile.

"*Otsukaresama deshita, mō chotto desu. Hai, settai desu,*" (You must be tired, there's just a bit more to go. Here's some *settai,*) she said, bowing. She gave me a small can of green tea, three hard candies that tasted like maple syrup, and a refill of my water bottle from her cold thermos.

Without another word she turned around and went back to work as I said thank you. Like a geriatric tag team, the other woman came over just as the first bent back to her work. The ritual was repeated, this time with a can of Boss coffee, a sweet bean cake, and offers of more water. Before she turned back, I caught her attention.

"Thank you, Grandmother. What are you doing?" I asked, hoping she would chat for a bit.

"We are cleaning the shrine. We do it twice a year," she said, and turned back to her work.

I shrugged off my pack, rested on a nearby bench, and watched the two women work. In their 80s, they cleared the area of unwanted vegetation bit by bit.

A small building off to the side housed a toilet. I sucked down my full bottle of water and looked longingly at the toilet, despite the stench. I had consumed at least five liters of water throughout the day but hadn't peed once.

The woods can make you paranoid when your body is acting strangely. I sat on the bench, trying to calm my racing heart down, and remembered a story I once read about a woman who died from over-hydration while running a marathon—not dehydration, as one might suspect. She drained cup after cup of water, never refusing a drink from the race volunteers. As the sweat continued to pour out of her, she drank more and more, her thirst increasing. She collapsed and died just a few miles from the finish line.

My soaked clothes clung to me, my heartbeat was erratic, and I had no urge to pee. Was I on my way to over-hydration? Was I being overly dramatic? I pulled myself up and shouldered my pack. I thanked the old women, before following the path around the right side of the tree and down into the next valley.

Almost immediately, I passed a thin *henro* hiking up the path I was walking down.

"You're walking the route backwards?" I asked as we paused in the middle of the narrow path to let the other by.

"Yes." His eyes seemed distant.

"You're almost done then," I said. Not without a touch of wonder.

His eyes got even farther away as he barely heard me.

"Good luck," we said at the same time, and both moved on.

I looked back, wishing that I were almost done as well. I still had one more mountain to climb and two and a half miles before I reached Temple Twelve. I began to worry if I'd even make it, as I contemplated the 730 miles I had left to go and the toll just two days had taken on my body.

The only things that cheered me up were the little signs hanging from thin branches on the sides of the path, encouraging me along.

"Good luck."

"You're almost there."

"Just one more mountain!"

"Thank you for walking," they read, red characters on white, flapping in the slight breeze. I almost cried from the kindness of the people who had put the signs there.

I lifted my head, took a good look around, and filled my thoughts with the surrounding beauty rather than the pain of my feet and the fierce beating of my heart.

Twenty minutes later, I stepped out of the forest halfway down a steep river valley and into a village defined by the passage of time. Old mud-walled homes clung to the sides of the valley. Their blue, red, and silver pointed tin roofs sat on older, traditional straw thatching that had become too expensive to repair due to the cost of materials and lost knowledge. In just two steps, the *henro* path changed from a mountain path to a trespassing dirt walkway. I wound my way between houses, through gardens, and along old rock retaining walls to reach a swift river below. The town was quiet, and I didn't see a soul while I crossed between mountains.

The village helped to reorient me back to the adventure I was on. I crossed the river over a crumbling concrete bridge. On my right, moss-covered steps led up the mountain, away from the *henro* path, to plum and cherry orchards. Sweet and sour scents mixed and drifted down the mountain. Unlike on the previous climbs, I was eager to get moving. This was my last climb of the day, and I only had an hour before the Temple Twelve stamp office closed at 5:00 p.m.

The forest seemed darker and the path narrower, but I moved with a light step up the steep dirt path, switchback after switchback. Small stone shrines poked out of the dark undergrowth. Silent Jizō statues hid in the shadows, ever vigilant. Jizō is a bald-headed *bodhisattva*, someone who has found enlightenment like the Buddha but who has chosen to be reborn over and over, rather than enter nirvana, until everyone is saved from the cycle of life and death. Jizō is a good guy. He protects children, the souls of the dead, and travelers—exactly the type of companion anyone would want on a walking pilgrimage.

In one mountain town I visited in western Japan, thousands of rock pillars lined the riverbed. Bereaved families build them, hoping to reduce the suffering of their stillborn children, who are forced to pile stones forever on the banks of the Sanzu River in the underworld for the suffering they have caused their parents. Jizō doesn't think that is fair and saves their souls by hiding them from demons, in his robes.

Jizō is not just relegated to sacred mountains and sad riverbeds. You'll find him at roadside shrines, in temples, at intersections, in the middle of rice paddies, in cemeteries, and along mountain paths. He may be the most prevalent Buddhist image in Japan. He was, at least, the hardest working *bodhisattva* on the path to Temple Twelve. Covered in moss or a red smock to keep him warm, he lines the path guiding travelers on their way or surrounding those who have fallen. Stone grave markers, displaying only the word *henro*, are a particularly popular gathering place for the little stone protectors on this path.

After seven hours and 16 hard miles, I emerged from the woods. I climbed my final flight of stone steps, lined with bright red lanterns, to the gated entrance of Shōsan-ji. Massive cedar trees, each as wide as a small car, shot straight into the sky. A nine-foot green statue of Kūkai, walking stick and begging bowl in hand, welcomed me.

I marched to the bell tower on a path lined with blue azaleas, grasped the rough rope attached to a thick log, and announced my presence. The temple complex was in flux. A large new administrative building was at odds with the ancient atmosphere of the forest. As if to correct the imbalance, construction workers were building a traditional temple using huge stones from a quarry I'd passed on my way up the mountain.

I attended to my pilgrim duties—chanted, prayed, lit incense, left name slips—and then reluctantly entered the new building to get my scroll signed. Two middle-aged men in blue robes sat behind a high counter, cooling under a fan and chatting. A TV blared in the background. One of them had hung up on me that morning, but now they were neither friendly nor dismissive. They were just doing a job.

Shōsan-ji seemed to be benefitting from its position and popularity. As one of the highest and most picturesque temples, it attracts hundreds of thousands of pilgrims and tourists each year. Most visitors use the paved road leading up from the other side of the mountain. Business had been good, as the new buildings attested.

I had conflicted feelings about the success, as it contradicted my own desires for a mountaintop temple untouched by the interests of society. I was planning to visit the cave, higher on the mountain, in which they say Kūkai sealed the fiery dragon from which the temple got its name. But the day was drawing to an end and I needed to find a home for the night. I paid my 500 yen and left. I couldn't ask about the *tsuyadō* again.

I left the temple, encouraged by the mountain views. I hoped that I was just being petty, and the temple was in fact a wonderful place. Perhaps next time I will not expect anything more than a beautiful view. That thought saddened me even more because I couldn't shake my own feeling that a temple was there to help people. Of course, temples also have to earn a living, and the balance was difficult to maintain.

Leaving Shōsan-ji, the *henro* path dipped back into the woods, through orange orchards, and right past the still-standing tool shed. I thought about ignoring the caretakers and just spending the night. After all, no one was likely to stop by; there was no one around. But I couldn't bring myself to stay, knowing that I wasn't welcome.

With the tool shed denied me, I decided to head for a toilet. It was not just any toilet, but a Western-style toilet. It sat at the base of a valley and it was so nice that I remembered it even after seven years.

The toilet was a Western sit-down model rather than a

Japanese squat style. If you haven't had the pleasure of squatting over a hole in the ground and trying to keep from peeing all over your clothes, you are not missing much. Japan has become famous for adding tech to Western-style toilets, and most houses in Japan have heated seats. Some even have remote controls for water that will wash any part of your junk that tickles your fancy. Why a remote is needed remains unclear.

But these technological marvels are rare in rural Japan, where the squatting hole reigns supreme. Add the increased space needed for wheelchair access, and you have a beautiful area to wash up in private. With its wood siding that mirrored the surrounding natural beauty, the toilet held more appeal than any mountain temple in the area.

I had no idea if I would find shelter as well. But the prospects of running water and sitting, even if my bodily functions never kicked in, would keep me going for the extra four miles I needed to get to the bottom of the valley.

Halfway to the toilet, I came across Jōshin-an. The Temple of the Cedar Staff marks the most popular origin story of the Shikoku pilgrimage. Beautiful rock walls, a clean gravel yard, and open views of the mountains beyond contrasted with the deserted, rusted tin temple in front of me. It was so unremarkable that I passed by, unaware of its importance, seven years ago, remembering instead the wonderful toilet. The most notable features of the temple are a large cedar tree and a raised green statue of Kūkai, standing over a wretch. Despite a lack of attention to the temple's construction, one does not get far into Shikoku before hearing about Emon Saburō, the poor soul at the saint's feet. In a fit of sin, death, and salvation, he became the first Shikoku pilgrim.

Emon Saburō was a wealthy man living near the western Shikoku city of Matsuyama with his eight sons. One day a disheveled monk appeared at Saburō's home begging for food. Saburō ordered the monk be sent away with nothing.

The monk returned the next day, and Saburō ordered his staff to put human shit in the monk's bowl. This continued every day for one week.

On the eighth day, Saburō went to the gate himself and struck the bowl from the beggar's hand, smashing it into eight pieces. The monk left and never returned.

The next day Saburō's eldest son died, then his next oldest each day thereafter, until they were all dead. Realizing his mistake, Saburō gave away all his possessions and set off to seek the forgiveness of the wandering holy man.

Saburō circled the island for four years, always just a few days behind Kūkai. Desperate to find the monk, Saburō turned around and started walking counterclockwise. With his strength fading, he struggled up the steep climb to Shōsan-ji and collapsed halfway up.

As Saburō neared death, Kūkai appeared just in time to grant forgiveness. Kūkai wrote something on a small rock and placed it in Saburō's hand before burying him and marking the grave with his walking stick. Legend has it that the staff grew into the massive cedar I now rested under, and Saburō lay somewhere underneath me.

It is ironic that this simple, solitary, and unacclaimed temple was the true heart of the pilgrimage. Unencumbered by the money flowing into the established temples, the Temple of the Cedar Staff is free to reveal its true character, a personal moment on the path, alone except for the presence of Kūkai.

This presence is the backbone of the pilgrimage. There is always the chance of meeting Kūkai. Countless *henro* stories speak of encounters at tenuous moments. The staff reminds pilgrims that you are never alone. Various pilgrim paraphernalia reinforce this and bear the phrase "*dōgyō ninin*" (two walk together). When walking over bridges, *henro* lift their staffs so as not to disturb a sleeping Kūkai underneath.

The land holds a symphony of miracles attributed to Kūkai. You can't walk more than an hour in any direction before seeing some plaque or marker explaining how Kūkai established this spring, built that temple, stopped a disastrous fire, or cured the diseases of countless believers.

I hoped Kūkai would be kind to me that night as I continued on my way to find the nicest toilet in the area.

The sun set at my back as I arrived at a silent hamlet just after 7:00 p.m. Clustered at the bottom of a river valley, a handful of houses huddled around a small concrete elementary school. A single road passed through the village. In the middle of this beautiful, remote settlement sat my toilet, just as I remembered it, bathed in the flickering florescent glow of a lamppost. On the opposite side of a large gravel parking lot sat my other salvation. I walked over to the "*Henro* Station," a tin-covered row of souvenir stalls with tables still set up, silent and unused during the low season— my home for the night.

I chose the cleanest table and unpacked right away. Sandals on, as I limped across the dark parking lot towards the toilet, I came face-to-face with a white-haired man who seemed to appear out of nowhere. He had a strong, chiseled face, well-ironed flannel shirt, and a small black Chihuahua on the end of a leash.

"Good evening." I bowed low. "Is it okay if I spend the night here?" I asked, concerned with being polite but unsure what I would do if he said no.

"Good evening. It's not my place to give permission." He bowed his head. His dog ignored me. "Although *henro* do stay here from time to time," he added, perhaps in response to my dejected expression.

"Thank you." I bowed. He had given me a precious gift— peace of mind.

The toilet had gathered considerable dirt over the past seven years but did its job. I used the faucet to wash my body. Waves of dirt and sweat poured into the floor drain. Next, I washed my clothes, as I needed to dry them at night to be ready for the next day. By the time I emerged, a billion stars shined down on the now pitch-black valley.

Sitting on a table, I was in the middle of eating dinner when a car pulled into the middle of the parking lot, blinding me with its high beams. A figure stepped out and we regarded each other for a few moments. Unable to see the driver past the blinding lights, I grew nervous, afraid someone had arrived to kick me out.

"Please come and bathe with me," the deep voice said.

He switched off the lights, and I recognized the man in the starched flannel with the small dog I had met earlier. Anywhere else in the world, getting into a stranger's car in the middle of the night, in the middle of nowhere, to bathe with him would seem insane. At that moment, it sounded like the only rational thing to do.

"Thank you!" I grabbed my small yellow quick-dry camping towel and jumped into the passenger seat. The ride took just under five minutes, but I thanked God for sparing my feet the walk. I thought we were heading to his private home, but instead we arrived at a beautiful traditional inn. Wedged between a thick, forested mountain and a swift river, it put my hawker's stall to shame.

"I have two other guests tonight, but they have both already taken their baths. Feel free to take your time," the man said. He led me through an empty dining room past a row of knee-high wooden tables on straw *tatami* mats. Bay windows looked out over a sculpted garden. Shaped bushes and stunted trees rolled over the garden into a frothy river below.

I took my time. There few places in the world as enchanting as a Japanese *ofuro*, or bath. Like most things in

Japan, there is a ritual for the *ofuro*: wash, soak, rinse, dry. I folded my clothes and placed them in a waiting basket next to a sign warning those with heart conditions not to enter. I stepped naked into the bathing room. A line of four shin-high wooden seats waited for me, each one assigned to a small hip-high shower and faucet. I sat, knees reaching my chest. Slowly, deliberately, I began. Warm water gushed into a cedar bucket, and once full I poured the water over my head. Refill, repeat. Refill, repeat. The warm water kneaded my tired shoulders. The ritual slowed my racing mind.

My hand towel, folded into a small square and soaked through with body wash, rested on my thigh. I used it to wash my feet, between each toe, my calves, my knees, my back, my face, behind my ears. No area escaped notice, and every inch received equal attention. The bucket refilled, I washed away the soap. I washed away my thoughts. I prepared myself for the bath. Wave after wave of hot water rolled off my head. My worries washed into the drain.

Cleansed, purified, I stood and walked to the bath. Big enough to hold four adults comfortably, I had it to myself. Soft, yellow cedar planks held hundreds of gallons of scalding, muscle-soothing water. Bracing myself for the coming shock, I stepped in. My instincts screamed to jump out, but experience kept me in. Inch by inch I lowered the rest of my body. I sat still, careful not to move and create any unnecessary pain from the scalding water.

Slowly, I grew accustomed to the heat and relaxed. I soaked. My hand towel rested on my head so as not to taint the water with soap or dirt it might still hold. I forgot the day, I forgot the pain, I forgot about the next day and the promise of pain. I soaked.

It didn't matter how long I soaked. There is no clock in the *ofuro*. Eventually I climbed from the bath, sweat pouring from my body, and sat down at the shower again, free to relax. I rinsed away the heat with cold water. The shock closed my pores and firmed my skin back up after the heat had softened my callouses to mush.

I took my time getting dressed, then drew in a deep breath before sliding the door open, prepared to face reality and my parking lot. The owner was waiting for me, ready to drive me back.

Now the dining room was in use. Two guests sat cross-legged, enjoying a beautifully arranged dinner with six or seven different dishes and as many colors. One was an older Japanese man with salt and pepper hair. The other was a middle-aged Western woman. Both wore the typical summer *yukata*, a thin robe held together with a simple cloth belt.

I walked by them silently, careful not to intrude on their dinner or overstep my bounds as a temporary guest at the inn. My night was destined for a solitary table, a dirty parking lot, and oppressive humidity. My toilet used to be the best in the valley.

4

BACK TO TOWN

Days start early on the pilgrim's path, and I was up and off my souvenir table by 4:30 in the morning. Nothing moved in the small valley as I looked up the steep forest walls to the ridgeline that would take me back into Tokushima city. My plan was to hit five new temples by the end of the day, finishing near Temple Seventeen, not too far from where the pilgrimage began.

The forest was silent, except for the normal creaks and groans of animals and trees stirring, the morning air stiff as the remote valley waited in anticipation for the mountains to release the sun. I was the only creature visible in the forest, the jingle of my staff's bell and the blood pounding in my ears the only sounds, as I wound my way up a steep earthen path. Silent green cypress trees lining the path were my only companions.

The tranquility of the Japanese countryside was a blessing as I left the busy roads behind. Now, as the temples started spreading out, and I contemplated the long road to the south coast, the enormity of my task set my mind afire with worry and self-doubt. I thought I heard faint bells from the top of the ridge. I stopped, straining my hearing to confirm the presence of other human beings. I was suddenly aware of a deep need for companionship. I sprinted up the steep, slippery path and stumbled out onto a narrow country road, into two surprised, sweat-soaked *henro* sharing tangerines. They stared at me and I at them, recognition from the inn last night hitting us at the same time.

The Japanese pilgrim was short, lean, and strong. Only his gray buzzed hair gave away his 60 plus years. I introduced myself in Japanese.

The woman's face brightened instantly. "You speak Japanese!" she exclaimed in English, while the Japanese man seemed to relax from some long-held tension. "This is magnifique!"

"Hello, my name is Yamada. This is Léonie, from France." The man returned the greeting and gestured to his companion.

Yamada-san offered me a tangerine, and I slid off my pack. I learned all about Léonie in a sudden rush.

She stopped and took a breath. "Sorry, sorry. I don't speak any Japanese and have not spoken to anyone in days!" she confided.

Despite not understanding any Japanese, she had dreamed of walking the pilgrimage after reading about it in a French spiritual magazine. Wanting to experience the "real" Japan, she set off without a map or any concrete directions. Her plan was to walk as far as Temple Twenty-Three, the last in Tokushima Prefecture.

Yamada-san had found Léonie, lost and walking the wrong way, on his first day. Worried about what would happen to her, he decided to accompany her, even though he spoke only a few words of English himself. He was on a four-day holiday and was walking the pilgrimage in stages, whenever he could get time off work. At the end of his career, this was considered a long vacation, the first he had taken in 40 years. Today was his last day, and he worried about her going on alone. The twinkle in his eye made it clear that I was his solution.

"We can't just let her wander around Shikoku with no idea

where to stay." Yamada-san said, glancing at Léonie. He lowered his voice, even though he knew she couldn't understand. "It just wouldn't be safe for a woman to sleep outdoors. I mean, you're different. You speak Japanese. You have a map. But she ... well ... you see my problem."

There were certainly some safety issues on the pilgrimage, but Yamada-san was being more paternal than genuinely worried about crime. Most likely he thought this was his duty, and once he had decided to help, nothing would stop him from carrying it out.

The care Japanese take of visitors seems to be directly proportional to how much time people have spent in the country. First time tourists receive a rush of presents, help, and concern, and leave thinking this is everyday Japan. It is a way of treating guests that is backed into the culture and is common etiquette for most everyone I have met. The longer you stay, however, the more you learn that being part of the system, being accepted, requires heavy levels of reciprocal obligations, until you are the one helping and doing your duty. No more presents, that is for sure.

Explaining to Yamada-san that I wasn't Japanese, especially since we were talking Japanese, was not going to do any good, and so I just said what was expected. I nodded, humming a response that didn't use any words but could have been a yes, could have been a no, and should have been taken as, "I see, but what exactly is your suggestion? I'm not committing to anything."

His worry over Léonie was touching. Once Japanese take responsibility for someone, they don't let them down, even if it disrupts their own plans. I am sure Yamada-san was not expecting to spend the beginning of his pilgrimage this way, especially during his first vacation in 40 years. But he had, and his kindness was at the heart of what I loved most about living in Japan. I was also sure that Léonie didn't understand the scale of Yamada-san's sacrifice. Of course, nor would Yamada-san ever want me to tell her.

I acted as a translator as we hashed out a plan, all three of us together. Léonie was okay to go out on her own; she wanted the challenge. This seemed to ease some of Yamada-san's fears. I consulted my map book, which listed inns along the path, and then Yamada-san made bookings with his mobile phone for her next two nights. We drew maps, wrote in explanations, and transliterated common Japanese phrases for her to use, while Léonie took it all in and tried to keep up. His duty complete, Yamada-san relaxed visibly. He walked ahead, alone with his thoughts, while I talked with Léonie.

"I love Japan. It is the most magical place on earth. The Japanese are so mystical, in touch with their Zen," she proclaimed. "You must know this. You've lived here for years. This is why I came to Shikoku—to find enlightenment."

I didn't know how to respond. The word "Zen" has become so misappropriated by the West that she was using it in a way that made absolutely no sense. But I still understood what she meant. In fact, I was just like her when I first arrived in Japan. I was attracted to Japanese spirituality, to Buddhism, and what I thought was a better way of living.

But six years of living in Japan had built up a lot of metaphysical gunk. The effort to live a normal life, to fit in, build a career, make relationships work, all in another language and culture, had taken its toll on me. It had stripped a lot of the wonder out of me. It was hard to relate to the person I once was.

And yet, just like Léonie, here I was on a spiritual quest in Japan. We walked along a high ridge, a bit behind Yamada-san. It was hard to dismiss Léonie's wide-eyed wonder when traditional thatch-roofed houses clung to winding terraced rice paddies all the way down to the river raging below. The setting was magical.

We caught up to Yamada-san, who was putting on his plastic-wrapped conical straw hat in anticipation of leaving the protection of the forests behind. I tried to tell him that the plastic was only for rain, and he looked at me like I was crazy. "It's sold this way for a reason, Todd-san."

Despite enjoying their company, walking at their pace was not an option if I wanted to make my own flight home in one month, let alone reach my goal for the day. I started outpacing Yamada-san and Léonie almost right away, and before I realized it, they were gone.

Each *henro* walks according to their own schedule. At times, paces align, and then soon break apart. It is rare to find someone to walk with for too long.

FOR TWO GLORIOUS hours I walked along the top of a wooded ridge. The road was flat, and the slight breeze wafted sweet smoke from the farms below. The road eventually descended quickly, depositing me onto a busy highway that hugged the banks of the Akui River. Like almost all rivers in Japan, millions of tons of concrete constrained the banks on each side, their purpose to prevent flooding, as Japan is one of the most disaster-prone countries in the world.

Eleven long miles later, the noonday sun beat down on me. No longer protected by the mountains I had left behind, I sucked in acrid exhaust fumes as compact cars and trucks whizzed by frighteningly close, inches from ending my journey permanently. Each car and truck was a miniature version of its Western cousin. Mini vans were exactly that. Small jeeps were no larger than two-door hatchbacks but appeared to be bigger against a narrow road lined by small houses.

I hobbled along until I reached a short staircase kissing Route 21 that led to Dainichi-ji, Temple Thirteen, the Temple of the Great Sun. A small temple, it sat squished between the valley's river and the busy road mere inches from the entrance gate. I prayed and received the temple's calligraphy on my scroll before turning my attention to lunch. I spent the next hour, shoes off, lounging on *tatami* mats in the noodle shop next door, slurping thick *udon* noodles from an oversized bowl. A group of retirees, dressed in uniforms of khaki pants, small daypacks, and brimmed hats, passed in and out of the shop on their way to and from the temple. Frequent loud sniffs were the only indication that they were aware of me at all. I smelled horrible.

Once my belly was filled with oily broth and slithering carbohydrates, I set out. Temple Fourteen, Temple of Everlasting Peace, sat just one and a half miles into the beginning of the residential maze surrounding downtown Tokushima, where I had started the pilgrimage. Like at all the previous temples, *henro* were in short supply. It seemed even bus *henro* found the heat difficult, as I had not seen one bus, usually packed with 40 or more *henro,* over the past three days. The peace and quiet was welcome, as was not having to wait in line to get my scroll signed.

The temple's grounds were cut by rows of rocks resembling a mountainous landscape. Said to have healing powers, the temple is visited by disabled people from all over the country who hope for a miracle. A pile of discarded crutches offered encouraging proof to newcomers. A young, out-of-shape pilgrim limped through the massive wooden gate, looking like he was in need of a miracle. We greeted each other with a now practiced refrain, "*Gokurōsama deshita,*" a greeting that all pilgrims, in fact all Japanese, use to congratulate each other after a long day.

Passing each other many times over the course of the day, I had watched him deteriorate physically as his limp grew worse and he slumped closer and closer to the ground. Weariness weighed down his face, and desperation clung to him as much as his sweat-soaked white shirt.

"Leave your pack here. I'll wait for you," I said. "We can walk together for a bit." I gestured to the sun-bleached bench next to where I sat. He shrugged off his heavy pack, murmuring thanks as he shuffled off. I watched him chant at each shrine, despite his weariness, and then collect his calligraphy and Buddha slip. He limped along, only just able to lift his feet over the exposed rocks.

"Where are you headed to today?" I asked. It was just about 2:00 p.m., and there was plenty of walking left in the day.

"I'm staying at an inn near Temple Sixteen. I'm not sure where it is. I only have the name," he confessed as we dragged ourselves down a deserted neighborhood street. He didn't have a map book and was relying only on the *henro* markers to guide him. "I've gotten lost quite a bit," he sighed.

I understood his desperation. Every step we took brought me closer to my greatest failure seven years ago, at just about the same state he was in. Maybe that is why I was taking the time to look after him.

"I'm staying at a *zenkonyado* tonight. It's free and you're welcome to join me if you want. It's near Temple Sixteen as well," I offered, sensing how close he was to the edge. I knew that edge all too well.

"I can't. My parents won't let me stay anywhere but at inns," he confided. "They're paying for my trip, and they think it's too dangerous to camp out or stay with strangers." He looked at me apologetically.

Yūto-san was 21 years old, from downtown Tokyo. A junior in college, he was exactly the same age I was when I first walked the pilgrimage. Like me on my first trip, he seemed depressed and, faced with the enormity of the miles ahead, ready to give up.

Yūto filled the silence as we passed through quiet backstreets that would soon be flooded with homebound workers. "I decided to walk because I thought it would make me stronger," he whispered, eyes locked on the road ahead. "My parents didn't want me to go. They said Shikoku is a dangerous, wild place."

I remained quiet, voicing only the appropriate murmurs of comprehension so he knew I was still listening.

"Now I don't know if I can continue. My feet are covered in blisters, one foot is swollen from . . . I don't know, really. And every step makes me want to scream."

I understood. "The blisters will heal, but you need to be careful of tendonitis. Maybe you should take a break tomorrow, let your body rest, and then walk less each day," I suggested. It was advice I wouldn't have accepted myself, my first time around, or even now.

"Maybe."

"In any case, I'll help you find your hotel."

Yūto nodded his thanks. We walked in silence for the next hour, left to our own demons, his in the present and mine in the past. After a quick stop at Temple Fifteen, we reached Temple Sixteen, Kannon-ji, named for the *Bodhisattva* of Compassion. It was a small temple, serving the needs of the nearby households. If not for its famed place as one of the 88 temples, it would have looked like any normal neighborhood temple.

After searching the map book, we found Yūto's inn a few streets in the opposite direction from my destination for the evening. I walked him safely there, and we exchanged name slips at the entrance, wishing each other good luck. I suspected I wouldn't see him again, that he would be bound for a train back to Tokyo in the morning. But I hoped he would find the strength to keep going.

A row of five black taxis greeted me as I arrived at my destination. A thin old man with white gloves and a black suit ignored me as he washed one of them. A curl of smoke rose from the cigarette hanging from his mouth.

"Excuse me, can I stay the night?" I asked. It was an odd question to ask at a taxi office, which added to my doubts as to whether I was at the correct place. Cars whooshed behind me on the busy street as the man puffed on the cigarette and motioned his head to the back office. I inched up to the dull prefabricated structure, which consisted of exposed steel beams and a corrugated roof that covered both the office and taxis.

"*Sumimasen. Itoue-san irasshaimasuka?*" I asked, poking my head into the office.

A middle-aged woman dressed in a striped knee-length skirt uniform ignored me in favor of a notebook. As I tried to ask again, she waved her hand to my right and said, "Stairs," without even looking up.

I looked through a small doorway behind me and found a staircase. I wiggled out of my shoes and left them in the rack at the bottom. At the top of the narrow stairs, I found a small, empty apartment.

Eight aging straw *tatami* mats filled the well lived-in room. Hundreds of name slips, dominated by white but with splashes of red, green, and the occasional gold, covered the walls. Photographs of visiting *henro* adorned the sliding door. One gifted traveler had pasted ink drawings of the 17 temples dotted throughout the city of Tokushima.

A laminated hand-drawn map showed the way to the nearest supermarket. It helpfully recommended buying dinner just after 7:00 p.m., when the staff discounted unsold *bentō* lunch boxes to help sell off the last of the day's stock.

This was Sakae Taxi, a *zenkonyado* offered up by owner of the company Itoue-san. *Zenkonyado* are like *tsuyadō* but are offered to pilgrims in people's homes, or offices in this case. This hadn't been included in my map book, but I learned about it from the list of free places to stay I had received at Temple One. Luckily, this listing turned out better than the last attempt at Temple Twelve. In some cases, *zenkonyado* provide both lodging and meals. Either way, they are almost always associated with receiving merit to eliminate bad karma or gain further merit.

None of the workers seemed willing to explain the rules of staying or to indicate whether Inoue-san was there to say thank you to. I was nevertheless grateful to take off my heavy pack. I gathered my scroll and small white *henro* pouch that held my valuables and temple essentials, and set off for Temple Seventeen.

The Temple of the Well hid in the suburban sprawl, just over a mile away. My feet were still sore from the long day but felt lighter, as it helped to not carry my backpack as well. My spirits grew brighter knowing that I had a place to sleep in safety, even if for just one night.

Despite my good mood, it was hard not to dwell on what had happened here seven years ago as I approached the temple from a narrow backstreet. Seven years ago, I was no better than young Yūto whom I had left earlier in the day, ready to quit.

I HAD COME to Shikoku at the age of 21 to become stronger, to have an adventure that would prove that I was ready to be an adult. Instead, just three days into the trip, I found myself huddled under the temple's overhang during a rainstorm, reduced to tears. The pain was too much, the loneliness was overwhelming, and the stress of not knowing where to sleep each night had gotten to me. Three days. That was all it took for me to give up.

A kind couple, observing the first anniversary of their son's death, noticed me. They approached me, and without a word, led me to the altar to pray with them. The mother wrapped a jacket around me, the father took my bag, and with barely a word spoken they drove me to their home. They lived halfway to Temple Eighteen and in the morning asked where I wanted to be dropped off. Weary and desperate to finish, even after just three days on the path, I asked for a ride to the next temple, skipping the ten-and-a-half-mile walk.

I gave up my plan to walk the whole way and was willing to start taking buses and trains, anything to help me finish as soon as possible. My plan to prove myself was ruined, and now I was just on a trip to get it finished. It was my greatest failure. It wasn't just that I stopped walking, it was that I stopped walking because I quit. After all, I was too weak mentally to tough it out. I was a scared kid who couldn't cut it.

The next day I found myself alone again, this time on a rain-drenched, dark mountaintop with nowhere to stay. Fate intervened, and I met a group of three walking pilgrims who, like the kind couple the night before, invited me to join them at an inn further down the path. They took me under their wing and taught me how to read my map book and how to live on the trail with less.

We walked on average a marathon a day—26 miles. Four days of that and all who remained of the original group were me and one other, a 60-year-old man named Matsushida-san. Day after day we slept outside and just walked. We pushed through injuries and thoughts of quitting, until we arrived, just 28 days later, back at Temple One, transformed. I couldn't stop thinking of the mere ten and a half miles I had missed and the weakness that had led me to quit. I walked back to Temple Seventeen from Temple One and then on to Temple Eighteen, completing the entire circuit by foot.

FOR SEVEN YEARS I felt like my first pilgrimage wasn't quite correct. I had now returned to walk it the right way. Somehow, I still felt like I hadn't fully walked the pilgrimage, all due to that moment of weakness when I accepted the car ride. This time around, I hadn't yet quit, but I was surprised at how weak I felt already. As I walked back to Sakae Taxi, there were moments when all I wanted to do was curl up in a ball in a safe, air-conditioned room and stay for days.

That is why I was back on Shikoku. Somehow, I had lost sense of that 21-year-old kid who was willing to jump feet first into a pilgrimage, unprepared, with little Japanese and no idea of what to expect, who would somehow come out stronger on the other side. Over the years since then, I had felt myself slipping, into a couch, a TV show, and the monotony of everyday life, unchallenged by its lack of adventure.

I had used teaching English in Japan as an opportunity for adventure, but I'd never regarded it as a career path. I liked learning how to teach, developing a skill, but once I found my rhythm, I wasn't satisfied with teaching English. I took on more responsibility until I found myself the head English teacher in an elementary school, working in Japanese and supervising staff. Despite the higher position, I was still paid the same small fee I had earned when I'd started out six years earlier. Stress after stress accumulated as I felt the system would never let me be anything more.

I asked for a raise, some type of recognition, but my boss in the Department of Education just said all foreigners had to be treated the same, even if some of us were doing more. Finally, the combination of dissatisfaction with the type of work and the restrictive environment, even one as beautiful as Japan, led me to quit, with proper notice of course. My boss almost broke into tears and promised me a raise right then and there. It turned out he was worried about how my quitting would make him look.

I left my job. I also left my long-term Japanese girlfriend of six years. That also wasn't easy, but something didn't feel right in our relationship. I was tired by 9:00 p.m. every night, and I was only 28 years old. Nothing felt right about Japan anymore, so I moved on to graduate school in the United States, and a new life. I was done with Japan. It was time to move on.

And yet, here I was, back again. Back to the place that had almost ruined me, but also back to the place that showed me who I could be when I first arrived. I was back to walk the path again—to do it properly, to prove I was still strong and to finally figure out what I wanted to do with my life.

I arrived back at the taxi shop, surprised to see I had a roommate for the night. Lanky, with a shaved head and wire glasses, Shunsuke-san was full of energy, smiles, and fast Japanese. He was from Saitama Prefecture, near Tokyo, had just quit his job as a real estate agent, and at the age of 28, was also searching for his next path in life, except he was cycling around Shikoku for a month. While he was ecstatic to find an American *henro*, I suspect he would have been just as excited over hot water or folded napkins. I liked him immediately, despite his one obvious preoccupation.

"Tell me, what's it like to have sex with American girls?"

Soba noodles threatened to shoot out of my nose as I tried to eat the dinner I'd bought at the local supermarket.

Unfazed, he continued to probe. "Is it easy? I bet it is, it must be," he concluded with no help from me.

"How long have you been riding your bike around Shikoku?" I asked, trying to switch topics.

"Hmm. If it is as easy as you say, how should I go about getting American girls to sleep with me?"

"How did you find out about Sakae Taxi?"

"You're right, you're right. I guess there is no formula, you just have to ask. You can't ask Japanese girls for sex like you can American girls."

I was saved from making up the secrets of luring American girls into bed when Inoue-san himself appeared. We stood up immediately to thank him for the roof.

"Please, please sit down and we can chat," he said. He motioned to the pillows surrounding the low table where the remnants of our dinner lay.

In his mid-50s, shoulders hunched and shirt disheveled, he slumped into a lounging position on the *tatami* mats. The stench of stale cigarettes assaulted us from across the table. After dispensing with the pleasantries of where, when, how long, and how come I was walking, I finally asked some questions of my own.

"Why did you build this apartment and start accepting *henro*?" I asked. He didn't strike me as the overly generous type. It turned out I couldn't read a person at all.

His eyes narrowed. Shunsuke looked like he was going to fall asleep from the civilized conversation. "I have four reasons. The first is that my grandfather passed away, and I wanted to do something to honor him and ensure a peaceful afterlife. Next, the train station nearby was full of sleeping *henro* and it was becoming a burden on the neighborhood.

"Third, I went trekking in Nepal a few years back. Camping out was tough, and often shelters for hikers were full. I came to understand how much walking *henro* suffer. During the hike I had a serious injury and thought I would die. Only my Buddhist practice and the kind people around me saved me."

He never mentioned the fourth reason, but three was plenty, and the last one, the unspoken one, seemed to kill the mood. Or maybe he sensed our weariness. Either way, the night was at an end. He wished us good luck and disappeared down the stairs. Relationships are like that on the pilgrimage—intense and over quickly.

We rolled out our sleeping pads and bags, ready to end a

long day but too weary to want the next to come once our eyes closed.

"Todd?" Shunsuke whispered into the darkness.

"Yeah?"

"Have you had sex with Angelina Jolie?"

"No."

"Does she fuck a lot?"

"I have no idea. I don't know her."

"I see. Have you fucked Jennifer Aniston?"

"Good night, Shunsuke."

"Good night."

5

A REAL HENRO

There is no escaping reality on the pilgrim's path. It took all of Day Four to get out of the city and past Temple Nineteen. My reward for the day was a downpour, and once again I had nowhere to sleep. There was nothing to do but give in and splurge on a small countryside inn where I bought a bit of sanity for just $80.

As I checked into my room, reality checked to see if I was paying attention and gave me a swift kick. There was no way my body could sustain my current pace. My feet were riddled with blisters and my ankles were swelling up. But my wallet and my fixed plane ticket were unforgiving travel partners. I had to be on a plane headed back to debt-inducing graduate school in 31 days. I pulled out my money, $1,500, which seems like a lot, but not in Japan. Just the calligraphy on my scroll would be $440, plus $30 a day to eat, leaving only $320 to play with. Basically, enough to last 25 more days sleeping outside six nights a week and splurging on a proper futon only once a week. So, what was I supposed to do? Quit? Not a chance. Continue on with no clue how to manage? Sounded like a plan.

On Day Five, in the morning coolness as I approached the mountain path leading to Temple Twenty, The Temple of Crane Forest, at the top, all obstacles seemed like solutions waiting to be discovered. I was feeling manic again, breathing in ecstasy-infused country air. The chorus of cicadas reverberated in rolling waves from deep in the surrounding forest. Glad to be off the unforgiving asphalt roads for a while, I marched up the snaking *henro* path, through cedar-filled forests, for almost two miles, to the ancient wooden temple sitting 1,600 feet above. Dehydrated yet again, I approached the imposing weathered wooden gate and was surprised to see the paved road ran right through it, a touch of magic lost.

Seven older *henro* chanted vigorously in unison in front of the *hondō*, flanked by a pair of elegant metal cranes standing over eight feet tall. I waited until they finished before sending my own chant on its way, swallowed up by the encroaching forest. This place felt sacred.

The attendant happily pointed to a hose where I could refill my water bottles and handed me a multicolored name slip.

"I received it earlier today," he said. "Keep it with you and it will help protect you."

"Thank you. Where is the path to Temple Twenty-One?"

"Just over there." He pointed behind me. "You can't miss it."

He was right. The tiny trailhead boasted no less than six different markers crowded into a one square foot area. Two small stickers were stuck to a guard railing protecting cars from a sharp drop off, and a five-foot inscribed log was lodged into the earth. A shorter, age-worn stone marker kept it company, with ancient carvings highlighted in red paint. Topping it all off, a wooden stake pointed towards the next temple. Unlike some other temples, this one knew how to take care of walking pilgrims.

The morning long past, the humid summer air ensured the forest shade made little difference as I fought gravity down the steep path and my body relinquished the last of its essential fluids. I took a quick swallow from my recently refilled water bottles, so desperate for a drink that I dismissed the strange taste as a product of the plastic bottle. Past ancient moss-covered stone statues, the *henro* path let me out into someone's backyard. No one appeared to be home as I trespassed through. The path wound its way between crumbling ancient stone walls to the river valley below, where a lone elementary school sat deserted in the depopulated valley. Elderly women, their husbands nowhere in sight, worked in small gardens, vigorously reshaping the land.

Japan is facing a population crisis that has been brewing ever since the end of World War II. 2005 marked the first year that the number of deaths exceeded the number of births, resulting in a negative growth rate and a perpetually graying population.

The Japanese government is, of course, worried about the situation and has pushed to make the working environment more hospitable for pregnant women. I witnessed the result firsthand when one of my colleagues was laid off when she told the school board she was pregnant. Graciously, her boss said she was not being fired but merely her contract was not being renewed. The new environment allowed her to avoid the social stigma of being fired.

The Japanese countryside, and villages like the one I was walking through, has been hardest hit by the decreasing birth rate, as most young people have moved to the cities to find work and escape the inconvenience of country life. Trains, malls, restaurants, supermarkets, mobile network coverage, arcades, and convenience stores, all the advances of modern Japan, were far from the slow-paced village.

I WALKED along the river until the path plunged back into the woods, leaving the farms behind, and started the 1,700-foot climb to Tairyū-ji, The Temple of the Great Dragon. Taking a preparatory sip of water, I spit it out, finally realizing that something was wrong. The water tasted foul, and as I examined my two bottles, I saw hundreds of brown flakes floating around. Toilets are few and far between, and it would be horrible to get diarrhea during the long hike in the summer heat ahead of me. The hose I used to fill up the water bottles must have not been used recently, with bacteria and algae incubated by the moist air. Reluctantly, I poured the water out. I still had a couple of hours of climbing left, and now no water.

The path started pleasantly enough, along a stream to a small rice paddy hidden deep in the mountain. Several abandoned, rusted cars squatting nearby ruined the magical moment. I took out my camera anyway and, as I had done with so many of my pictures, I excluded the trash and misled my viewers with the curated beauty found all over Japan.

The trail left the stream far below as it mercilessly climbed the mountain. Full dehydration set in shortly after, and I started dry heaving my way up the path, stumbling often. Dizzy and soaked with sweat, my legs began to stiffen and cramp. Eyes downcast, I froze just in time as a pit viper, *mamushi*, slithered out from under the leaves below my raised foot. I used my staff to keep my balance until the viper passed safely to the edge of the path. Adrenaline burned away my fatigue, and two hours later I came to a lone gate marking the beginning of the expansive temple that covered the mountaintop further up.

As is customary, I stopped just short of the entrance, bowed, and asked permission to enter. I stepped over the large wooden beam at the center of the gate and into the sacred grounds. Evil spirits have many powers, but apparently lifting their feet 10 inches is not one of them, and they are unable to cross the barrier. Another series of steep steps greeted me before I reached the top of the mountain, where Kūkai visited in his formative years. Before I could worry about my spiritual needs,

I locked my mouth around a nearby faucet, gulping down a few liters before even noticing the beauty around me.

A two-story pagoda sat further up, hidden inside the forest-covered mountaintop. At the edge of a nearby cliff, a large statue of a sitting Kūkai juts out into the surrounding mountains to mark the place he meditated and performed esoteric rituals on his quest for enlightenment.

Despite countless stories associating Kūkai with various temples around Shikoku, Tairyū-ji is one of the few temples where he actually confirmed his presence himself in his book *Sangō shiiki*. According to his own account, between the ages of 15 and 19, he performed the Morning Star Meditation and chanted a mantra one million times: "The valley reverberated to the resounding echoes of my recitation until the morning star Venus appeared in the sky." He failed to achieve enlightenment and set off farther down the coast in search of more wild lands.

I wondered how accurate his count could have been. Who can count to a million before getting a bit thrown off? I'm sure I was focusing on the wrong part of the story.

Today, the modern pilgrim need not bother with the difficulties of ascetic discipline or laboring up the steep path. Just below the pagoda sits a cable car, the longest in western Japan at 9,104 feet, which transports *henro* and tourists up to the top of the mountain so they never have to break a sweat. For those feeling slightly more adventurous, a road winds two-thirds of the way up the mountain to a parking lot, from which they can struggle for enlightenment at their own pace.

It was at this parking lot, on my way down, that I encountered Yūto puffing his way up the back side of the mountain. I was shocked to see him again, so far ahead of me and coming from the wrong direction.

"Todo-san, good afternoon!"

"Good afternoon. How are you?" I said, stealing a look at his feet to see how his limp was.

"I am good. Sorry, I am in a rush to get to the top. Good luck," he called back to me, as he pushed past without even pausing. His limp was gone, and he looked tired but healthy. It was a remarkable turnaround, just like I had pulled myself together years ago. I was amazed to see him doing so well.

I continued for another 45 minutes and eventually reached a roadside rest stop, seemingly designed just to house the six vending machines before me. My drink of choice was Pocari Sweat. The name evoked images of a little mythical creature being squeezed of all its sweat in some horrible factory hidden deep in the mystical Japanese mountains. If you can get past the name, the drink itself is great. A sports drink, similar to Gatorade, it rehydrated and provided much-needed sugars. The other machines were filled with hot and cold coffee and tea, sodas, and fruit juices that contained only 1 percent actual juice. Vitamin drinks dominated another corner, promising vital vitamin D or 1,000 lemons' worth of vitamin C.

Sticking to my Sweat, I set off and was almost run over by a cycling *henro* as I stepped out onto the road. Quickly turning around for another pass to finish me off, the *henro* careened towards me, manically ringing his bell. *Chring. Chring. Chring.* He slammed on the brakes just before crashing and lifted his hat-covered face. Yūto beamed with pleasure as he rang the bell once more.

"You bought a bike!" I exclaimed, not without a bit of sadness as comprehension flooded over me. He had taken the easy way out rather than pushing through the pain.

"Yeah. I was about to give up on the advice of my parents. I was walking towards Tokushima station when it suddenly hit me. I called them, they agreed, reluctantly, and I was set." He couldn't hide his pleasure, and his smile infected me too. "My feet don't hurt anymore, and I will be able to finish in just 10 days or so. Isn't it great?"

"Yeah, wow." Before I could add any more, he was back on his bike, riding circles around me before finally waving his staff in one hand as he rode away. *Chring. Chring. Chring.*

I was happy, sad and jealous all at the same time as I set off on the hot, deserted road for Temple Twenty-Two and then on to my home for the night, a small gazebo next to a dam.

I WAS NOT DISTURBED EVEN ONCE by a passing car. Quiet and flat, I enjoyed the stroll through the backcountry roads until the *henro* path left the road and turned off into the woods again. I crossed ridges covered in cedar, and the path dropped suddenly into a tunnel of green bamboo as thick as my leg. The breeze sent the towering stalks clacking into each other as I floated my way along the soft leaves that covered the path.

I exited into a quaint farming village surrounded by bright green rice paddies, before rounding the corner and getting my first glimpse of Temple Twenty-Two, The Temple of Equality, and its unusual guest. Standing at the base of stone stairs leading to the temple was the scruffiest looking *henro* I had seen yet. Shoulders rolled in a perpetual slouch, he stood with a bowl and prayer beads in his left hand, staff in the right, chanting the Heart Sutra repeatedly. A straw *henro* hat, the tip ripped and frayed, covered his graying hair, and a wispy mustache framed his murmuring mouth. Baggy jeans met his green, fashionable classic Adidas Superstar shoes and hid the contours of his lower body. His white *henro* shirt, sleeves rolled up to the shoulders, was open wide at the chest, exposing his ribs and revealing a scrappy, lean body.

I watched from a safe distance as an older *henro* couple dressed in flawlessly white *henro* paraphernalia descended the temple stairs and dropped a 1,000-yen bill in his bowl, before driving away in a luxury van. Once the couple were safely out of sight, the begging *henro* deftly slipped the note into his jeans pocket, took a few coins out of the bowl, and bought a hot can of coffee from one of the vending machines.

As I approached, he yelled without turning around. "Hey. Where ya headin' today?" he grunted at me in the rough Japanese that has been adopted by tough guys nationwide. Coffee can in hand, he slouched against the stone staircase leading up the mountain.

"Hi," I said. "A little ways further to the dam." I did not want to give him precise details. Japan is a relatively safe place, but something about his demeanor and the fact that he was begging at the temple set off warning bells.

"Ah, yeah, the gazebo . . . don't go there, it's no good," he said. "There's a place right around the corner from here; it's free and has a shower."

"Well, it's still early and I have more walking to do today." It was only 2:00 p.m., and I had walked just 12.7 miles. Half of that covered two mountain peaks. "Thanks, but I'll be okay." I ended the conversation and headed up the stairs.

As I left the Temple of Equality, the begging *henro* was waiting for me.

"Here, I drew you a map to the rest house," he grunted as he pushed a torn piece of paper into my hands.

"Yeah, but this place isn't listed in my places to sleep, and I have more to walk today," I countered. "I am better off just having lunch here and then heading to the dam."

"There's no water at the dam. No toilet either."

"The map says there is."

"Map's wrong."

"Thanks. I'll think about it." Not intending to do anything of the sort, I dug into my pack for a 100-yen coin to drop in his bowl for the information and the map, and probably to placate him.

"Keep it. I don't accept money from walking *henro*, only those pretty white *henro* who drive."

"Stay safe." I shouldered my pack and was two steps past when I heard the incomprehensible mumbling chants start back up behind me.

To regain some strength, I headed towards the only restaurant in the small hamlet. I found it shuttered and dark, the note on the door advising me to come back in the fall. The lack of food affected my plan significantly, as there were no more shops on the way to the dam. Nowhere to get lunch, dinner, water, or breakfast for the morning killed any idea I had of moving on for the day.

I looked at the hand-drawn map and decided to give it a try. After a short 200-yard walk, I came to a traffic light. A prefabricated building sat at the intersection. A sign on the door directed me to seek permission at the small hardware shop across the street that sponsored the *tsuyadō*.

"Sure, but there might be others staying the night," the old man in a blue apron said as he squeezed his way in between the shop's two aisles.

I limped to the rest house and entered a small room with wall-to-wall *tatami* mats that could sleep three to four people comfortably. The room was sparsely furnished with a bookshelf, plastic coffee table, and a small TV with rabbit ear antennae. The shower was outside in the back, and a small washing machine sat next to the front door. I still needed food. I consulted the map and found a small supermarket about a half mile in the opposite direction from the path. I decided to give myself an early day and bought lunch, dinner, and breakfast for the next morning.

Back at the house, I washed my clothes, took a shower, and attended to my feet. Blisters covered both heels and had found their way between each toe, as well as on each pad. My feet were in bad shape and getting worse with each step. I hoped the unexpected early end to the day would help them heal faster.

A few hours later, as I lay on the *tatami*, feet elevated and throbbing, the sliding door crashed open and the oily, somewhat musty odor of the begging *henro* assaulted the room.

Suzuki-san had been begging at the temple for the past three days, trying to support his next section of the walk. He was 30 years old and from a small farming village in Tokushima, where he helped his parents work the land. For the past year he had walked the Shikoku pilgrimage and was on his fourth and final time around the island. I felt like an imposter on the trail, compared to Suzuki-san. Here was a guy who didn't care about time or money. He was just walking and living a pure *henro* life.

"When did you first start begging?" I asked, secretly peeking into his bowl to see how much he had pulled in.

"After one and a half times around, I ran out of money, so I put out a bowl on the advice of another *henro*. It's good money if you have the time, but you have to stay in one spot if you want to make enough coin." He cinched his belt, securing it at the last of a series of handmade holes. As he settled in, he pulled out a dog-eared, faded magazine about hot springs and fancy hotels in Shikoku. Despite having reviewed the same options hundreds of times before, he lovingly read each page as we chatted about life on the trail.

Once you get past initial formalities, *henro* typically begin to silently rank each other. Are you walking or driving? In a bus or in a car? If you are both walking, then you keep exchanging information until one of you is determined as the toughest. Do you sleep in hotels or outside? How many miles do you walk each day? How many times have you walked?

Those who walk and camp outside each night are

performing the pilgrimage in its most traditional manner, the closest to ascetic discipline, and the ranking decreases from there depending on physical exertion and difficulty. Despite leaving society behind and donning the white shirt, pilgrims still structure themselves in a way that mirrors Japanese rankings and cultural norms that they seek to escape.

Suzuki-san was a poor rural farmer, far removed from the Tokyo elites who sat behind desks 14 hours a day. On Shikoku he commanded the highest of respect in the *henro* pecking order, walking over 40 miles a day when he did move, and circling multiple times. After a year of being broke and homeless, his obsession with luxury hot springs made sense.

"When I finish my fourth circle, I can get certified as a guide at the first temple." He flipped through the magazine and then went back a few pages as if to confirm something.

"So, you'll be a guide for bus tours?"

"I don't know. Maybe I will just go back to the farm." He lit a cigarette and turned on the TV.

I was exhausted, hot, and it was past my bedtime. It was 8:00 p.m. and Suzuki-san was just getting started after standing in one place all day. All he wanted was to stay up late watching fuzzy TV.

Before I tried to win a losing battle with the noisy TV and sleep, we made plans to meet the next day at Hashimoto-san's bus, near Temple Twenty-Three, the last official temple in Tokushima Prefecture. I'd leave first and then he'd catch up later, once he woke up. It was nice to have someone to talk about the walk with. Still, before nodding off, I slid my money and passport out of my bag and into my sleeping bag.

6

FREEMASONS ARE BAD

Some days don't go well, no matter how hard you try and how well you plan.

Suzuki-san slept peacefully as I left early in the morning, turning my attention to the south. From here the temples spread out at probably the same rate the population decreases. Temple Twenty-Four sits on the southeastern point of Shikoku, on Cape Muroto. Almost 59 miles away, the distance weighed on my mind. Only Temple Twenty-Three, my destination for the day, was left to break up the walk. Leaving the mountain paths and the busy city behind, the trek down to Cape Muroto is a hard slog along the hot pavement of Route 55. This meant that planning ahead became all the more important as the population and access to food thinned out.

I had agreed to meet Suzuki-san at Hashimoto-san's bus, near Temple Twenty-Three in the beautiful bay town of Hiwasa. Where to sleep is probably the most important decision walking *henro* face, and the availability of decent places sets each day's pace and destination. To help me reduce the stress of uncertainty, I needed to get better at picking my destination each day, and even planning where to sleep two or three days in advance. I planned to walk 13 miles, then 22, and 16 miles over the following days, spending the night in a bus, a free inn, and then a gazebo with a toilet just past Cape Muroto at Temple Twenty-Five. Each place marked my goal for the day, breaking the enormity of 750 miles into manageable segments.

Picking where to camp outside was a strategic choice, balancing the availability of shelter from possible rain (i.e. a roof), water, toilets, privacy, noise, and the feelings of your host neighborhood. I had to be welcome first; after that, a roof and water were my next priorities. Nothing beats being able to wash off the grime and car exhaust of a long day and refresh weary feet—except, of course, not waking up to a sudden downpour with nowhere to take cover. All things being equal, I tried to choose places away from the main road yet still along the *henro* path to avoid extra steps.

Due to scheduling conflicts, I never stayed in train stations. I needed to sleep by 8:00 p.m. and get up by 5:00 each morning. The schedules of commuters went well past 8:00 p.m., making a good night's sleep all but impossible.

Hashimoto-san's bus was a *tsuyadō* and thus preferable to all the nature-based options. It was a converted commuter bus filled with *tatami* mats, blankets, and even a TV. Parked in front of Hashimoto Restaurant across the street from Temple Twenty-Three, walking pilgrims who stayed received the added *osettai* of a free dinner. To get there, I first had to make a choice: follow quieter roads along the coast through quaint villages and backroads, or trudge along the busy Route 55 and shave almost two miles off the trip.

The decision came quickly as I reached the base of the dam where I had planned to spend the night in a *henro* hut, a recent class of gazebos erected by local communities to support walking *henro*. Suzuki-san was right—there was neither water nor a toilet at the hut, making it nearly worthless for a walker, except as a pleasant place to take a break. Across the dam, a remote temple had a toilet and water, competing in practicality if not accessibility.

To save my feet, I chose the shorter route and plodded along the narrow, busy main road, praying nothing would hit me from behind. Without warning, a plain white van whizzed past, knocking my hat off. It screeched to a halt at an alarming angle just in front of me.

A man wearing a light gray jumpsuit jumped out of the driver's seat and rushed towards me with all the intensity of a kidnapper. He stopped just before crashing into me and bowed. "Good morning, *ohenro*-san," he said. "We can give you a ride to Hiwasa." He gestured to the van, just as a bald, crinkled old head popped out of the passenger side window.

"Thank you, but I'm walking only." I bowed back, praying silently that the temptation would disappear quickly over the next rise.

"It's dangerous to walk on the road, plus it's a long way to Hiwasa."

"Thank you, but it's just as dangerous on all the other roads around Shikoku, and it's even further to Temple Eighty-Eight." I shrugged helplessly, showing off my staff to punctuate my argument.

He looked disappointed. "Be safe," he said, then turned around and jumped back into his van in a magnificent leap. He sped away, leaving me with a gift of exhaust.

I hit the first of many tunnels at the top of a pass before Route 55 began winding its way down into the fishing village of Hiwasa. I flicked on a blinking red bicycle light I attached to my pack earlier and plunged into the darkness of a rural Japanese tunnel, the pinpoint light at the end my only reference point. There were no lights to guide cars and trucks safely through, and there were no walkways for pedestrians. The tunnel became a death trap towards the middle as it narrowed even further.

Despite all the drawbacks, I liked tunnels and looked forward to them. The cool air provided a temporary reprieve from the humid, sun-scorched air, and the acoustics were great for belting out the songs that had started getting stuck on repeat in my mind over long days lost in thought. That was until a speeding delivery truck forced me to quickly press myself flat against the cool concrete wall.

It was only 10:30 a.m. as I reached the outer fringes of Hiwasa and came across the shocking sight of Hashimoto-san's bus. It had been moved to a deserted dirt parking lot on the outskirts of town. The only sign of life came from a vibrating washing machine, which sat outside in front of the silver bus. I poked my head in to find the owner of the wash, but no one was around, just his or her laundry set on spin.

I continued and a mile later arrived at Temple Twenty-Three, The Temple of the Medicine King, and its long stone staircase leading to views of the rooftops and the small bay bobbing with aging fishing boats. The temple is famous for dispelling evil forces working against you. As I climbed, women and men were busy placing one-yen coins on each step to protect them from bad luck during dangerous years. In Japan, people believe there are certain years when misfortune is more likely to strike. For men, things get hairy starting at mid-life, through ages 41, 42, 51, 52, 60, and 61. Women, it seems, need to be careful for most of their lives, through ages 19, 30, 33, 37, 51, and 61. Women placed coins up to step 33, while men continued to the last, 42nd, step.

I ate lunch at Hashimoto Restaurant, across the temple, where I overheard Mr. Hashimoto talking to two young men, dressed in head-to-toe leather, touring Shikoku on their motorcycles. When you offer free lunch, you become a popular guy, and after they exchanged hugs the issue of the bus came up.

"Yeah, well, I had to move it," Hashimoto-san said. "Too many people were staying in it, and with the new rest stop opened up next door, I have been losing a lot of business." He shrugged his shoulders helplessly. "Plus, one night a couple of drunken *henro* broke into my restaurant looking for more beer. I had the bus towed to the outskirts of town the next day."

Plans change quickly on the *henro* path, and I had another decision to make. After filling up on beef *udon* and ice water, I decided it wasn't worth staying at the bus. The prospect of backtracking a mile seemed like the worst idea available, and it was still early in the day. My three-day plan was shot, and I needed to find a new place to camp for the night.

While I thought about what to do, I decided to do some minor foot surgery. My feet were in constant pain, and I popped two pain pills that were becoming like candy to me. I had been medicating morning, noon, and night for the past six days, which was not a sustainable solution. I had lost my needle the previous night, so I pulled out a bent, dirty nail I found on the ground and sterilized it with my lighter. I had just started lancing my blisters when I caught the two bikers staring at me like I was injecting myself with heroin.

After an hour's rest, I began to feel better about my decision to hike another twelve and a half miles. Suzuki-san would understand. He had been walking long enough to know these things happen. I doubted I would ever get the chance to explain why I didn't wait for him.

BESIDES THE TWO red-butt monkeys playing by the side of the road on my way out of Hiwasa, and the dramatic drop in car and truck traffic, there was little to mark the new stage of my journey away from Tokushima's 23 temples and on to Kōchi. The road shyly avoided the coast. Salt air, carried through occasional gaps in the surrounding mountains, was the only proof of the ocean on the other side. There was nothing to do but push on, one foot in front of the other, for hours on end. I examined every passing item in detail.

On long walks you become a part of the environment and notice things that others, who live in the area but pass by in cars, might ignore every day. A rusted sign becomes a curiosity, a broken tree sets off a 20-minute mental debate on how it met its fate. You think of family members and friends and, wish they were with you. You realize how important they are and vow to never take them for granted again.

Since graduating from university, for six years I had spent my time and money traveling around Japan and Southeast Asia. I rarely sent out notes to friends, and at one point I forgot to call my parents for two years straight. My mom was not impressed. It all seemed perfectly normal at the time—interesting experiences were everywhere, and there was only so much time. Now, I thought about my family constantly. I wanted to let my parents know how much they mattered to me. Of course, I had isolated myself on the pilgrimage, and that was not going to happen.

You sing songs, you wish someone would stop to chat, and you never forget the throbbing pain in your feet. But the mind comes up with a million topics and ways to keep you from thinking about your life right now and what you want to do in the future. Decisions are pushed to later; there is plenty of time.

When you discover the world on foot, everything you used to know in life changes. You no longer think in terms of time spent traveling but in distance covered. A mile becomes a long way and each step is a calculated decision. You avoid stepping up on curbs as you will have to step back down, and over a month those extra steps add up. Time slows down and life becomes simplified to its bare essentials: water, food, shelter, and companionship. There are no appointments to keep, you don't have to worry about your stressed-out boss or buying the latest gadget. Actually, the last thing you want is more stuff.

Days of the week mean nothing, and time is dependent on the sun, not the mechanics of man. The world becomes a bigger place, and your life but a speck in the infinite universe.

And so, I walked, wrapped in the colors and smells of the road. My staff bell jingled and thumped rhythmically. This was now my job; it was what I did and, increasingly, it was who I was becoming.

Emerging from a tunnel, I was immediately comforted by a strong sea breeze as I reached my destination. Deep blue sea blended seamlessly with blue skies, broken only sparingly by distant evergreen islands and sharp brown rocks bursting out of the ocean, gasping for air. I walked on a bridge over a small rock-strewn beach. Below me a family was packing up after a long day of swimming.

Two young boys ran around naked, their mother desperate to catch them in towels. The grandmother began to pull off her heavy black bathing suit. Thinking better of it, she took a cautionary look around until our eyes locked. Without a care in the world, she turned around and dropped her bathing suit. I hurried on, embarrassed and blushing.

I increased my pace until a stone *henro* marker directed me down a small road to *Bangai* Four, Saba Daishi, the Temple of the Mackerel Daishi, where a *tsuyadō* awaited me.

Bangai are literally "outside the number" temples that are not included in the official 88 temples but are affiliated with the pilgrimage route. Officially, there are 20 *bangai*, which means there are 108 total temples to visit if you include them. One hundred and eight is an important number in Buddhism and represents temptations that humans have to overcome in order to reach nirvana. Most *bangai* receive few pilgrims because they are off the main path. Others, like Saba Daishi, have marketed themselves well due to location and a creative sense of history.

If you read the temple's founding story today, it says that while visiting the temple, Kūkai (who was given the posthumous name

Kōbō Daishi) asked a fishmonger for some dried mackerel. The seller refused and moved on, when suddenly his horse collapsed. Realizing his mistake, he begged Kūkai for forgiveness, threw in some free mackerel, and miraculously, his horse recovered. Going a step further, Kūkai took one of the dried fish and brought it back to life, releasing it into the picturesque bay across the street. In reality, it was a monk named Gyōki who supposedly cursed and then cured the horse. It was not until sometime in the 18th or 19th century that the name gradually shifted to Kūkai in the founding legend.

The shrine was an uninhabited worship hall until 1945, when an enterprising young pilgrim turned monk moved in and marketed it to the passing *henro*. Add in two fire walking ceremonies a year, a lodge for the 100,000 bus pilgrims that pass right by on Route 55, one large body of water, and a national coastline park, shake well and bake for 55 years in the subtropical heat, and you get a large, thriving "unnumbered" *Bangai* Number Four. Confusing, right?

Despite the reportedly historical liberties, the staff at Saba Daishi were incredibly friendly. They let me stay in their wonderful one-room *tsuyadō*, complete with an electric mosquito repellent, soft futon, and fan. It felt so good I stayed awake as long as possible, trying to keep the morning from coming too quickly.

KŪKAI WALKED this rocky coastline over 1,000 years ago, picking his way over mountains, forced to descend into small bays in search of food on his long trek down to Cape Muroto. The geography limits the potential population of the area, as towering mountains rise steeply from the rocky ocean, leaving no beach to traverse. Route 55 clings precariously to the side of the mountains, only occasionally moving through sparsely inhabited villages thankful for the little flat land available. Even the train, the consistent symbol of Japanese ingenuity that travels through the remotest regions, gives up halfway down the coast and returns to Tokushima, humbled.

Just before I entered Kōchi Prefecture, a deserted *henro* rest station showed me that little had changed in the past millennia. A hand-drawn map warns walking *henro* to be careful and highlights a "dead zone" of roughly eight and a half miles where there are no toilets, water, or shops. Located right in the middle of the zone is the Bukkai hermitage, where I planned to camp out on the advice of the accommodation crib sheet I'd received at Temple One.

As I passed out of Tokushima Prefecture, I left the Land of Awakening Faith and entered the Land of Religious Discipline. Symbolically and physically, the pilgrimage is divided into four stages corresponding to the four prefectures. Symbolism never hurt so much. Basically, the first week kicks your ass and wakes you up to the fact that you need more than just strength to continue. The next stage, the one I was entering now, is where you live with the pain, come to accept it, and let it go. The final two stages, the Lands of Enlightenment, and then Nirvana, were too far ahead both mentally and physically to give much attention to. My greater concern was the 21 miles that I planned to hike that day—not an overly ambitious day but still one that deserved a fast pace.

The view as I walked the road down to the cape was monotonous in its beauty, revealing itself all at once, secure in its enormity and endlessness. It was hard to tell whether I was moving at all as the rocky coast, rolling sea, and enclosing mountains stretched endlessly north and south. Only the appearance of weather-beaten hamlets, clinging to the rocky coast, helped to mark any progress. Wearily, I passed the day pounding my body against the asphalt, until I noticed a handwritten sign inviting walking *henro* to rest, which appeared as suddenly as the town that housed it.

Attached to a small guest house, catering to surfers looking for quick access to the reef break just off the rocky shores, was Da Hawaiian Kitchen. Its surfboard-shaped sign proudly announced it was at once a burger joint and an internet café. The relaxed, soulful sounds of Jack Johnson flowed out of the café as a Sponge Bob balloon waved happily at me in the wind, convincing me it was time to take a break. Burgers, music, and internet—proof that God really did exist.

Another *henro* was already taking advantage of the picnic table and free oolong tea in a dispenser nearby. He was dressed in shorts and a sleeveless white *henro* shirt that was ripped and retied on one shoulder. Prayer beads hung from his neck, while a pilgrimage-themed bandana, like my own, covered his head. Busy drawing a large ink pen Buddha, he didn't notice me until I stood at the table with a drink in my hand.

"Hey, you're white!" he exclaimed. His face broke into a nearly toothless grin. The few teeth he'd managed to save were stained dark yellow and framed by a wild three-day facial shadow. Long, oily rivulets of gray hair shot out from his round head.

I complimented him on his keenness of eye.

Taizan-san was from Tottori Prefecture, on Japan's northern coast, and on his second pilgrimage. The first time around he drew pictures of the temples and was responsible for the decorations plastered on the walls of Sakae Taxi. This time around he was drawing all of the temple Buddhas. He was on day 12 and had already inked more than 100 drawings. His relaxed attitude seemed limited to his own lifestyle. It didn't take long before he found fault in the way I was walking and living my life.

"You're walking too fast. Slow down. You need to enjoy

where you are." Walking in straw sandals helped ensure that he wasn't going to break any speed records.

"Where are you sleeping tonight? Here at the inn?" I asked, trying to change the topic.

"Bah. See, this is what is wrong with you. I don't know. I never know where I am going to sleep at night. That's your problem. You keep wanting plans to be made and set. You can't live like that." He never looked up from his painting.

I took his words in and thought them over. I had limited time and money and had to do the pilgrimage in my own way. What other choice was there but to adapt to my circumstances?

"All other *henro* are too concerned about getting from point to point. Every day you try to reach a certain point. That's not a good enough reason to walk. You need more. I walk until I stop, and then I sleep when I get tired." He rounded off the halo over the Buddha's head.

Instinctively I fought back to defend my choices, my way of life. "Yeah, but you need to have a place to sleep if it rains."

"Animals don't care if it rains. We need to be more like them. If I'm on a step and I get sleepy, I stop and sleep, right there. If I'm on the side of the road, I do the same thing."

I was too tired to argue.

I kept quiet and started nodding politely. I wasn't convinced by his strategy to get hit by cars and picked over by stair-climbing monkeys and wild boars. I enjoyed talking with him, but we just had very different views. As I got up to eat the burger I had ordered earlier at the café, he gave me some final parting advice. "Don't worry about where you are going or how far you get. Just enjoy where you are. You'll make more friends that way."

Either influenced by the artistic *henro* or feeling confident in the few miles I had left to walk, I took my time to really enjoy the cheeseburger and a double helping of french fries. Watching the surfers rise and fall on the break below, listening to music from home, and stuffing my face with grease made me never want to leave. For a brief moment—two full hours—I felt that I had stepped back into the comfortable embrace of society.

I left to the artist's protests that I should slow down and seek enlightenment. Easy to say for the guy content to hang out at the only burger joint for miles.

IT WAS hard to let his criticism go, and I spent the rest of the day, mind spinning, trying to justify my pace and decisions. Four hours later I neared my destination and began looking for the small road leading to the Bukkai hermitage. I limped into a small valley in the middle of the "dead zone."

Village houses huddled against the back of the valley, built as far away from the unpredictable coastline as possible, forming an arc around the community's rice paddies. The whole town seemed to be out working the paddies dressed in knee-high rubber boots and gray jumpsuits. The warmer weather on the southern coast pushed up the harvesting timetable, and rice cutters drove back and forth across the yellow-green landscape, while other villagers gathered discarded rice stalks and hung them to dry.

The hermitage was easy to spot, its enormous trees and crooked wooden building an oasis in the middle of the rice fields.

I approached a middle-aged man in a gray jumpsuit who was supervising his elementary-school-aged son busy driving the rice harvester, possibly for his first time. "Excuse me," I said, "I'm a walking *henro*. Is it okay if I stay at the hermitage tonight?"

My innocent question set off a flurry of activity as the father sent the boy off to find someone, anyone, else.

"Sorry," he said, clearly agitated, "I don't live here. We rent this land from someone in the village. We aren't from here and are just down to harvest the rice." He turned back to his task.

Eventually, I found the caretaker raking leaves behind the hermitage. He looked to be about 90, but his body was still taut and muscular from a life of constant work. He had barely looked me over as I started to bow, and he shouted "*Dame!*"

"I'm sorr...."

"Bad!" he repeated again in Japanese to eliminate any doubt. Then he turned and walked away without another word.

Stunned by his rudeness, I didn't know what to do. It was not common practice to show such emotions in Japan. Maybe this was why the first man had been so agitated? It was just past 4:00 p.m. and I had taken my time walking just over 20 miles, as the free-room sheet indicated that the hermitage was a safe place to sleep.

I turned to the rice farmer to see if he could help. But he had quietly returned to his son, looking anywhere but in my direction. Maybe it was my imagination, but the rest of the farmers shifted their bodies away from me. Reality sucked the wind out of me. There was no help to be had here.

There was nowhere else to sleep close by. In fact, the map didn't show anywhere within a 12-mile radius until Temple Twenty-Four. The dead zone was living up to its name. I had promised myself at the beginning of the pilgrimage that I would accept it when help was not given, and now that promise was being tested. Tired and sore, I had no other choice but to move on. The map at least showed a bathroom five and a half miles away, perched on a cliff next to the ocean. I also hoped for some water and flat ground to sleep on. It was the only lead I had, so I set out once again, hoping to find something sooner.

Blisters continued to form on my feet, and my pace slowed dramatically. The sun quickly withdrew behind the towering mountains as I trod through lonely stretches of nothing but rock and water.

After four miles, as night settled in, I found myself in a small harbor village. I came across a quiet middle school, the gates closed and the grounds deserted. It would have been simple to climb the fence and collapse under the tin roofing of the bicycle parking area.

I couldn't bring myself to do it, despite the pain and a worsening limp. I had worked in both elementary and junior high schools, and I knew that the fear of strangers was real to teachers and parents. Over the years schools have been the target for bizarre crimes.

One year, while all the seventh graders at the rural junior high school where I worked were taking swimming lessons, a pervert slipped into the girls' changing room. They returned from the pool to find holes in all of their panties. The creep cut out the bottoms and presumably sold them on the now illegal used panty market. That there used to be a legal used panty market is disturbing enough, the fact that they were profitable even more so.

I moved on, limping through a tunnel that let out into a group of prefabricated houses on the right and a 20-foot concrete storm wall on the left. Being boxed in with nowhere to go but forward dampened my spirits even further. It had been a long day, 15 hours walking. The idea of quitting was starting to become a real possibility. But before I could venture down that dark road, I heard someone yelling. From the window of a passing car, a young boy, no more than eight or nine years old, popped his head out from the back window.

"Good luck, *henro*-san," he yelled, waving me on before he disappeared around a corner.

The kind words worked their way into my spine. I lifted my head, straightened my back, and limped on. Joy swelled, and I was convinced God, or Kūkai, or something had reached down and touched me. This was my first touch of what is known as pilgrim's mind. It is a common effect of pilgrimages, in which you start to enter a new state of reality where everything is connected, and small things take on larger mystical significance.

A mile and a half later, I rounded a corner, and a rocky promontory, dropping sharply into the ocean far below, lay before me. A narrow dirt road led to the base of three natural giant rock towers, two of which were married with rice straw ropes. Folded paper in the shape of lightning bolts swayed in the wind, marking them as sacred in Shintoism. The rocks represent the union of the creator god Izanagi to Izanami and, by extension, the marriage of men and women. The third rock, towering over the others, stood stoically alone, giving no indication as to why it was unsuitable for marriage.

I rounded the newlyweds to find a wooden gazebo perched at the edge of a 50-foot cliff. Uninterrupted seas spread infinitely into the distance. Salty, sticky air filled my nose as waves crashed in my ears. It was the most beautiful sight I had ever seen. I stumbled down the hill to the waiting embrace of my new home, into the arms of its peculiar resident.

A short, muscular pilgrim with a shaved head was hanging up his laundry along a line strung from one gazebo pole to the next.

"Excuse me," I said, waiting for him to turn around. "Is it all right if I stay here tonight with you?" I thought I was just being polite but was shocked by his answer.

"Sorry, there is only one bench." He looked nervous and began to twitch. He turned away, as if that would be the end of it.

After such a long day and with nowhere else to go, I was not about to be kicked out. I shrugged off my pack. "It's okay. I can just sleep on the concrete floor." I smiled and turned to unpacking, leaving no room to negotiate further.

He went back to hanging his laundry.

A stiff, steady wind blew off the ocean, promising a cool night without mosquitoes.

While being ignored, I tended to my feet. The extended walk had caused new blisters to cover my heels, and they had relentlessly taken over all my toes. The toilet was broken, but someone had rigged a black hose to the water supply, so I could at least wash my feet and body. Camp sandals are essential and allow for a bit of luxury after a difficult day. Nothing feels quite like slipping off your shoes after a long hike, allowing fresh air and water to bathe away the sweat and heat. Your feet swell from the day's effort, and their freedom from confinement, at least until morning, can't be beat.

Accepting the inevitable, the bald pilgrim greeted me when I returned from washing up. His large black pack rested against a wheeled pull cart stuffed with clothes, books, and various personal effects any sane pilgrim could do without for a month. Hashimoto-san was no ordinary pilgrim, not least because his sanity was certainly in question.

At 53 years old, he had been walking the pilgrimage for the past seven years, never stopping as he circled Shikoku. He slept outside each night and accumulated an impressive amount of possessions for a walker. When he acquired too much to move, he shipped items back to his brother in Nagoya, who rented out Hashimoto-san's apartment to help fund his brother's lifestyle. When he needed more money he simply begged at a temple.

"I know how to live long by eating right," he said quickly, as he rummaged through his cart for a book. Beaming, he held it up like a small child. "See, see, here it is. I told you I had it." The book was called *The Natural Diet*.

I listened politely as he described in agonizing detail the exact number of carbohydrates and vegetables one had to eat at exactly what time of day. Disgusted, he looked at the processed fish sausage I stuffed into my mouth, the only protein I could find at the small mom-and-pop store 15 miles back, before the start of the dead zone. It was disgusting, but my body craved protein and fat.

"Nuts are better for you. I am surprised you don't know all of this. You are American after all!"

"What does being American have to do with it?" I asked. No one in Japan had ever extolled the virtues of America's diet to me before, especially given the evidence that half of Americans are overweight, and a substantial percentage are considered obese.

"Of course, the book was written in America. It was a best-seller. I'm sure you know it."

"Sorry, but I haven't ever heard of it." I was convinced that he had fallen prey to a slick marketing technique, the same kind that once convinced the Japanese that Americans eat Kentucky Fried Chicken on Christmas Eve. For years, young men reserved a seat at KFC well in advance to make sure they could bring their girlfriends out on a romantic dinner that night.

There was a childlike innocence to Hashimoto-san that made conversation difficult. It could have been his personality, or the years walking alone, but he didn't seem to be used to being around people or engaging in normal conversations. Everything out of him was a stream of consciousness, jumping from thought to thought without waiting to hear a response. He was earnest and sweet, yet paranoid at the same time.

"I know another pilgrim who has been walking for 11 years. He's a great man. I will walk until 2011. Then I will stop. Hopefully I will have attained enlightenment by then."

"How do you manage to hike all of the mountains with so much stuff?" I asked.

Hashimoto-san shifted uncomfortably. "I don't." He gazed out across the ocean. "For the past two years I have only visited 55 temples each time around. But more and more I think it is important that I visit all 88, just like Kūkai wants us to. I've seen him before. So have others. You need to meditate. Let me tell you how. I will send my stuff to my brother so I can walk to all 88 temples next time around." On and on, his boyish face lit up as he discussed Kūkai, meditation, and a multitude of topics that popped into his head, never in any clear order.

I listened, too tired to respond. He was cute, but I hoped that I would be able to sleep sometime soon. Without warning, his whole demeanor changed.

He grew quiet, leaned closer, and whispered, "You know, the Freemasons control the world. I have a book right here that explains it all. It's a bestseller."

"Yes, I've heard of the..."

"Oh, tell me, how much do you pay each year to be a member?" he asked, suddenly very excited and close to yelling.

"Well, you see . . . I'm not a member. I have no idea how much people pay."

"But you're American, right? This book was written in America." He held up the book accusingly.

"Sorry, but I haven't read it, and like I said, I'm not a Freemason. Sorry . . ." I shrugged my shoulders helplessly, hoping he would calm down.

I'm not sure if he believed me, but he suddenly decided he wasn't going to stay the night in the gazebo. Not with a Freemason sleeping over him. "There's another spot eight miles down the road. I was planning to sleep there tomorrow but I might as well walk there tonight to keep cool. I'm going to meditate in the cave for a week or so."

He threw his wet laundry over his cart, muttering the whole time.

Seven years is a long time to be alone, and I think our talk was too much for him. Having to relate and speak to another person for so long made him uncomfortable. We exchanged name slips, wished each other good luck and safe travels, and then he disappeared up the ramp to the main road, dragging his cart behind him with one arm and clutching his staff with the other.

I settled onto the bench he had left and had the best night's sleep yet, as the wind cooled my body and crashing waves erased my thoughts and fears. I too was glad for the privacy as night descended, and I was no longer forced to make small talk. As sleep overtook me, I was convinced someone was looking out for me and had provided me with exactly what I needed so that I could grow.

Something had happened today, but I needed time to work it out. Surely a large hand was at work to deliver me to this small wooden gazebo, overlooking the most magnificent of watery vistas, in the shadow of wedded rocks. I wondered if the third rock was jealous or happy for their love. Not for the first time, I wondered who I really was.

7

ABANDONED

It never ceases to amaze me how well people in Japan live with conflicting realities. Not everything needs to make sense, and just because history tells us one thing, it doesn't stop everyone from believing the exact opposite. And yet, both can be considered true.

Take the pilgrimage itself as an example. The pilgrimage is a gift from Kūkai. We follow in his footsteps, and at any moment we may meet him, just like Emon Saburō, the first pilgrim from the origin story. This is the common reality on Shikoku. A blend of folk belief and miracles set the residents of Shikoku and the influx of pilgrims on a mad rush around the island to ensure guaranteed enlightenment at death, or some other spiritual quest.

On the other hand, the temple's monks spend their days in lifelong pursuit of enlightenment through meditation and mantras, performed in dimly lit temple halls at dawn, in the attempt to leave worldly desires behind. Many pilgrims seek more immediate rewards, hoping Kūkai will deal out miracles to relieve physical struggles in the here and now. All the temples peddle miracle stories, despite Kūkai's own writings and the historical records indicating a more subdued account.

Kūkai was one of the most accomplished writers of his time,

even developing the hiragana script (one of two syllabaries in Japanese) that is used together with Chinese *kanji* characters in the Japanese language. And yet, in his own words, Kūkai only confirms his presence at three areas of the pilgrimage: his birthplace, Zentsū-ji, Temple Seventy-Five; the mountaintop of Temple Twenty-One; and the windswept Cape Muroto where Temple Twenty-Four digs in its heels.

Despite numerous claims to the contrary, no other proof exists that Kūkai circled the island in any shape similar to today. While his early life was spent searching for enlightenment in the wilds of Shikoku, his later life was spent in the established religious centers of Kyoto and Nara. He ended up on the remote Mt. Kōya, in the middle of the Kii Peninsula, where the center of Shingon Buddhism still sits. It is also the area where the Japanese believe their gods first lived.

Pilgrimages on Shikoku existed long before Kūkai started wandering. The current route incorporates many sites linked to *Shugendō*, a Japanese mountain ascetic religious tradition, and the mountain areas where *yamabushi* (mountain mystics) performed spiritual rituals in secret. Over the years, Shinto animism and spirit worship mixed with Buddhism as it spread from stuffy aristocratic centers to the common folk.

Two monks, En no Gyōja and Gyōki Bosatsu, predecessors of Kūkai, helped expand the common appeal of Buddhism. Like Kūkai, they both found part of their spiritual answers on Shikoku. En was born in 634 CE. He became an unlicensed priest who wandered the countryside doing charitable deeds, preaching a mixture of Shintoism and Buddhism. En is said to have gained his mystical powers by performing ascetic rituals on the summit of Marozan, above Temple Twelve. This practice encouraged others to travel to Shikoku, seeking powers from the gods on remote mountain peaks. En himself was, in the end, exiled far from Shikoku by the imperial family on charges of sorcery.

Gyōki's name is almost as common on Shikoku as Kūkai's, as 30 temples claim him as their founder, even though most scholars doubt he ever visited the island. Born in 670 CE, he was a shaman as much as a Buddhist priest. Like En, he rejected the established government system and preached spiritual awakening to the masses as he wandered the countryside, establishing temples, building bridges, and helping villages develop. Attracting thousands of followers, he alarmed both the Buddhist hierarchy and the government, and was arrested in 717 CE. So as not to waste his talents, he was eventually put to work raising funds for the great Tōdai-ji Buddha in Nara, the world's largest bronze statue of the Buddha.

Kūkai helped to cement the practice of performing religious austerities on sacred mountains due to his years seeking enlightenment on Shikoku. After his death, pilgrims began to travel to Mt. Kōya in Wakayama Prefecture to visit his mausoleum and, eventually, the important places of his life on Shikoku. For almost 800 years, the pilgrimage fermented in a heady mixture of folk belief, esoteric Buddhism, Shinto mysticism, and ascetic austerity.

When the Warring States Period ended in the 1600s after 200 years of near-constant military conflict, the pilgrimage began to take shape as more and more commoners felt free to move about the country. By 1680 the first guidebooks appeared, marking the route that we walk today. Sign markers were gradually added and *henro* lodges built to aid pilgrims, especially commoners, who gradually increased in number and became wealthier once they were granted their own lands. Stories of Kūkai and the miracles he performed spread, and legend turned to fact.

IN A SMALL CAVE cut into the eastern base of Cape Muroto, on the southeastern tip of Shikoku, I looked out across the parking lot to blue skies and frothy seas. History and reality converged in the tiny, damp cave. Behind me incense rolled into the darkness above, shadows danced to the flickering of candles, dripping steadily on the stone shrine. Impossibly bright crabs clicked their way over my feet, their red shells moving over every inch of the wet rock floor. The wind howled outside, battering the temple sitting 50 meters above me through a million tons of rock.

This is where the young Kūkai meditated for three years until he achieved enlightenment, over 1,200 years ago. Kūkai described it as a merging with the universe and wrote, "The morning star, which shines in the sky, entered my mouth." After enlightenment, he took the name Kūkai, which means "sea and sky." It would not be until after his death that the government renamed him Kōbō Daishi, The Great Teacher. What is clear is that Kūkai was here, and that he gained some sort of truth from the universe. It must have been difficult and utterly lonely.

I climbed the steep steps up to Temple Twenty-Four, clutching my hat as the wind fought to rip it away. Cape Muroto is a wild place of jagged, rocky cliffs and stubborn, gnarled vegetation. Lashed constantly by the forces of nature, it is one of Shikoku's two great capes; the other, Cape Ashizuri, marks the southwestern-most point of Shikoku. Both capes are said to be the gateway to the dead as well as the Pure Land, a realm of enlightenment in Buddhist mythology.

Temple Twenty-Four is weathered and worn. After eight days and 148 long miles, I felt the same way as I took shelter under its cedar overhangs. The bones in my feet felt as twisted and deformed as the rocky outcrops. Pain was my reality now, both mental and physical. Every inch of my feet was covered in weeping blisters. A pronounced limp from tendonitis in my left ankle tightened its grip with each step.

I turned the southeastern-most corner and began the even longer 180-mile walk across Kōchi Prefecture to the next cape, Ashizuri. There is a reason this section is called the Land of Religious Discipline. The miles between temples become longer and longer, while the enormity of the task is reflected in the long coastline ahead.

But the path doesn't care how you feel. I picked myself up and headed west along the south coast to Temple Twenty-Five, reminding myself to take it one temple, one day, one step at a time. The paved road covered any sign of the ancient *henro* path and led me towards the port town of Muroto and the Temple of the Illuminating Seaport. The temple sits on a high hill overlooking hundreds of bonito fishing boats, a constant beacon of safety in a perilous business.

Bonito, a skipjack tuna, is smoked, dried, and then shaved into flakes to make *katsuobushi*, an important ingredient in Japanese cooking. It is used to make a broth called *dashi,* which is an essential ingredient in *miso* soup.

But I wasn't in the mood to take in the sites or fish. I let gravity drag me down the smooth stone steps into the waiting embrace of the small town. Seeing another *henro* of roughly the same age, I decided to push my normal shyness away and make the first move. Most of my life I have waited on others to invite me in, worried that I'd be rejected or made to look like a fool. The result, of course, was that I was alone more often than not. If I couldn't fix my feet, maybe I could at least fulfill my need for companionship.

I approached the short *henro* as he left the stamp room at the bottom of the hill. "Excuse me," I said. "I know it's early, but would you like to grab a bite together?"

His blank face brightened instantly, the rest of his teeth suddenly joining his protruding buck teeth in a wide grin. "Yes! How about we take a walk first to Temple Twenty-Six together and find a place to eat nearby?"

Ishii-san was 24 years old and from Osaka. A journalist for one of the main national newspapers, he was quiet but determined. He had been walking for the past two days, covering about 35 miles a day. He only had six days off from work and was determined to get as far as possible. Last year he began from Temple One, and he figured it would take him another two trips back to complete the route. It was the only time he got off of work, and he chose to spend all his vacations pushing his body to the breaking point. After just two days, the miles were wearing him down, and he looked worse than me.

Two miles later we turned off the busy main road and into recently harvested rice paddies. Near the base of a mountain path leading up to the next temple, we found a dull concrete restaurant filled with tourists and rice farmers. Across the street, the farmers' hard work showed in row after row of drying rice bundles, woven together with fiber twine and hanging from large bamboo racks.

It is always risky taking off your hiking shoes during the day, as the feet might swell, making it impossible to put them back on. I decided it was worth it and released them on the unsuspecting diners nearby, confident they would pretend not to notice.

Ishii-san wasn't as brave. "I know how bad my feet are. Better to keep the pressure on them or else I won't be able to continue," he said, turning quickly to the plastic menu.

We savored the 40-minute lunch break. It was the longest break I allowed myself each day, and I was at once happy to have it and sad it would soon end. Deep-fried breaded pork cutlets with egg and onions cooked in *sake* and sugar overflowed from the large bowl in front of me. Underneath, the rest of the bowl was filled with soft Japanese rice. A garnish of spring onions topped it all off, sending me into further bliss as I snapped the wooden chopsticks apart and dove in. Warm miso soup filled with clams and bonito flakes soothed my throat. We filled out bellies without speaking, content to have someone close who understood pain.

It was difficult to leave. It was even more difficult watching Ishii leave without me, but he didn't want to waste any of his short vacation time.

I stayed back for an extra 15 minutes to care for my feet. As always it was painful work, and I downed another three painkillers. The bottle advised only one every six hours. I was up to nine a day. The nearly empty bottle rested reassuringly next to me as I looked at my map and decided to add seven and a half more miles to my day's plan so that I could reach a bathroom by the sea.

It was a hard decision to extend the day by another two hours. It meant I wouldn't arrive at my camp until at least 7:00 p.m. But the following day I would be climbing a mountain, and it was better to walk more miles on flat ground now.

Of course, rational planning didn't make a difference to my body. I was on the edge of collapse. My feet and left ankle throbbed, even after I forced them back into my shoes and started limping towards the next temple. Somewhere in the repressed recesses of my mind, I knew this couldn't continue, but pride pushed me on. I couldn't fail like I thought I had the first time.

I waded through a sea of white-clad bus pilgrims, the first I had seen, as I tried to find Ishii. Two bus tours had converged on Temple Twenty-Six, congesting the alter areas as the tour guides processed the calligraphies and stamps of 60 people. Mass synchronized chants rolled in waves off the mountain top as I struggled against the white eddies of flowing elderly pilgrims, until I found him.

"You're going farther today?" he said. "Can I join you for the night? I don't have a map book and have been staying in hotels each night. I have no idea where to stay."

My heart sang. "Of course!" I gushed, excited by the prospect of sharing the night with someone.

I pulled out my map book before he changed his mind and gave him directions to the toilet by the sea.

"I am going to stay here and rest for a bit, though," Ishii said, finally giving in to reality himself. "My feet are killing me, and I need to rewrap them."

"Sure," I said, "but I need to keep going. I would rather rest at the end of the day."

Two steps later I was lonely again, my staff the only thing holding me up, and the prospect of seeing Ishii later keeping me going.

NOT FOR THE FIRST TIME, I wondered where such weakness came from. A pattern was emerging in my life where I put myself in difficult situations and then chastised myself for not being strong enough to deal with them. Was I in the process of growing, or was I in over my head?

Despite coming to Shikoku with the goal of finally deciding what I wanted to do with my life, I spent the rest of the day distracting myself with pity and repetitive singing rather than really thinking about what type of job would make me happy.

For years I had been trying unsuccessfully to figure out what to do with my life. Before quitting my English teaching job, I had made a list of interests, activities I loved, and possible jobs. The closest I got was something to do with international relations. With a vague idea that I wanted to work internationally and help people, I started studying international aid and conflict resolution at graduate school. It turned out there are hundreds of different career tracks that could bring me on.

I sought professional help and took a personality test offered by my school's career services. After I had spent

$40,000 for the first year, they unhelpfully told me my ideal job was either an adventure guide or a missionary. The tuition I had already paid for the second year was looking less than satisfying. So, where the experts had failed, I was hoping the pilgrimage would help bring clarity. If I had been seeing clearly, I would have noticed that I decided to go on a spiritual adventure to find my answers, seemingly the same answers my personality test gave me.

Instead, the hours passed by in mind-numbing pain, punctuated by expansive views of the rolling blue ocean and sudden gusts of wind as cars and trucks sped by. The landscape was devoid of color, the road and cheaply constructed prefabricated buildings were all gray until a blurry, bright orange shirt cruised past on a bicycle and then was gone just as suddenly around the next corner. I quickened my pace to catch one last glimpse, and as I rounded the corner, I found the smiling girl waiting for me beside the road.

"Hi," I said. "I'm Todd."

Her smile was incredibly bright, lending color back into the weary road. "I'm Kanako," she said quietly, pulling out a water bottle and a small bowl from bags strapped to the back of her bicycle. She pulled off the white towel covering her bike's wire basket on the front to reveal two squirming young salt-and-pepper puppies. "I found them four days ago, abandoned in a sack on the side of the road. No one would take them, so I'm bringing them with me until I can find them homes."

She was unconcerned about where I was from or why I was walking, and we slipped easily into a comfortable conversation about almost everything else. She was 17 years old and was riding around Shikoku for five weeks before she had to return to high school for her senior year in Hiroshima. Open and honest as only innocence can be, she laughed easily, and her personality sparked through her eyes each time she smiled.

"I'm not doing the pilgrimage, just trying to see as much of

Shikoku as possible," she said. "My parents weren't happy with my decision, but they let me go. To be honest, I wasn't prepared for how lonely things could get."

We eased back onto the road, and she pushed her bike next to me. We walked together for the next hour, enjoying the day once again. The miles slipped easily by until we were close to my toilet for the night. We stood outside a small, deserted shop that had been boarded up. Marked in the map book as the last store with food, there was nothing else close by. I would have to backtrack over a mile to buy dinner and breakfast. Dejected, we crossed the street to an equally deserted beach where we sat together in silence as the puppies played in the sand.

The waves rolled on, never breaking their commitment to the beach. I, on the other hand, was losing my grip. My feet were in no shape to walk back to another shop. Kanako's presence opened a new possibility to my situation.

"Can I use your bike?" I asked, a bit too desperately. "I could ride back to the last store and buy food. It won't take long, I promise." I didn't know what I'd do if she said no.

"Of course," she said gently, resting her hand on my shoulder. "We'll wait for you here."

Relieved, I smiled my thanks and got on the bike. I had no other choice. Besides, I was riding back, not ahead, so I was still walking the pilgrimage fully. Desperation fueled my rationalizations as I peddled away.

After walking for over a week, the speed of the bike was a shock. Cool air tickled my hair as I moved seemingly effortlessly. My feet didn't hurt, and I shopped and rode back easily. The constraints of the road, my pace, and my strength were instantly transformed into an overwhelming sense of freedom and mobility. I arrived back at the beach bearing gifts of chocolate for Kanako and a dinner of seaweed encased rice balls for dinner and breakfast.

Feeling better, we hit the road again. A short 10 minutes

later we arrived at what I hoped would be our home for the evening, a parking lot jutting into the ocean on an uninhabited peninsula. A small bathroom sat in one corner, surrounded by tropical palm plants. A hill rose sharply behind, directing all attention to the vast ocean beyond. There was nowhere to seek shelter from the rain or to sleep, other than on the asphalt.

We rested on the ground as I unpacked. The puppies occupied our time and attention as they tried to run away in every direction. The sun sank closer and closer to the end of a long day. I avoided talking about sleep, unwilling to face the fact that Kanako might leave.

For a time, nothing interrupted us, until a blue and red blur rode by, slammed on its breaks, and then cycled back. "Hi, I'm Jun," a young, bespectacled guy said in perfect but accented Japanese. Without waiting for a reply, he climbed off his bicycle and joined us.

Quick to talk and slow to listen, he told us his whole story in one long sentence. He was 22 years old and from South Korea. He was riding all over Japan on a six-week cycling trip, sleeping outside in his tent. He was as lonely as the two of us.

"I'm really glad I found both of you! I haven't met anyone in a few days," he confided.

We laughed and shared stories of the road, about the many kind people we had met and the occasional mean-spirited ones. I was happy. All I needed was for Ishii to arrive and make it a perfect evening.

However, as the sun kissed the horizon, Jun became restless. "Where are you sleeping tonight?" he asked.

"Here," I replied, spreading my hands outwards. "I'm walking and this is the only place close by with running water."

"I see. Well, I'm riding farther tonight," he said. "Do you want to join me?" he asked Kanako.

My heart skipped a beat.

"Sure," Kanako said, without pausing.

Within five minutes we were saying our goodbyes, and I was left alone with the setting sun and the crashing waves. Circumstances had changed quickly, and my rollercoaster emotions even faster. I felt abandoned by both of them. It was irrational, petty, and if I was being honest, rooted in years of feeling inadequate, worried I'd be ridiculed or rejected. Jun had rolled in and ruined everything, but really, I was the problem.

Even lonelier than before, I wished I was stronger and more outgoing. To make up for my shyness, I have sometimes coped by pretending to be outgoing, forcing myself to do things I was uncomfortable with, as if I had something to prove.

The sound of high tide crashing into the rocks below was all that kept me company as I set up my sleeping pad and mosquito net. By 8:00 p.m. Ishii had not arrived, and I was too tired to wait any longer.

I crawled into my tight mosquito tent. My sleeping pad, being only two-thirds size, was light but impractical. I had learned to keep my blistered heels off the ground by lumping half of my clothes under my ankles. The other half were stuffed into my sleeping bag case for a pillow. I fell into an uneasy sleep. As I had done over the past few nights, I dreamt of walking and nothing else. I walked the next day's 20 miles and felt the anxiety of finding a place to sleep. I experienced every jaw-clenching step, unable to escape reality even at night.

At 3:30 a.m. I was jolted awake as a large, bright yellow van with plastic fire wings attached to the back screamed into the parking lot. It threw its high beams on me and revved its engine 40 feet from where I lay, encased in mosquito netting held up by my staff, my pilgrim hat resting on top. Three more deafening revs and the van squealed towards me, drowning out my shouts to stop. At barely five feet away, I rolled off the asphalt onto rocky ground, caught up in my netting, as raucous laughter escaped the windows. The van cut away quickly, fish tailed around two times, and then squealed off the parking lot and out of sight.

Adrenaline coursed through my veins as I disentangled myself from the mosquito net. Unable to calm down, I collapsed on a flat rock hidden from the parking lot, hiding in case they came back. I couldn't stop thinking about being left by Kanako and Jun, and Ishii not showing up.

I probably could have handled the "attack" and brushed it off if I had been feeling confident. But I felt vulnerable and weak in so many areas. Kanako leaving and Ishii never showing up added a sense of paranoia I equated with mental weakness and compounded the physical sense of inferiority that was driving me to punish my body to become stronger. I was missing a piece of life that everyone else seemed happy to accept. I couldn't be happy at home, and I kept looking for purpose somewhere else. Every time my family asked me when I was coming back to "real life" or when I was going to finally "settle down," it just intensified my struggle. I wanted more than a steady job, a family, and a house. That struggle also made me feel guilty and selfish for leaving everyone behind.

If I had been more aware, I would have seen the inevitable push to get myself into hard situations was really just a way to prove I could survive them. They were proof that I was strong, that I was competent. They were needed because I didn't feel either.

Sleep never blessed me again that night. Instead, I worried how I'd make it all the way in time to catch my plane. I didn't realize it at the time, but I had gambled my self-worth on an unrealistic timetable. Luckily, the pilgrimage is an excellent teacher, even for stubborn students.

8

MAMA'S CHARIOT

W hen you live outside, nowhere is completely safe. There are no walls to protect you or doors to lock. Anything can happen in the middle of the night. I was still shaken from the previous night, not only because of what had happened but from what might have been. It was my first encounter in Shikoku with *bōsōzoku,* a type of young Japanese gang that usually hangs out in cities.

Bōsōzoku, which means literally "violent speed tribes," are something like pseudo-*yakuza* (organized crime). They are a young, reckless subculture of thugs looking for a good time by getting into fights and causing havoc on the fringes of Japan's generally mainstream, regimented, and polite society. A favorite pastime is ignoring noise and traffic ordinances as they cruise through town in illegally modified motorbikes, cars, and vans with gigantic exhaust pipes, bright colors, and aero kits. Easily recognizable, they harken back to the days after World War II, with greasy hair, elaborate jumpsuits, and kamikaze style headbands. And when they are on a rural vacation it seems they also enjoy late night games of chicken with sleeping *henro.*

They are a product of Japan's relentless pressure to succeed by high school or be sidelined. Not all of their crimes are as innocent as skirting the traffic code. In one act of aggression and boredom, three *bōsōzoku* beat an elderly homeless man to death with metal bats in Tokyo. When asked why they did it they responded, "We were stressed, and beating the old guy made us feel better."

I was stressed out too as I limped past a small enclosed bus stop. I jumped back as the door slid open and an older *henro* forced a large pull cart right into my path.

"Oh, sorry about that," he whispered from inside the small corrugated tin hut. I helped him wiggle the heavy metal cart onto the road.

Short and unassuming, he was wafer thin, with slight stubble the only rough area on soft, supple skin. An unspoiled white towel covered his head, setting off his tanned, gentle face. He hung tightly onto his cart with one hand as he looked calmly at the ground in front of me, each of us waiting for the other to speak.

"You slept here last night?" I asked. "It's not on my map."

"Where were you last night?" he said.

"In a parking lot."

"That's no good. It's dangerous outside. You need to be more careful."

I wished I had met him yesterday.

"Let me see your map," he said, extending his free hand.

I handed it over, and he spent a few minutes marking safe places to sleep up to Temple Forty that weren't shown. It was clear he had been walking for a long time, but he wouldn't talk about it.

"You need to be careful. Shikoku is not as safe as it seems. *Henro* are attacked all the time. Sometimes by people pretending to be *henro*."

"How long have you been out here?" I asked, unsure if I was pushing too far.

"A long time. There are more of us than you think, and not

all of us wear the white," he said, referring to the pilgrim's outfit.

The "us" he was talking about were the homeless, or those cast aside from normal Japanese life. Unable to fit into the "real" world, they choose to walk around Shikoku, where their lifestyle doesn't draw as much attention. It was clear he didn't want to talk about it.

I brought the conversation back to a more comfortable topic. "What else should I be careful of?"

"Well, let's see," he said as his eyes lifted and reflected a new brightness. I wondered how long it had been since someone had looked at him and treated him as an expert in something. "First off, don't trust everyone in white. Some thieves will follow you for days and pick up your name slip out of the box at the temples. They'll approach you towards the end when you're tired. They'll claim to know you, showing your slip as proof, and then rob you blind in the evening."

I nodded to keep him talking, but I also didn't want to believe what he was telling me.

"When you are sleeping in *zenkonyado* and *tsuyadō*, always sleep with your money in your sleeping bag with you. Those places attract the worst thieves." He shook his head and winced in remembered pain.

I thought of Suzuki-san, the scruffy looking begging *henro*, and how I might have misjudged him. But I had still decided to sleep with my money down my pants back at the *tsuyadō* near Temple Twenty-Two.

"I see you're carrying a scroll. Well, watch out in the last prefecture. Those are worth a lot of money back in Tokyo. Gangs steal them, complete the last few temples, and ship them to their boss for a quick buck." He was right, about the price at least. A completed scroll, done by walking, fetches between $3,000 to $4,000 in stores in Tokyo, for those who want the spiritual protection without having to suffer.

My money strapped firmly to my body and my scroll clutched in my hands, I thanked him for his kindness and left him behind, expecting highway bandits to jump out of the trees, until my paranoia disappeared around the next bend. Despite my night with the gang, I hadn't seen anything as bad as he described. Of course, after a few years walking and sleeping outside, it seemed he'd had his fair share of attacks.

I struggled through the humid air until, a few hours later, a growling stomach forced me to rest for lunch. I jumped off the main road before an overpass bypassed what looked like an unremarkable town below.

The upside was the lack of both foot and vehicle traffic, and a bright, shining convenience store beckoned to me like an oasis in the desert. It was the first real convenience store I had seen for over a week, and I shouted with joy.

Japan has perfected the convenience store and turned it into an acceptable place to buy breakfast, lunch, and dinner. Rows and rows of Japanese *bentō* boxes filled with sushi, grilled chicken, and buckwheat noodles dazzle the taste buds and tempt the waistline. Rows of refrigerators hold every type of beer and soda Japan produces.

I rushed into the clean, bright sanctuary, unable to contain my excitement.

"Excuse me, where are your *bentō* boxes?" I asked, looking around frantically.

The shopkeeper looked at me like I was crazy. "We don't have them." He went back to ignoring me.

I didn't understand. This wasn't convenient at all. Dejected, I searched the rows of packaged breads promising freshness through the end of the decade. In the end I settled on a deep-fried ham sandwich, sold in the bread section, with a shelf life of two years. It tasted worse than it looked, which was an achievement.

While I was struggling to accept the lack of choices, a toilet flushed, and out of the bathroom came a man with a droopy face in a long-sleeved denim shirt, large black-framed glasses, and an uneven haircut that touched a week-old beard. He approached the cashier slowly as he wiped his hands on a pocket towel.

"Thank you for letting me use your bathroom," the man said with a slight bow.

"Huh? Sure," the cashier replied without looking up.

"It's very clean. Thank you," the denim man pressed.

The cashier looked annoyed. "That's fine. Don't worry."

"You let me use your bathroom my last time around. Thank you."

The cashier looked up for the first time and nodded quickly. "It's just a bathroom, don't worry," he replied. He turned towards an imaginary task, ending the conversation and leaving the denim man nothing to do but bow to his back and leave the store.

The honest gratitude of the man made me realize how simple my life had become. I understood the value of a clean, sit-down toilet. It was a highlight of my own day. Things had become so basic in life that a clean bathroom, a bathroom in general, was something special. I appreciated its existence, how much it cost to build, that someone cleaned it each day. I marveled at the engineering skill and the effort taken to design and craft the pipes.

I left the store, angry with society and ready to get back to the trail where things really mattered and everyone was equal.

The denim shirt man was waiting for me. "Where are you from?" he asked.

"America." I was too tired to get sucked into this game.

"I've never met a foreign *henro* before. Can I ask you some questions?"

I glanced down at my fried ham sandwich to hide my grimace. I was in extreme pain and only wanted peace and quiet. "Sure," I replied. "But I don't have much time, so I'll have to eat my sandwich while we talk."

We sat hunched on the curb separating the road from the sidewalk, not once disturbed by a passing car or another convenience store customer. I popped the last of my pain pills and settled in for a long talk.

"Why would you come to Shikoku?" he asked. He probably thought it was a simple question.

But for me, it got right to the heart of everything in my life. "That's a difficult question to answer quickly," I replied. I wasn't up to delving into my soul to explain myself, but the earnestness on his face made me try. "Well, this is my second time walking. The first time I came to find some strength in life, to prove myself as an adult. It worked. At least for a time. But I never completely left Shikoku. Almost every day since then I thought of Shikoku and the freedom I found here, outside of society's pressures."

"So why did you come back?" he pressed.

"Well, once you experience complete freedom, you become restless. Somehow life got away from me. I don't feel strong any longer, and I have no idea where I am heading in life," I confessed. I took a bite of my sandwich and thought carefully how to put my feelings into words.

"I feel like I locked myself into a life other people wanted for me because I needed to make a decision. Everyone seems to just want me to come back home, get a job, and act like everyone else they know. So, I left Japan and started school again so that I could get a different type of job.

"But the truth is, I'm not sure if I am happy with my decision to move back to the US and go back to school. If I don't figure it out, I could get stuck for another 10 years doing something just because it's expected of me, rather than because I want to."

I was exhausted, in pain, and too wrapped up in myself. I

switched topics without thinking. Without taking the time to see the person in front of me. "What do you do for a living?" I asked.

"You shouldn't ask that question," he murmured back quickly as he dropped his eyes.

I felt ashamed that I hadn't realized. "I'm sorry."

"It's difficult," he said. "I left Osaka seven years ago when I lost my job. People are kinder here. If you walk around you get *osettai*. People see you."

I didn't know what to say, and I didn't have the energy to give more. I swallowed the rest of my ham sandwich and then pushed my way out of the conversation. We said our goodbyes, wishing each other safe travels, and meaning it.

Out of sight, he continued to weigh on my mind. He was so grateful for the toilet, and to speak to me. I grew ashamed when I realized I hadn't even asked his name. Why not? He had very little in life. All he wanted was to be seen, to be valued as a human being. Why didn't I ask his name?

I was being selfish, distracted by my own unanswered questions in life. I had ignored his immediate needs. It felt horrible. How many other people had I phased out, thinking only about myself and what would make me happy?

Why didn't I ask his name?

I ARRIVED at the road leading to Temple Twenty-Seven, The Temple of God Summit. New sharp pains wrenched my calves, leaving my legs stiff and my mind defeated. There was no way my body could sustain my current pace. I shrugged off my pack next to a stone Shinto *torii* gate marking the beginning of the road up the mountain. I couldn't walk through it as someone had parked their SUV right in the middle of the gate, forcing pilgrims to walk around.

Temple Twenty-Seven is a *nansho* (perilous place), and like Temples Twelve and Twenty, is meant to prevent self-indulgence. These days the *nansho* seemed to have lost its meaning, as a paved road runs right to the main gate at the top. The road carried bus and car *henro* easily past me as I struggled up the mountain. Sweat poured down my face and into my eyes, blurring my vision as my legs seized up. With each step forward, my body shut down further until I was moving inches at a time.

This wasn't how it was supposed to be. Sure, I remembered the pilgrimage being hard, but not like this. It wasn't supposed to break me.

I reached the top and was presented with a choice: to the right, stone stairs led to the simple Shinto stone gate, or to the left, stone stairs led to the massive wooden Buddhist temple gate. Located just a few feet apart, the religions shared the mountain in a harmony that belied past conflicts. In 1868 the Meiji Restoration swept through Japan, ousting the previous feudalist model and beginning the process of "modernizing" Japan while elevating Shintoism.

The *haibutsu kishaku* movement, literally "abolish Buddhism and destroy the Buddha," sought to drive Buddhism out of Japan, and between 1868 and 1874 as many as 36,000 temples were destroyed across the country. Temple Twenty-Seven, where I now stood, was burned to the ground and the main Buddhist image was moved. Kōchi Prefecture showed a particular zealousness, as seven of the sixteen temple sites were either destroyed or shut down. For two decades, Temple Twenty-Seven lay in ruins, until it was restored in 1887. While the shrine and temple reconciled and merged once again, most temples on Shikoku were left separated, causing Shintoism to be all but expunged from the pilgrimage as it exists today.

I gulped down a liter of water gushing from the waterfall enclosed by bright green moss-covered stones, said to have healing powers. I wasn't sure if that was true, but it was cool and refreshing and exactly what my overheated body needed. The temple buildings are located on different levels of the mountain, sunny terraces linked by steep stone staircases that shuttle pilgrims and tourists about. It was serene, set within the protective embrace of the cedar forest and enveloped in the drifting chants of pilgrims, punctuated by the regular beat of bamboo on bamboo to frighten wild boars away. I collapsed on the highest point, the expansive view reaching all the way back to Cape Muroto. I sat alone, trying not to let my own mental cacophony affect the hard-won peace that had returned to the temple and shrine. Bus pilgrims passed by in a blur as they rushed from shrine to shrine, chanting quickly, making sure to stick to the bus tour's schedule.

I had made it to the top of the *nansho* and passed the most recent test. But my mind was looking to the next day, and along the way a plan had begun to form in my mind. It started as a small idea, slowly building until it had taken hold and I knew it was the right move. With a heavy heart I decided to stop for the night in the next large town and buy a bicycle.

I could have tried to push on walking, but my body would pay a heavy price. My tendonitis was getting worse, and I had developed an unhealthy reliance on painkillers, just to keep moving. This wasn't the reason I came to Shikoku. I hadn't come here to punish myself, but to find out who I was.

The plan was a relief. It meant I could stop worrying about the pain and the taxing mental anguish of how I could finish in time. And yet, I felt a deep sense of shame at the same time. I was giving up on the image of myself I had built up and what it meant to walk the pilgrimage correctly. If I stopped walking, I wouldn't be doing the pilgrimage the hardest way any longer. I took pride in the fact that I had walked the pilgrimage in only 30 days the last time, pushing my body beyond what I thought was possible, despite the consequences—shredded feet, damaged ligaments, and severe malnourishment. In that pain I had found strength, and adulthood. Of course, this time around I was seven years older.

This time I was supposed to find myself and release my past regrets that continued to weigh on me. Others would be stronger than me, others would be more accomplished. I couldn't shake my dark thoughts, even though everyone I had met had advised me to walk slower, to enjoy myself, to be happy with where I was. It still felt like failure.

Uneasy about my decision but committed at the same time, I walked slowly down the mountain. As I rounded a bend, a monk shuffled out of a parking lot, leading 30 elderly bus pilgrims. He was young, dressed in black flowing robes, with a large, dark, well-crafted bamboo hat shading his whole upper body. A huge hip pack was strapped to his waist, threatening to push me over as we stopped to greet each other.

"Good afternoon," I said in Japanese.

"Hi," he replied in perfect English. "It's hot isn't it?"

"Wow," I said, not even trying to hide my shock.

"Yeah, wow," he said with a smile. "I lived in San Diego for a few years before I became a monk. Are you okay? You don't look so good."

I smiled back weakly. Without thinking, I spilled out my bike plan, explaining quickly my reasons and rationale. I was still trying to convince myself it was necessary.

"You shouldn't push yourself too hard. You need to take care of your body," he reassured me. "I've been around Shikoku 20 times now and haven't walked even once. I take groups around by bus and don't have any desire to walk it."

He moved to catch up to his clients, then stopped, and turned. Switching to Japanese he looked me in the eyes and said, "You can only ever be where you are."

He didn't stick around to explain what he meant, and the next moment he was out of my life. What I took from it was that we can wish things to be different, but reality is what it is, and we need to accept where we are. Acceptance is not always easy.

It would be okay. I was still doing the pilgrimage. I had a fully fledged monk to back me up. I let his words sink in a bit further to dull the immense pain in my feet and encourage me along.

I ENDED my 12-hour day at the seaside city of Aki.

Hot, lonely, and low on money, I followed the only natural course. I broke out my credit card and checked into an expensive (for my budget) hotel. I cranked the air-conditioning as low as it would go, blared the TV, took a shower, took a bath, washed my clothes, took a nap, and then took another shower while lying on the ground to keep the pressure off my feet. There was nothing particularly special about the impersonal business hotel, but it was an oasis, four thin walls shielding me from the harshness of the pilgrimage and life on the streets.

I left my staff and hat at the hotel in an attempt to blend back in with society. The walk to the local Home Center, a mix between The Home Depot and a Walmart, took just 10 minutes. I unsheathed my credit card once more and bought the cheapest bike they had, a $98 *mamachari*. The workhorse of the Japanese transportation world, it immediately conjures up images of women ferrying small children to school, one on the front handlebars, another in the back, and a basket laden with groceries. It has a low crossbar for easy mounting and a massive seat big enough to cushion butts.

There is an ongoing debate about where the word actually came from. The *mama* obviously comes from "mother." The *chari* is either borrowed from the English word "chariot," or from another slang word, *charinko*, based on the "*charin, charin,*

charin" sound the bell makes, combined with *ko*, the Japanese word for child.

Either way, this was not a Ferrari. My bike was dull silver, with a black wire basket on the front and only one gear, designed for quick trips around town, rather than mountain-trekking pilgrimages.

"How many times would you like to pay for that?" the young salesclerk asked.

Japanese credit cards work differently and offer a variety of charging options aimed at separating future pay checks from their owners right away. If you reply, "Three times," the shop will charge your credit card an equal amount for the next three months . . . for a nice service fee. You can even delay the charge until bonus time and pay it all off several months later.

"Just once, thanks," I replied, and walked my bike out of the large warehouse.

The evening air whipped against my face as I raced back to my hotel at what was surely the fastest speed any human had ever traveled.

Things were never going to be the same.

9

THE KINDNESS OF GRUFF STRANGERS

God was speaking to me again. "It is okay. You are doing your best." God doesn't speak in contractions. "This is what is supposed to happen." For a billion years God shaped the world, gently nudging life into place, a little amino acid here, a walking fish there, a couple of mass extinctions to reset and reboot. Over the millennia the inhabitants of Japan, of Shikoku, gradually grew more sophisticated, learned to speak, to read and write, to build tools, houses, and eventually, divinely inspired automated vending machines, complete with hot coffee cans, beer, whiskey, batteries, and porn.

He speaks in mysterious ways and I was beginning to see parts of His master plan. I knew I was being sent a message. How else could I explain the convergence of the *henro* path with a paved bike path beginning mere feet from my hotel? "You did the right thing," He said, as the bike path opened up before me. Or maybe it was Kūkai, or whatever mystery you subscribe to. It was something.

For two glorious hours I cruised along the bike path, the ocean my constant companion, surfers blending and cutting through the steady waves on my left. Beach goers soaked up the sun, tempted me to take a break, and ignored me all at once.

Worry and self-doubt about my choice still nipped at my mind, but the salty wind and speed of the bike soon left it all behind.

I looked ridiculous. My pack was strapped to the back of the bike with bright yellow bungee cords, my staff threaded between the bike's frame so as not to fall off, and my conical pilgrim hat was tied tightly to the front basket but managed to flip constantly in the wind. I was still dressed in white and the wind rippled through my beard as I rode.

Free from the pain in my feet, I could really see things, be present. However, loneliness soon replaced physical pain, as I worried that riding my bike would separate me even more from other pilgrims. When I saw a *henro* walking slowly in front of me, I knew it was time to get off and talk.

His name was Yori-san, he was about my age, and he spoke fluent English. We connected instantly. In a twist of fate, he had just completed his master's in international relations in the United States, in a program almost identical to my own. God was speaking to me again, but I was polite and listened to Yori-san first.

I got off my bike and walked with him, our backs to the ocean as we were slowly swallowed up by the city of Kōchi's suburbs.

He was returning to Tokyo after being on the path for two weeks. He worked for an opposition Democratic Party politician and was being called back suddenly to help defeat a vote to privatize the Japanese postal service. He didn't want to stop but felt he didn't have a choice. Japan Post was a behemoth, a government-owned corporation that employed one-third of Japanese government employees and held the world's largest stash of personal savings, at $2.1 trillion.

"Actually, I quit my job a few weeks back and came to Shikoku to discover what I want to do in life." He sighed and shook his head. "But . . ." He looked down, almost said something else, and then continued, "I can't refuse. I probably won't get back to Shikoku again."

"I'm sorry," I said. "You can always come back after the vote."

He looked at me patiently, like I was a child. "No, if I go back, I can't leave again. I'm trapped. Anyway, what are you doing here? Are you Buddhist?"

The change in topic caught me off guard and showed he had already made his decision.

"No, I'm a lapsed Catholic," I said. "Or at least that's what other people call people like me. I still believe in God, or at least something like God, but the church doesn't really speak to me anymore, nor the rules we create to justify our understanding of something infinite."

"Why not walk a Christian pilgrimage?"

I thought carefully, wondering how much I wanted to open myself up to a perfect stranger. "I don't think we can ever really know God fully," I began. "How can people who are finite begin to understand something that is infinite? I think our experiences are filtered by our cultural lenses, and we can only glimpse a limited part of God. For a long time, church, and, I guess, culture in the States, hasn't given me a way to experience God. Plus, I'm feeling trapped at the moment and have no idea what to do with my next step in life. I came here hoping to reclaim a bit of my strength."

"Yeah, but what do you expect to find here?" he quizzed, still not satisfied. "This is Buddha and *kami* country. Don't get me wrong, I'm not really Buddhist or Shinto either. I just want to understand why a foreigner comes."

We walked in silence for a few minutes. I wasn't usually comfortable discussing my relationship with God, and I hated it when others preached about theirs or what they thought mine should be. Maybe it was my loneliness, maybe a deeper need to be understood, but I decided to open up for the first time.

"I've met God before," I began, waiting for Yori to react. When he didn't, I let it all pour out.

There was a girl; there always is. Up to that point she was the love of my life, and I was convinced that we would get married. I loved the idea of marrying my college sweetheart. Looking back on it now, it was the kind of love that is fueled by youth's overcharged emotions, where self-worth gets entangled in the approval and validation that a relationship brings. The fact that I didn't understand my own value pushed me to leave and seek answers. Despite being in love, I had just graduated from university, while she had two more years left, I needed a job, and more importantly, I needed an adventure.

I moved to Japan to teach English just a month after graduating, enticed by a life of adventure, and left her behind. Barely four months later, our relationship was in its death throes. In a desperate attempt to salvage it, I bought a ticket home. The night before my flight I stayed with a friend who lived closer to the airport in Osaka.

Even looking back now, I'm still not sure what happened. I must have been feeling nervous about my trip, and I started drinking with my friend, despite having an early flight the next morning. We stayed up drinking until 6:15 in the morning, just 15 minutes before I needed to leave for the airport. When you are that drunk, everything seems like a good idea, and I thought I could take a quick 15-minute nap before heading out.

Four hours later my buddy stumbled into the living room and woke me up.

"What the fuck are you still doing here?" he asked stupidly, looking at me like I had just confessed to loving his mother.

I jumped up from the *tatami* mat, swearing for 10 minutes straight. I got dressed, still drunk but determined to get to the airport even though I wouldn't arrive until two hours after my flight had departed. I had to try. I had to do something. If I didn't make it home, we would break up and it would be my fault.

There is a feeling that overwhelms you when you think something is your fault. It is a type of stress that churns in your stomach and makes you want to throw up. I raced to the train station and caught the first bullet train out in an attempt to make up some time. It would still take two hours to reach the airport. As I sat in the train, the stress grew, my stomach sank further and further, and I felt physically sick from both fucking up and drinking too much.

An hour into the train ride, the pressure continued to build, consuming my body and mind with raw, unrelenting anxiety. I felt like I was going to explode, and then suddenly it all dropped away, and an overwhelming sense of peace spread throughout my body. Everything I was worried about just a second ago disappeared as my mind shifted from my head down to just below my stomach. Called the *hara* in Japanese, it felt like my whole being, including my thoughts, were coming from exactly two fingers' width below my belly button. It made perfect sense at the time.

Yori stopped walking and looked into my eyes as I continued.

It is hard to explain without sounding crazy, but I was already too far in to stop.

"I realized, I felt, that God and I were the same," I said.

I wasn't sure "God" was the right word, but it was the only term I knew for whatever force was running through the universe.

"In that moment, it was perfectly clear to me that I had a soul, and that soul was a part of God, connected to me, inside of me, here," I said, pressing my fingers to my stomach.

I was God, Yori was God, everyone was God, as we were all part of the universe. There was no distinction. Praying to something outside of us made no sense, as we were all God. All the barriers in the world fell apart and I was connected to everyone. Everything was related and a part of God. With this clarity, I *knew* that everything was going to be okay. I knew that I was going to make my plane and there was no reason to worry. It would all work out.

The sense of peace stayed with me, even though my connection to God slowly faded as my mind took back control.

An hour later, two hours after my plane had supposedly taken off, I walked calmly to the airport counter. The ticket agent knew my name right away, as I was the only one who hadn't arrived. I told her it would be okay. She looked at me strangely and confirmed that my plane had been delayed by two hours and was just about to board. I was drunk and tired, but everything was okay.

That was the first time I ever told someone about my experience with God, and I was unsure how Yori would take it.

"What happened to the girl?" Yori asked.

"Ha! The trip was a disaster. For two straight weeks we fought, played with each other's emotions, and then she broke up with me on the last day, at the airport.

"It has been five years since that experience, and I've tried to get back to that feeling. I've meditated, prayed, hiked, drunk, and tried to slow down to feel the connection again, to experience God under better circumstances. I'm hoping this trip will do the trick."

"It sounds more like you experienced a piece of enlightenment. You're a very tolerant Christian, Todd," he said, and started walking again.

We walked together a little while longer, but there wasn't anything else to talk about. Society was dragging him back to the world of the living, and he was letting it. I was sinking further into the pilgrim's mindset, into my search for God, and the feeling that everything would work out in the end. I got back on my bike, we said goodbye, and I rang my bike's bell until I rounded the next corner.

THE TEMPLES SLIPPED by as the day wore on. I rode through lunch, still pushing myself for some reason, until I found myself in the center of the city of Kōchi, society now calling me back. I realized I hadn't checked in with my family since arriving in Japan almost two weeks before. I knew they must be worried. Dropping off the face of the earth tends to worry my excitable parents, probably because I had been doing it to them throughout my adult life. Taking advantage of my newfound mobility, I set off in search of an internet café, down a busy four-lane road away from the *henro* path.

I parked my bike under a gigantic red neon sign that simply said *"Manga"*. Nothing goes together better in Japan than the internet and comic books. Order a coffee and you have access to thousands of comic books, the internet, or even video games.

The clean sliding glass doors made me acutely aware of my grimy appearance and an unholy smell that would have stood out in a bovine slaughter factory. Gripping my straw hat and staff, I took a tentative, self-conscious step inside.

The café was a cavernous room filled with rows of books and secluded nooks to read and use the internet.

"Welcome home, Master," a lithe young woman said while succeeding in bowing and curtsying at the same time. What the fuck?

Another young woman rushed forward to accept my hat and staff.

"Um, thanks," I stammered. I looked around and remembered to close my mouth as I was suddenly surrounded. Innocent eyes begged me to give an order as four Japanese French maids, dressed in short mid-thigh black dresses with petticoat, pinafore, bows in their hair, and black tights, surrounded me like groupies.

Most young Japanese still live with their parents until they get married. The decision is partly financial, as it is expensive to live on your own, and it is partly cultural, as a son may be expected to continue living with his parents even after marriage, and a daughter only moves out to join a new family. Either way, leaving at 18 is not very common for young people, and few have the experience of living on their own. Instead, they engage in part-time or even full-time jobs to help them pay for cars and mobile phones, and to assuage an insatiable thirst for branded clothing and accessories. I wondered what type of conversation you can have with your father after a long day in a French maid outfit.

Dad: "How was your day?"

Maid: "So-so. Only three guys wanted to take a picture with me today. I did get touched by an old guy, twice." (Each picture costs an extra $5.)

Dad: "Hmm. Better luck tomorrow, pumpkin."

Of course, that assumes that the father is home before midnight, because his boss, who hates his own life, has made him go out drinking each night for the past 20 years. The "salaryman" culture is incredibly destructive in terms of family life and healthy relationships. The term is a take on the English term "salaried worker," a white-collar worker who shows over-riding loyalty to his company, which is now his other family, with the boss as head.

"Master, what would you like?" the head maid asked in a high-pitched, squealing voice that was supposed to be sexy in a cute, innocent, and way too young way. How could I possibly answer without getting arrested?

"Uh, can I use the internet?" I asked.

"Of course, anything you want, Master." She curtseyed again and led me to a back booth.

Surprisingly busy for a weekday afternoon, the café was filled with *otaku*, obsessive fans of *anime* (cartoons) and *manga* (comics). Antisocial by nature, they prefer fantasy roleplay to the complicated rules of Japanese societal interaction. Then again, that sounded pretty normal to me. Throw in refusing to get stuck in a business suit for the rest of their lives and a predilection for French maids in short skirts, and their life choices seemed more than rational to me. The bigger question was how more Japanese people *hadn't* chosen this lifestyle. I could have finished the pilgrimage right then and there if any of the girls had been brave enough to ask me to marry them.

Geeky faces peeked from around corners, angry, no doubt, that someone was taking attention away from them. They tried to cut me down with eyes like *katana* (swords), shot energy balls from their hands, and silently transformed into monstrous beasts ready to smite me back to 136 different Buddhist hells. I looked back at them and smiled, causing them to flee back to their cubicles of solitude.

Seated, I waited for that moment of ecstatic release that had eluded me for two weeks. In a fluffy black swirl, my maid got down on her knees. I tensed in anticipation as she said sweetly, "Here you are, Master. Would you like milk or sugar?" I nodded as she stayed on her knees and slowly mixed my coffee. Nothing is quite as satisfying as the first sip of coffee, and I hadn't had any for the past two weeks. It was, in fact, horrible coffee spewed from an impersonal machine, but as it slid down my throat, the room suddenly burst into color. I felt awake again for the first time in ages.

I gripped the firm, warm glass lovingly as I typed away to my family, regaling them with the highlights of life on the road, conveniently leaving out the subservient maids. I told them how much I loved and missed them.

I have spent the better part of my adult life running away from home, not calling for months at a time, and even spending two years without setting foot on US soil or contacting any of them. Caught up in my own life and the high of seeing what's around the next corner, I left everyone behind, assuming that, as friends and family, they would still be there when I got back. It was only in the desperation of pain and loneliness that I realized how important family is and the effort it takes to stay in each other's lives.

When friends and family are not right in front of you, it's easy to let relationships slide into disuse, and sometimes when you go back to dust them off, you realize there is nothing left. I found this out the hard way. I figured I could pick right back up with everyone when I returned to the US for graduate school.

The truth was that I was just as horrible at keeping in touch, even when I returned. Friends had gotten married and moved out of the city, family had moved across the country, and I dived right into the work that was in front of me. Before I knew it, a year had passed, and I was back in Japan because doing something new was easier than breathing life back into friendships that had run their course.

I see now that it was also a cycle that was keeping me on the move. It becomes easier to stay abroad, where norms ensure you are always an outsider, comfortable in your role. There is minimal emotional investment needed. If I was paying closer attention, I would have seen how this contributed to my continued loneliness.

But I wasn't paying attention and I had wasted enough time on society. I needed to get back on my bike. Temple Thirty-Two sat on top of a hill three and a half miles away and it was almost 5:00 p.m.

I finished my coffee in a gulp, paid the counter maid, and left to cries of, "Don't go, Master! Come back soon!"

If my attempts at finding my calling in life failed, at least I would have one place I could return to.

I reached the base of the hill with only five minutes left to run up before the office closed. It didn't seem fair that I was rushed, even with the bike, and had to run on my poor feet. I had compromised my trip, and I was still behind. I clearly had time management problems, especially since I hadn't even stopped for lunch. Or perhaps I had an inability to stop. The memory of coffee and maids sustained me as I raced up the stone path.

Zenjibu-ji, the Temple of the Ch'an Master's Peak, sounds as cool in Japanese as it does in English. Not really a master's peak, it was in fact just a small hill. The path was steep and wound its way through twisted rock formations straight out of a Chinese ink painting. Through the large wooden gate, past the stern-eyed *nio* guardian statues, I raced straight for the stamp room. No one was there. "*Sumimasen!*" I yelled into the back room.

I couldn't hear anything through the blood pounding in my eyes, perfectly in sync with the throbbing in my feet. I yelled again, and 10 minutes after 5:00 p.m. a woman in a blue and white apron shuffled out. I prepared myself for a fight.

"*Onegaishimasu,*" I said, and held out my scroll with both hands, head and body bowed at the appropriate 45-degree angle. She stared blankly for a few moments and then broke out in laughter.

"Why so formal, *henro*-san?" she teased.

Was this a trick? It was after 5:00 p.m. and the office was closed, but she didn't seem to care.

"Sorry, it's just that I'm in a rush. I need to get to Temple Thirty-Three before it gets too late, so I can ask to sleep in their gazebo."

She waved her calligraphy brush at me and said, "That's no good. The ferry is out of service and you won't make it in time."

My heart sank.

"Ah, cheer up. Have a jelly. It's *settai*," she said with a wink, and reached into a pocket to produce a green apple jelly carton.

She went back to signing my scroll as I fidgeted, impatient to move on. I thought I could still make it. I had to try, as I didn't have any other place to sleep. I was about to leave when I was called back.

"Why don't you stay at Yamaoka's *zenkonyado*?" She rummaged behind her desk and handed me a flyer with a map to his house and his telephone number. "Just be sure to call so he knows to expect you." Without another word she giggled again and disappeared into the back room.

I broke down into tears. People had been nice to me here and there, but she was the kindest woman I had ever met. She was gentle and nonjudgmental. Judging by my tears, these were two qualities I was sorely missing. People in Japan can be incredibly nice, but the structure of everything and the attention to detail can build up until you find yourself a blubbering mess in a now dark temple office. It is these micro differences that build into what we recognize as culture shock.

I pulled myself together and prayed at each shrine of the lotus-shaped temple grounds. Yamaoka-san's *zenkonyado* wasn't listed on my sheet of free places to stay, nor on my map, which was strange since he'd gone through the trouble to advertise. I shot off another prayer of thanks that the temple hadn't adapted to the modern world just yet and hobbled over to the rare public telephone. It probably won't be long before city dwellers and tourists searching for "old" Japan will marvel at the curiously stationary telephones with little slots for change.

"Yes."

"Excuse me. I'm a *henro* and I was wondering if I could . . ."

"What?" the gruff voice barked into the telephone.

"I received your flyer at Temple Thirty-Two . . ."

"Where? What are you talking about?" he yelled.

This wasn't going well. "You know, Zenjibu-ji . . ."

"Where?"

I began to wonder if I had the right number. "The temple. Zenjibu-ji."

"You mean Mine-dera." His voice was like sandpaper rubbing against my ear.

"No." Desperation flooded my voice. "I mean Zenjibu-ji!" I hurried on before he could yell at me again. "I'm at Temple Thirty-Two and was told you have a *zenkonyado* where I can stay. Is it okay?"

"No." My heart sank, again. "You're at Mine-dera. Bring your dinner." The conversation ended as abruptly as it had begun. The grating voice was replaced with the stinging sound of a disconnected line.

The beeping telephone was replaced by the rhythmic buzzing of the cicadas as I rested on the same style of faded blue bench found at every temple. Two young girls burst out of the singing forest, giggling as their father struggled to catch them. As dusk settled in, even the usually fierce *nio* guardians seemed to soften while the girls raced around the temple grounds.

I was invisible to them. I didn't exist, and the only open arms waiting for me were those of a gruff old man. I wasn't looking forward to staying with him, but the approaching darkness took away any other options.

It didn't take long to reach Yamaoka-san's house, nor was it difficult to spot. The house was an unremarkable, prefabricated clone found everywhere in Japan. What made it unique was the large open-air wood hut in the front yard, with signage inviting pilgrims in. I dropped my bag on the log bench, walked past the faucet, and waited as the doorbell echoed into silence. I rang again before trying the door to yell inside. It was locked. I tried to look through the windows, but they were shuttered. It didn't matter. I had a bench to sleep on, a roof to protect from the rain, and water to wash away the day.

I had waited for an hour, relishing the fresh air on my still-blistered feet, when the sound of crunching gravel startled me into a standing position. That was a big mistake, as the shooting pain sent me promptly to my knees. Embarrassed, I used my staff to pull myself up just as Yamaoka-san stepped out of the car.

I bowed deeply. "Thank y..." I began.

"Follow me," he said, turning his back before I could register his face. I fumbled with my bag and limped into his house, uncertain of what was happening. After taking off my shoes, arranging his along with mine facing out towards the door, I tried to follow him into the kitchen, where he was putting groceries away.

"Go upstairs and take a bath. You stink." He never looked up.

"Excuse..."

"Take the room on the right. Hurry, someone else is coming soon."

A *room*? I had expected to sleep in the gazebo. For a room I could deal with all the gruffness in the world.

"My name is Todd. Thank you for the room," I called as I climbed the steep steps.

"Ugh. You were at Mine-dera. No one calls it Zenjibu-ji, and no one knows what number it is," he yelled in return. As introduced as we were ever going to be, I got naked in the strange man's house, checking the bathroom lock three times, just to be safe.

After I was clean, I found my room and unpacked. I had just turned my back when someone ran down the hallway from the second room, and into the bathroom. I wanted to lay down and rest, but I went downstairs to be polite, not wanting to seem selfish to our host or to the new *henro* who had suddenly appeared.

This time, I was allowed to enter the dining room. Yamaoka-san was busy preparing his dinner of sushi, sashimi, miso soup, and rice. Maybe he didn't notice me. I pulled out my convenience store curry *bentō* box and put it lovingly on the table.

"I—" I began.

He cut me off.

"We'll wait for the other *henro*." Conversation closed.

I sat in silence, burning each aspect of the cluttered kitchen and dining room into my mind. I shifted in my seat 32 times, sighed heavily 22 times, until exactly 23 minutes and 12 seconds later, a young, tanned, fit, handsome man entered the kitchen. I had looked at the cheesy, fake wood wall clock 157 times.

I tried to introduce myself but was shushed into silence as Yamaoka-san joined us at the dinner table.

"So, my name is Yamaoka." He spread his hands and pointed in my direction. "As you can see, we have a bit of a problem."

"Nice to meet you. I'm Tayano," the other *henro* replied while bowing deeply. "I'm sorry, but I don't speak English either."

"Saaa, I was afraid of that. He hasn't said a word since he arrived. What if he is expecting dinner?" our host asked Tayano-san.

My dinner was sitting in front of me on the table. I examined Yamaoka-san as he accomplished the astounding feat of not seeing me while looking directly into my eyes. It was the same skill restaurant staff have when you are frantically waving your hand to get their attention.

Yamaoka-san looked just like he sounded—rough, with a pock-marked face that was too long and full for his diminutive stature.

"Um, excuse me, but I can speak Japanese. I'm speaking it right now. We spoke in Japanese over the phone," I reminded him.

Yamaoka-san stared back at me like I was a museum piece. Maybe I needed a placard explanation.

"Eh? What did he say?" he asked Tayano-san. I tried to reply for myself, but he cut me off.

"It seems that he speaks and understands Japanese." Tayano-san confirmed.

No sign of change touched Yamaoka-san's dull face as he turned to re-evaluate me. Then, like a rising tsunami of emotions, he exploded. "Ha! I knew you could speak Japanese."

There was never a doubt. I now fit into a category and I was safe; he knew that I could be trusted to live up to my responsibilities as a guest. He let go of his own preconceived notions about foreign pilgrims, and it was time for me to face mine. Yamaoka-san turned out to be one of the sweetest men I'd ever met.

We shared our stories in turn, as those on the road do. Tayano was a truck driver from outside Tokyo. He quit his job six months ago and decided to walk the pilgrimage to figure out where he wanted to go in life. This was his third time around; the first was in winter, the second in spring. He was on his last time around but wasn't any closer to figuring out his life. Or maybe he just didn't want to share it with us.

Yamaoka-san was linked to the pilgrimage in a completely different way. A cigarette was never far from his mouth as he told us his story in his gruff manner that was quickly becoming endearing. "I'm not from Shikoku. I lived all my life just outside of Kyoto, working for a factory." He paused to pull another long drag into his lungs. "Somehow, I got cancer in my throat. Had to have a tumor removed, twice. That got me thinking."

Obviously, that thinking didn't include quitting smoking. He poured a long pull of whiskey into his glass and continued. "I wasn't happy. No one I knew was happy. So, I sold everything, moved to Shikoku, and built this house for *henro*. That was five years ago. It turns out that personal happiness only comes from helping others to be happy."

He didn't say it, but I suspected that he was also hoping to gain merit from his acts and that Kūkai would heal him. I wanted to believe that it was working.

The night passed slowly for those who wanted to sleep and quickly for Yamaoka-san, who enjoyed the company. When the late hour of 9:00 p.m. rolled around, it was finally time to go to bed.

As we walked up the stairs, Yamaoka-san stopped us. "You know, things are changing," he said.

We looked back politely.

"The pilgrimage, I mean. There used to be *zenkonyado* everywhere. But too many people came from Osaka and Tokyo looking for a cheap vacation, getting drunk and causing trouble for the owners. Ten years ago, you could have found a *zenkonyado* in just about every town. Now, I'm one of the last left. It's sad that people can't learn to respect each other more."

The irony was not lost on me that, as a foreigner, I was often a big worry for inn owners. They would assume a foreigner wouldn't know the rules of the inn, how to take a bath, how to be respectful of others. But what happens when the Japanese themselves don't follow the rules?

"And the temples," he said. "Bah, better off not even visiting those anymore. Money-grabbing bastards, all of them. Except Mine-dera. Good people there, of course."

We shifted on the steep steps, but Yamaoka-san wasn't done yet.

"You know what gets me riled up?" he asked.

Please don't ask. Please don't ask. Please don't ask.

"What?" Tayano asked politely.

"Those high and mighty temple monks. They are worthless. They are supposed to help people, but all they worry about is sucking in money from pilgrims. They won't even let you pitch a tent!" He was gaining volume. "They wouldn't even exist without you paying your money into their pretty little boxes and paying for your cute calligraphy and stamps. I just wish they'd think about that a bit. Don't you?" he grumbled, talking half into his whiskey glass.

He didn't wait for a response and retreated into the kitchen to get more whiskey.

The wonderful thing about the pilgrimage is that nothing ever goes according to plan. On a day when I was convinced I would be separated from other *henro*, I found two shining examples of what made Shikoku so precious.

Both Yamaoka-san and Tayano thought I did the right thing buying the bike and that my path was my own. All this time I had been looking at walking and cycling in terms of which was better. My new friends helped me see that neither was better or worse, they were just different.

As I lay in my bed, I broke down into tears again. Sobs racked my body, exhausting me even further. Kōchi was the land of spiritual discipline, and it wasn't going to let me coast through. Rather than pushing my physical limits, my challenge was becoming apparent—to control my ego and stop comparing myself with others. I needed to stop trying to gain something that I could measure, compare, and feel proud of. Instead, I needed to release that part of me that judges, competes, and criticizes in an attempt to be the "best." As I let the last tears soak into my pillow, I knew the physical pain would have been easier to deal with. Realizing who you really are is not a pleasant experience.

10

BICYCLE GANG

Eleven days after beginning the pilgrimage, I rolled into Temple Thirty-Six, the Temple of the Blue Dragon, around lunchtime. The temple is hidden among the foothills of Mt. Utsuga, on a peninsula across the quiet bay of Usa, where only fishermen's boats disturb the calm waters.

A long stone staircase cut a straight line through the dense, lush forest. Bright green bushes and towering cedar trees cooled the warm midday air. I wasn't alone as I began my ascent. To my left, an ascetic dressed in spotless white robes sat in a moss-covered stone enclosure as freezing mountain water pounded onto his shiny, shaven head. Prayer beads were wrapped around his left wrist, like my own beads. His hands were together in front of his chest as he chanted, eyes closed, unaware of my presence.

Originating from *yamabushi* (mountain ascetics) practices and Shintoism, *misogi* is an ancient Japanese purification ritual that asks the gods (*kami*) to wash away sin from the six elements that make up the human body: the five senses and the mind. While almost all of Japan's citizens toiled in cities, ensuring their place in the 90 percent of society that made up the middle class, this guy sat under a freezing waterfall. I wondered what had pushed him to the fringes of Japanese society, how he had found the courage to break from the norm and form a small minority of extreme religious practitioners. I'd never know, and I moved on without disturbing him.

On my way back down the mountain from the temple, I was close on the heels of two young pilgrims. While performing our temple duties, they never indicated they saw me, nor did they spare a look as they bounded past me down to the parking lot. All that changed when they saw my ride.

"What?! You're the guy on the *mamachari*? How'd you get here so fast?" one of them yelled.

I pushed the oversized U-shaped kickstand up, allowing my back wheel to drop back to the ground. There is nothing more uncool than having a kickstand. I felt every painful second as the two young guys, with their fancy mountain bikes leaning against nearby trees, watched every detail.

"What do you mean? I just rode normally." I grinned at their indignation.

"No way, man! We left before you at the last temple. There's no way you could have caught up to us on *that* thing."

They were young, full of energy, and tried hard to look hip in their bike shorts. One was tall while the other was a head shorter with wire glasses. Both wore full hip packs cinched at the waist and black cycling gloves with the fingertips missing. They examined my bicycle, trying to figure out how the thing worked. They had only seen old ladies ride them and couldn't believe it was capable of making it up a slight hill, let alone the mountain passes of Shikoku.

"Seriously, man," the tall one said. "What's your secret? We've been busting our asses to stay in front of you, and here you are."

I didn't realize I was in a bicycle race, but it made me feel good that I outpaced them.

They were from Tokyo and in their third year at Waseda University, one of Japan's best, the equivalent of Princeton or Yale in the US. Hearing the name of the university usually elicits a pause as you think about the lower-level school you went to before you gush at how smart they must be.

The tall one was practically jumping up and down with frustration. "Can I take it for a spin?"

I waved him on as I got more of their story. Shinichi was the tall one and Ichiro the shorter friend. They were both born and bred in Tokyo, but they loved the countryside. For the past three years, every school vacation, they had taken off on their bikes to explore a part of Japan together. They camped outside, usually in public parks or in rest areas.

They had no particular feeling for the pilgrimage other than using it as a way to cycle around Shikoku, although Ichiro carried a small stamp book that he would give back to his aunt once it was completed. Temples were a mild distraction that helped dictate their route and were meant to be hit hard and fast, so that they could get back onto the road as quickly as possible.

"Whoa, Ichiro, you gotta check this thing out! It's got no gears. Crazy." Shinichi tried to kick out the back tire to spray us with parking lot gravel. But the heavy bike didn't cooperate, and he just came to a wrenching stop. "Crazy!"

"Peppy and cute" is the only way to describe them, and I dubbed them the Tokyo Boyz, a name they readily accepted with high fives all round. The pilgrimage route was filled with bikers, especially university students on their summer breaks. I was now one of them and slipped easily into talking about 100-mile days rather than the blister-inducing 20-mile stretches of a walking pilgrim.

Bike and age aside, a significant difference between us was our choice of maps. I was using the pilgrim's walking map that included walking paths and car routes. They were using the "Mapple" motorcycle cruising map.

Unlike my map, it didn't show the quickest routes to each temple. It only showed the roads and left the reader to guess the shortest way. It didn't care about walkers or cyclists either, as it showed main roads and left out the small backroads I had used to catch up to the Tokyo Boyz.

"Where did you get this thing? How much was it?" Ichiro asked, flipping through my map book.

"Back at Temple One, but I'm sure you can find it in other places. It's only about $20."

They whistled in unison. Like I said, cute.

"Too rich for us, man," Ichiro said. "We're on a budget." He handed the map back to me.

"Alright, let's get going, Ichiro. It was nice to meet you, Todd-san. Good luck and be safe," Shinichi said. They bowed in unison, straightening with huge grins and hands extended for high fives.

My hand met theirs. "I'll probably run into you later today," I said.

"Yeah, right!" Ichiro scoffed. "We're headed to Temple Thirty-Seven today, man. That's over 36 miles from here, over some of the steepest mountains on the island. There's no way you'll be able to make it by closing time on that one gear, mama."

It was a long way to ride after lunch, but I couldn't let them feel too smug on their mountain bikes. "I'll see you there," I called as they left the parking lot.

The wind stole most of their words, but I understood the laughing and "... crazy *gaijin* [foreigner]."

THE CLIMB out of the small city of Susaki, along Route 56, was short but steep as the road shot up almost 1,000 feet over just a few miles. My body bent forward between my enormous Y-shaped handlebars, I kept constant pressure on the pedals, knowing that if I stalled, I would never get enough momentum to continue biking and would be forced to walk and push. Large trucks and cars whizzed by, mere inches away, replacing cool, lush mountain air with fumes.

The biggest blow to my determination came out of nowhere as I labored up a mountain pass. A young woman dressed in a *henro* outfit passed me on her mountain bike. As she passed, she shook her head and pointed to my bike, "*Dame*. [Bad.] That's not the correct bike."

She yelled as her gears allowed her to outpace me. "You should go back."

I was pissed off. My frustration had been building during my previous six years living in Japan. Why did everything have to be in a box? Why couldn't people let someone be different? I wasn't going to give her the satisfaction and I peddled harder.

The climb was no longer about getting to the top, but proving that everything in life didn't need to follow a set equation. It was a small advancement for the lovers of *mamachari*, which belonged on the mountains as much as any society-approved road bike.

The reward for climbing a mountain is the hurling force of gravity that pushes your stomach into your throat as you scream down the mountain. Pure, unadulterated joy filled me as I descended one steep slope after another. The lack of proper brakes and the wobbling aerodynamics added an extra kick of adrenaline as I easily passed the same trucks that had passed me on the way up. I was having fun.

I wasn't supposed to be having fun. This was supposed to be about finding my purpose in life, and everyone knows that your purpose is not about fun. It's about settling down, taking on responsibility, and having a family. Guilt fought adrenaline on the battle ground of my stomach. Joy won, and I left behind the pains of walking, and the pains of trying to conform.

I was also confused. Pain has always been a constant companion for me on the pilgrimage. Walking despite the pain defined my first time around Shikoku, and it was hard to change the association that I had formed. If I was not pushing myself harder and further, was I still even doing the pilgrimage? Or was I a tourist like the Tokyo Boyz?

As I rode, the pleasure of the sun's warmth on my skin and the tingling of the wind as my eyes watered filled me with a profound sense of freedom. By the time I reached Temple Thirty-Seven I was convinced I was allowed to have fun and that everyone I had met along the way had been right. I needed to slow down, enjoy the walk, and not be concerned with where I ended up each night. Such freedom did come with a price, though, and I had limited resources in the currency of choice— time. The bicycle helped, but I knew that if I was to get the most out of my pilgrimage, I couldn't stay on the bike forever. I needed to go back to walking at a slower pace and learn to enjoy it as much as I had the plummet down the mountain. The question was when, as my destroyed legs were still taut with tendonitis.

As I passed through the temple's large wooden gate and into the protection of the religious grounds, I heard Shinichi yell his first English words—"No fuck!" He continued in Japanese. "Hey, Ichiro, the *mamachari* made it."

We ignored the stares of *henro* disrupted from their chants, and we hugged, high fived, slapped backs, and laughed our way to the faded blue benches found at each temple.

Finally, convinced the *mamachari* was worthy of a cycling tour, we stayed close to each other for the next few days, my basket and bell never more than a few turns away from their proper bikes ahead. Each night, we slept outside, close to natural hot springs (*onsen*) where, for a small fee, we could wash away the grime from the road and soothe our aching bodies. The bikes gave us a larger selection of places to spend the night, a luxury a walking pilgrim didn't have, and I enjoyed it to its fullest.

11

REDEMPTION

O n the southwestern tip of Shikoku, Cape Ashizuri juts defiantly into the endless churning blue ocean. Few places are as wild and remote. Temple Thirty-Eight, Kongō-fuku-ji, the Temple of Everlasting Happiness, waited for me at the end of the cape's edge, high up on a cliff that drops dangerously to the crashing waves below.

The *henro* path overlaps the concrete Route 27 as it makes its way down the coast towards the temple. My bicycle gang had separated based on pace, and I'd catch up, overtake, and fall behind on my way down the coast. Lush green mountains protected me from the cape's harshness until I suddenly came to a tunnel. I pushed through salty air until I emerged from under the mountain to sweeping views of the Pacific Ocean. Open endlessness released my thoughts from the worry and confines of my mind. Pure joy engulfed me as I twisted and turned around sharp corners, the road holding tightly to the green mountain on my right, at the mercy of the plunging cliff on my left. The smell and sound of the ocean filled and consumed my senses.

Facing south, the layout of the Temple of Everlasting Happiness was modeled after the Indian mountain Potalaka, believed to be a dwelling place of Kannon (Avalokitesvara), the

Bodhisattva of Compassion. It is from these cliffs that the endless blue horizon captured the imagination of the ancient Japanese. The cape has long been believed to be a merging point between the physical world and the spiritual. For centuries ascetics have journeyed to this southern tip in search of enlightenment, a place where one is able to break free from the confines of our physical world.

The temple was reportedly founded by Kūkai in 822 CE. Convinced this was the gateway to the Pure Land and enlightenment, countless ancient Japanese set out in rickety boats. None returned.

Over the years the high cliffs became a favorite spot for suicides as the young, in love, and distressed hurled themselves over the edge. Suicide is still a preoccupation that grips Japan to this day, with more than 20,000 people taking their lives each year across the country. As I stepped to the edge of the cliff, I fought my own urge to jump.

There is something coercive about heights, like a drug urging you to just take a step and feel the rush of air against your skin and a surge of adrenaline. I wasn't suicidal in the least, but there was still something compelling about the cliff's power. Something that it apparently shares with San Francisco, as one Japanese guidebook on the Shikoku pilgrimage oddly notes: "It is a favorite spot of suicides, like the Golden Gate Bridge of San Francisco. Do not miss the beauty of the sunrise here."

There is only one way down to Temple Thirty-Eight and one way back. I climbed back on my bike and retraced the 14 miles up the coast to where the pilgrim path split. I would start heading north along Shikoku's western coast. Someone should have told the guys in the boats heading south that they were going the wrong way, as heading north out of Kōchi Prefecture leads to the next phase of the pilgrimage, Ehime Prefecture, the Land of Enlightenment. If they could see how beautiful the road through the mountains is, accompanied by cool rivers stocked with delicious eel (*unagi*), they might have reconsidered.

Just after crossing into the Land of Enlightenment, I stopped for the evening near a hot spring with the Tokyo Boyz. Two days in a row of soaking in thermal waters helped me to have my first full night's sleep in almost two weeks. I hadn't touched a painkiller in three days, and it was clear my body was healing. We slept outside under the roof of a nearby sports park, and no one even questioned why we were there. The peaceful night helped clear my head and reminded me of my original purpose.

It was time to leave the bike and return to the life of a walking *henro*. Riding the bike had been a way to continue, to let my feet heal. But in my heart, I was not on a cycling pilgrimage. I was a walking pilgrim, and it was time to get back to being myself. I just hoped my new outlook on life, feeling the joy the of journey, could weather the renewed pounding my feet would take.

WE SPED alongside the ocean once again, up and down mountains and past the seaside city of Uwajima, famous for bullfights and sex. Well, famous for the sex museum, Dekoboko Shindō, at least. Founded by the former head priest of the Taga Shinto shrine, Morimaru Kubo, he supposedly gained enlightenment and distilled his understanding to: "Sex is religion, sex is philosophy, sex is morality, sex is science, sex is both life itself and human life."

A three-story museum holds Kubo's private collection of tens of thousands of sex items from Japan and around the world, including possibly, hopefully, the world's only collection of pubic hair. Several thousand strands of pubic hair from all over the world are preserved, categorized, and laid out for the world to investigate. How Kubo managed to collect so much boggles the mind and brings forth images of a Shinto priest scouring hotel showers for used bars of soap.

I left the Tokyo Boyz to catch up and rode ahead to the remote Mima valley, where Temple Forty-One, Ryūkō-ji, the Temple of Dragon's Ray, is lovingly cradled in deep green mountains. Heavy stone stairs and carved images of the fox god Inari Ōkami blended beautifully with the surrounding forests, mountain, and wooden beams of the temple's buildings. The mix of Shintoism and Buddhism was strong here, as the temple was also the center of worship for the mischievous Shinto god. Each of the temple's buildings rested at different levels, requiring extra effort to climb the various steps. I took my time, feeling no particular rush.

I relaxed on a bench and watched tourists get out of their cars and mix with chanting pilgrims. A steady stream of people entered and left, some praying, some snapping pictures, others just out for a walk. To say the temple, or any of the 88 temples, is part of a "Buddhist pilgrimage" felt like too heavy a label for Japan, as I sat surrounded by an equal number of Shinto shrines. Religion as a concept, compared to the West with its prescribed ways of belonging and exclusion, is very different in Japan. The pilgrimage seems less a product of Buddhism than it is a product of Japanese society. In fact, most religion in Japan, at least in how it touches the vast majority of citizens, is more akin to a culture. It is woven into the Japanese lifestyle and is not a separate activity.

I was once in a family house in Tokyo just before New Year's Eve, when everyone heads to a temple or a shrine to cleanse themselves for the year ahead. Of course, the family insisted they were not religious, that this was just something everyone does. Just before we left for the shrine, there were moments of intense activity, and I was ushered upstairs to a small back storage room.

A candle was lit, I was given incense, and then we all proceeded to pray to the spirits of the family's deceased parents. Housed in the closet was a beautiful Buddhist shrine made for the home (*butsuden*) that is passed down to the eldest son to take care of his family members who have passed on.

Religious activities are done by professionals. They live in temples, have gone to school, and know what they are doing. Pilgrims end up blending these activities together, around the common theme (at least on the pilgrimage) of ascetic training (*shugyō*). But it is also a common theme across Japanese culture, of working hard, setting a goal, striving for perfection, and gaining something invaluable in the process that is not necessarily religious but might be spiritual. Others visiting the temples might be just participating in tourism, cultural reification, or anything in between.

There was something special about this temple—the harmony, the quiet, the acceptance of two different religions. Nothing could disturb my sense of peace, of purpose. Until the Tokyo Boyz arrived and we met the head monk.

The monk, head shaven and wrinkled with age, was dressed impeccably in black robes. He sat slouched behind the counter, waiting to sign our books and scrolls. The Tokyo Boyz were in front of me as I and another female *henro* waited patiently.

"Excuse me," Ichiro said. "Could I please have an envelope to hold my Buddha slips?"

The calligraphy brush continued, with no response from the monk. Ichiro tried again but the monk cut him off as he ended his stroke. "You wasteful, stupid kids. You don't need another envelope. You can fit 100 easily into just one."

We all shifted uneasily in line as the monk chastised and lectured him on wasting resources and being impatient, laying all that is supposedly wrong with youth on his shoulders.

Ichiro didn't argue or get upset, even though his current envelope was torn to pieces after getting wet in a rainstorm the day before. He accepted the barrage in good measure, took his book and slip, bowed, and said, "Thank you."

None of us fared any better as the cantankerous monk decided to teach us all a lesson.

I presented my scroll with a bow, trying my best to not get on his bad side. It didn't work.

"You lazy, arrogant kid. The proper way to hand me the scroll is to roll it into two sections so that it is easier for me to sign." Of course, this would bend the scroll in the wrong direction. At every other temple the staff had been fine with unrolling the scroll to the unsigned section only, but I didn't dare explain this.

"I'm the only one on Shikoku who teaches people, the only one who is truly like Kūkai." The monk twisted and bent my precious scroll, treating it like it was nothing. I always imagined Kūkai to be kinder and less attached to his own ways.

I reached to take back my scroll before he destroyed it any further, and I received another tirade. "What do you think you're doing?" he yelled as I turned to dry my scroll. "Don't you care about the environment? Don't you have any patience? There is no need to use the blow-dryer. You can wait until it dries."

I was tempted to ask why there were two blow-dryers sitting on the table. But I kept my mouth shut and picked up a paper fan instead.

He snapped for the next person to step up. The woman was a middle-aged pilgrim, dressed immaculately in white, her gaze slightly lowered in polite meekness. She was going to be fine. Then she opened her mouth. "Excuse me, but is there a toilet?"

"Are you stupid? You kids don't know how to speak proper Japanese!" She stared at the floor, her cheeks turning red. "Ask your question directly: '*Toire wa doko desu ka.*' [Where is the toilet?]" he said slowly, to her humiliation.

She asked where the toilet was and shuffled off.

Whether the monk intended it or not, his rant on drying my scroll made me realize that I was moving too fast, too eager to get to the next place. It was time to get off the bike.

I met the Tokyo Boyz in the parking lot and broke the news. "Today's my last day with you guys. At *Bangai* Eight I'm giving up my bike and walking again."

Bangai are unnumbered temples. But there are so many of them that they have now been numbered.

"What, are you crazy?" they said in unison.

I smiled. I knew they didn't understand, and I couldn't explain it to them. They were on a vacation, but I had other things to work out. I still needed to figure out what I wanted to be when I grew up. As much fun as riding was, I realized that I could never figure it out if I continued on the bike. It had served its purpose, and now it was time to get off.

We shared one last mountainous drop, and I reveled in the speed. By 5:00 in the evening we were in the middle of the quaint castle city of Ōzu and had arrived at *Bangai* Eight, the Temple of the Bridge of Ten Nights. According to legend, Kūkai found himself at this bridge during winter and was forced to sleep under it when each house in the town refused him lodging. Cold, he penned a poem:

They will not help a traveler in trouble
This one night seems like ten.

A statue of a lying-down Kūkai is part of the shrine under the bridge, and the temple nearby has taken on the role of helping walking pilgrims. I planned to spend the night in a small *tsuyadō* it offered to pilgrims.

After saying our goodbyes, good lucks, and hope to see you

agains, I entered the temple's main office to ask permission to sleep and to offer a gift.

The monk on duty had no problem with me staying but warned it was small and that others might come in the middle of the night.

"Thank you. I'd also like to give the temple my bicycle." I tried to hand him the keys to the lock, but he made no move to accept them. My hand hung awkwardly in the space between us. "Don't worry, it's in great condition and is only four days old."

"No, thank you." He turned to leave.

This whole scenario had gone completely differently as I cooked up the idea in my head on the ride to the temple.

"Please, wait," I begged, not understanding why this was so difficult. "It's okay. I don't need it anymore, and I'd like for it to be used by someone rather than thrown away."

"We don't need a bike," the monk replied

I tried another way. "Do you have a bike?"

"No."

"Would someone use it if . . .?"

"Why do you want to give it to us? What's wrong with it? Is it stolen or something?" He looked at me with suspicion, like this was some sort of elaborate plan to get him or the temple in trouble.

I tried to explain everything, that I only needed the bike while my foot was injured, but now I was ready to walk again.

The monk still didn't want to believe me. Sweat ran down his bald head. I assured him it wasn't stolen a few more times and then tried to offer it as *osettai*.

"I'm not a *henro*. I can't accept *osettai*," he said.

I was getting frustrated, and he was getting ready to leave.

"It's a present from America," I blurted out.

The monk paused and considered this for a moment. Somehow, this absurd logic was okay, and he accepted the keys, if reluctantly. He didn't say thank you, and I got the feeling that that was supposed to be my line as he turned and walked away without another word. Everything has its place in Japan. *Henro* do not give presents to monks. But it turns out Americans can.

The *tsuyadō* was small, just big enough for two adults to sleep on its worn straw *tatami* mats. No one was there but the mats were covered with, um, reading material. Pictures of underaged girls in bathing suits and suggestive poses made up the bulk of them, others were naked women with their lower region pixelized in accordance with Japanese law. All were commonly found on magazine racks across Japan and showed the odd juxtaposition of sexualizing kids while adult anatomy was a no-no.

As I was putting the magazines to one side the door slid open.

"Todo!" I heard someone scream.

It was Kanako, the high school girl I had befriended almost one week ago. "How did you get here?" She entered quickly and gave me a big hug. Then she noticed the porn. "Gross."

This was uncomfortable.

"They're not mine!" I said. "They belong to the temple." That sounded like a lie.

"Yeah, right," she said with a laugh.

We pushed the porn aside and caught up. She had found homes for all the puppies and was lonely. It was her last night before she returned to Hiroshima and the pressures of high school.

Age differences didn't matter on the pilgrimage, and I couldn't think of a better way to transition off the bike than with the person who got me on the *mamachari* path. The universe was speaking to me again, and I might just be ready to listen.

We slept peacefully next to each other, surrounded by Japanese porn.

12

ENLIGHTENMENT

Kanako left early, and I got a late start at 6:00 in the morning. Before I left the temple, I made a quick stop to the men's bathroom. Just as things got going, in walked an old woman. I checked again and the tiny urinal assured me I was in the correct bathroom. I shifted to block her view as she started cleaning the urinal next to me. There were no privacy dividers. In fact, there were no doors to the bathroom at all and the windows were wide open.

"*Henro*-san, you look like something's wrong," the woman casually said as she scrubbed yellowed porcelain less than a foot away from my exposed manhood. I shifted and turned my back further still. Any further and I'd be peeing on the floor.

"Excuse me." I didn't know how to respond. Of course there was something wrong—she was in the bathroom. It was a common occurrence in Japan, where most of the cleaners are women, but I had never become comfortable with it. Nor did I understand why someone wouldn't wait to clean until the urinals were free.

"You are standing strangely. Something's wrong with your legs, eh? Follow me." She strode out of the toilet, taking off her elbow-length, pink rubber gloves, the sound of latex smacking off withered arms as she disappeared around the corner. I shook and followed. It was an odd thing to do, but by this point I was used to having weird things happen to me.

She led me back to the *tsuyadō* and told me to sit. I took off my shoes at her request and she ran her hands up and down my bare legs. Her eyes closed and her face scrunched in deep concentration as she listened to something no one else could hear, and she, just barely. She was performing *kikō*, an ancient practice of energy healing. It isn't something that most people run across much in Japan anymore, but there is still a deep cultural belief, at least in the idea of a universal energy, *ki* (*chi* in Chinese), that is fundamental to our health and wellbeing.

She was sure that my pain was due to an imbalance in my *ki*. I thought it had more to do with two weeks of constant walking and pounding them into mush against the unforgiving road. But I had to admit that it was soothing, and as I was about to start walking again, it couldn't hurt.

Spunky, with an energy that belied her 92 years, she seemed like the ultimate example of Japanese longevity. But she wasn't always like this, she said. In her 70s she became ill and was close to dying. Despite her family warning her to stay in bed, she came to the temple every day to pray, limping the few miles each way.

"It's my prayers that saved me and keep me healthy still. They will keep you healthy too." She smiled, snapped her pink gloves back on, and handed me her business card before wandering off. I called out a thank you just before she disappeared around a corner. I flipped over her white card, which simply said, "Kikku, Temple Cleaner."

I was soon alone again and back in the countryside. Ten minutes after turning off the busy main road, I felt like I was in the middle of nowhere. I followed the country road into the mountains, along a small river. There was an odd mix of dilapidated, abandoned houses, brand new rest areas, and silent recreation centers built for an aging population that never quite got as big or as energetic as expected.

It was hot, and I was thankful for my straw hat, secured back in place on my head after so many days tied to the bike. It was impossible to wear while riding the bike, and the top of my head had suffered for it. Despite wearing a bandana, my shaved head was blistered and oozing from a severe sunburn. But things could have been worse. Weeks of living with pain have a way of normalizing it.

My feet were still covered with painful blisters, but the tendonitis seemed to have gone. I walked slowly, enjoying the solitude, feeling like I had a new lease on life. I let myself enjoy the experience.

"*Henro*-san," someone called.

I stopped and looked into a dark wooden garage. Inside, an older woman, with a kind face and smile that lit up the earthen floor where she sat, was surrounded by bright green pears. Two other elderly women and one man in a gray jumpsuit were also hard at work preparing the newly picked fruits. In constant, if slow, motion they pulled off individual paper bags that had protected the fruits from bugs. Next, they wrapped each in Styrofoam webbing, ready to be shipped all over Japan as gifts.

This was the face of rural Japan. The elderly worked long hours in the fields and garage factories, unable to stop even if they wanted, which they probably didn't, as it went against society's notions of productivity and their own values. In many ways, this is the magic of Japan. As cities swelled and rural communities drained, economic links remained stable, in part by promoting the shipping of fresh, seasonal specialties to relatives as gifts. There might not be enough workers in the villages, but there was plenty of work.

"*Osettai*," she said as she handed me two perfect pears, protected from the bugs and perfectly ripe. They were delicious, crisp, juicy, and only slightly sweet. I gratefully ate them both as I walked deeper into the countryside on my way to Temple Forty-Five. The farther I walked, the older the towns became, the more elderly people I met, and the more hand-grown food I was offered as *osettai*. This was perfect, as the countryside didn't have any shops, and at one point I found myself eating a raw onion like an apple.

THE NEXT DAY was hot and muggy, just like all the rest, and I struggled up and down a long mountain path. The trees magni-fied the stuffiness, as the canopy trapped the humid air favored by the thick green moss that brightened the forest. Perhaps I had gotten too confident from the previous day's easy roads and the abundant food and help, as I now found myself lost and out of both food and water. A typhoon had swept through the area before I arrived, washing out paths and *henro* markers.

A network of crisscrossing logging trails confused me, and I spent two hours trying to find my way out. The *henro* walking map is invaluable, until you move off the paths. Then it is just extra weight in your bag. The world was beginning to spin as I dry heaved every few steps from the lack of hydration needed to fuel a long hike under such conditions.

I pressed on despite not knowing where I was headed. Slowly, the trees thinned out and the dirt path turned to asphalt as I stumbled into a lonely village, made up of a handful of houses surrounded by terraced vegetable gardens. I thought I was on the other side of the mountain, but with no markers it was impossible to tell where I was. The houses were traditionally constructed with wooden beams but had steep aluminum roofs. These covered up more traditional thatch roofing underneath. It was too difficult and costly to repair the thatch or even remove it as the skills became obsolete and harder to find, so most people just covered them over.

Desperate for water, I approached the only two people I could see. Hard at work in their garden, they were in their late 70s and had lived in the valley all their lives, watching it depopulate as children moved to the cities and their friends and neighbors slowly passed away. They were kind, easygoing, and generous. They offered me tea, three tomatoes, and liters of the best tasting water to ever come from a dirty hose. We sat together on a rough wooden bench and took a much-needed break.

I ate the tomatoes straight away, devouring them one after the other. I couldn't stop praising how good they were.

They waved off my compliments. "America, eh? Well, if you walk a third time, stop by and say hello. We don't get many visitors here and it gets lonely sometimes."

I asked them why they stayed if life was so lonely.

"This is where we belong. Without our farm we would have no purpose, nothing to contribute. We can't move to Matsuyama to be with our son, as his house is too small, and we would just be extra mouths to feed." Everything they said was with a smile.

They seemed to enjoy living out here, but I wondered how much was just for show.

The Japanese are known for their longevity—well, supposedly. The statistics are all based on death records. The problem is, Japan appears to have lost track of many of its centenarians. In celebration of Respect for the Elderly Day, Tokyo officials paid a visit to 111-year-old Mr. Sogen Kato, Tokyo's oldest male resident, only to find him mummified. It turned out he had died 30 years earlier. His family never reported it, so they could continue to collect his pension.

It could have been an isolated incident, but when officials went to check on Tokyo's oldest living female at 113 years old, shockingly, she wasn't living at her address of record. Her daughter claimed she lived outside the city, in what ended up being a vacant lot. Maybe the elderly mother was taken to *obasute yama*, the mythical mountains of folklore where supposedly elderly Japanese were dropped off to "live" out the rest of their lives. In most cases this probably ended in starvation or death by exposure.

It's not clear if *obasute yama,* which translates literally to "mountain to throw away old women," was ever really practiced, as no written record exists. It's also not something one would write about enthusiastically, but the idea has been passed down and many see it as a loving, warm tradition. The elderly sacrifice themselves for the family, as they are no longer useful, and the family grieves because they love their elders. No one wants to do it, but they do it because they love each other.

Shocked by their findings, the police launched an investigation and realized they had lost track of over 230,000 centenarians. Most of this was due to poor record keeping, as one man was still registered alive at 186 years old, but it was also due to the elderly moving away from their families and dying alone. The modern version of *obasute yama,* it seems.

Assuming a few missing centenarians won't throw off the math too much, Japan's longevity is still causing a crisis. Combined with the low birthrate, Japan is graying faster than any society in the world, with over a quarter of the population over the age of 65. At its current pace, by 2040 about 40 percent of all municipalities will become depopulated, and the world will have 20 million fewer Japanese people. One university in northern Japan went a step further and developed an extinction clock. It predicts there will be only one Japanese person left on August 16, 3766. The good news is that we have over 1,700 years to turn things around.

Of course, most young people now leave the village for the excitement of the city, and once thriving towns are in decline. Where the village was once the center of activity, it has become a remote afterthought, forgotten while rushing through subways and shopping for the latest fashion.

The countryside has become a narrow strip of amenities geared toward day trippers, for soaking in hot springs with sweeping views, and packaged tours to see how life used to be in idyllic, reconstructed traditional villages. The real countryside, where there are no rest stops, convenience stores, or tourists, is increasingly avoided. It is a place where the elderly eke out a simple existence of subsistence farming and rely on handouts from children too busy to leave their jobs and growing families. Yet, they remain obligated to send food and provisions through the mail to mark important holidays.

As I said goodbye to my saviors, I wished them well and promised to visit the next time I walked the pilgrimage—something we both knew would probably not happen.

I was back on the main road, which, out in the country, was more a lane. When you walk, you see the world in a completely different manner, and when I arrived at the intersection of Route 153 and Route 209, all I saw was the wonderful wooden bench on the corner, complete with an overhang to protect me from the sun.

I sat, I praised the makers of the bench, I eased out my tension, rubbed my sore legs, and said, "Thank you," out loud to the bench when it was time to continue walking. As I pushed on, with each step the mountains and forests slowly closed in, squeezing out the bright green rice fields that had accompanied me for the past hour.

An elderly lady, head covered with a large white hat, stopped me with the whack of her cane across my chest as I said hello. I winced more at the image of the attack than the actual force behind it.

"You're going the wrong way," she said.

I was sure I wasn't. "I want to climb this mountain," I explained as I pointed to the *henro* path on my map leading to

Temple Forty-Five. I knew exactly where I wanted to go—the most perfect path in the world that leads to the back side of the temple. It is funny what you remember from trips, and what I remembered most from my first pilgrimage was this path. I had thought about it constantly since my last pilgrimage, a perfect ridgeline path shaded in tree cover, narrow but not so much to make it dangerous. I knew I had to walk it again.

"Yes, you're going the wrong way. It would be better if you turn right here and follow the road to the temple." She pointed her cane down a road that didn't even appear in my map book.

I thanked her and started moving in my original direction. She whacked me again. "Crazy foreigner," she grumbled, before letting me pass.

The map showed two ways of getting to Temple Forty-Five. The first way followed the road and led directly to the front of the temple. The woman was trying to get me to go that way. I wanted to walk on the old *henro* trail that climbed over, not around, the mountain where the temple sat. I picked up the pace before she assaulted me again.

As I moved further into the wooded valley, the road narrowed into a windy lane, shaded by lush forests. Rundown traditional houses broke up the encroaching forests, and small fields of overgrown grass hid crumbling houses in the distance. Nothing was taken care of in this village. The gardens were overgrown and rusted out cars were left tilted in ditches. I didn't see anyone moving in the village until I was almost run over, not by a speeding car, but by a mechanically aided maniacal old man. As I turned a corner, he came whizzing down the road on his electric cart, laughing wildly.

He was bald, had a thick face that hid his age, and a big belly pushed against the cart's steering wheel. He was naked except for large tighty-whities. I stepped out of the way and he backed up. He stared at me. I stared back. Captivated, I couldn't help looking at his white underwear. What did he want? Who was he? Clearly, he was a bit mentally ill, and he looked at me with a determined expression and came at me again, laughing wildly. I stepped aside, he veered, trying to knock me down, and then disappeared around the corner, the electric motor buzzing almost as loudly as his laugh, until both were swallowed by the forest.

In less than 10 minutes of walking through the one-lane town, I encountered no fewer than six elderly cyborgs zipping around the town on electric carts, showing them off like tricked out custom cars. Someone must have figured out how to get the insurance company to pay for it all, or maybe after one person got one the rest felt like they needed to keep up with the new trend.

As I walked out of the valley of the electronic elderly, I came to a last old woman sitting on her own electric cart. She had a huge grin on her face that I assumed was because of the awesome wheels she was sporting.

"You're going the wrong way, *ohenro*-san."

I tried to explain where I was going, but she pointed to a sign just a little way up. It read "Taihō-ji, Temple Forty-Four" and had an arrow pointing straight ahead. My heart sank and I thought about stealing her electric cart.

Walking *henro* came at Temples Forty-Four and Forty-Five differently. Those in cars didn't care about distances and visited them in order. For pilgrims on foot, it was shorter to walk first to Temple Forty-Five and then move on to Forty-Four, followed by Forty-Six. I should have turned down a different road back at my lovely bench, but had missed the signs. Both women were correct, and I had been too stubborn to listen.

I was five miles out of the way and losing precious time before Temple Forty-Five closed for the evening. The kind lady on the cart showed me where I was on the map, and I had two choices. I could take the now shorter route and walk two miles along the flat roads to Temple Forty-Four, or I could backtrack

another five miles on the road and then up a mountain path to
the trail of my dreams.

I was exhausted, I'd gotten lost twice already, my body was
malnourished, and my answer was clear. I decided on the
longer mountain route. After 15 days on the pilgrimage, I
wouldn't forgive myself if I took the easier way when the path I
had dreamed about for seven years was just an extra five miles
away.

As I HIKED up the steep mountain path, no amount of hunger
could take away my excitement. I had chosen the more
rewarding path, the one that would make me happy despite the
extra work. This was a major change from just a week ago,
when all my decisions were based on conserving steps and
minimizing distance.

I crested the top of the rise, and the path was everything I
remembered. I stopped and admired the narrow ridgeline track
laid before me, shaded by straight cedar and pine trees lining
the steep slopes on either side. Slowly, I took a step forward and
felt loose leaves slide against the hard dirt beneath. I breathed
in the bright, slightly sharp pine scents, while a light breeze
rippled through sunlit leaves, cooling the sweat off my skin
with a tingle. Birds flittered from branch to branch, singing in
response to the jingling of my staff.

In that moment, as the whole forest entered through my
mouth, ears, nose, eyes, hands, and feet, my brain suddenly
popped, and the universe became clear once again. My
thoughts and feelings became one, finally at peace with each
other. I realized that my search for what I wanted to do for the
rest of my life had missed the point completely. The answer
had been staring me in the face the whole time. It was so

simple, and yet I hadn't been able to see it. I was already the person I wanted to be.

This was what I wanted to do for the rest of my life. This was already who I was. I wanted to have the freedom to walk a pilgrimage if I wished. I wanted the choice to pick up and move to another country when I wished. Learning new things, meeting new people, and making a difference in the world by developing new skills—those things were what made me happy. It wasn't about a specific job or career path but about the ability to change and grow. If something didn't make me happy, then I wanted a life where I could choose to do something else.

How had I missed this during my long search for a career, for a purpose to my life? It was in front of me all along.

I sat down in the middle of the path as my past came flooding back to me with a new clarity. What defined me were my choices and my actions. By choosing not to stay home, get a "normal" job, get married right away, have kids, and settle, I was already being the person I was searching for. Without realizing it, I had already accomplished what I wanted to do with my life.

The struggle was really about letting go of what other people expected of me. For the six years I had lived abroad, I had always assumed that I would return to the US at some point, having gotten the search for excitement out of my system, ready to settle. But I only felt this way because my family, my friends, everyone I knew expected it. No one they knew moved abroad and traveled the world. The one or two people they had heard of did it for six months or a year, at most, a short-lived adventure before they returned to real life.

The way forward was now easy to follow. It didn't matter what exactly I was doing as long as I was not stuck, as long as I could experience life unburdened from the pressure of what society expected. I wouldn't let myself believe that I was still immature, naive, or going through a phase. I had a new outlook on life, where each day was appreciated throughout the whole range of pain and pleasure. The ability to pick up and move on when needed is an amazing thing. It is not easy to leave the comfort of home behind and strike a new path. But this is what I wanted, to always be in it, to make my actions matter, and in the end be able to set my soul free to see everything and experience everything that is right around me.

I listened to the breeze wind its way through the forest, and the echo of birds chirping fade into the distance. My pilgrim's mind was no longer restricted to isolated events. I could see that the universe wraps itself in a veil of fake randomness. But by learning to let go, learning to listen, you begin to see structure. It turns out that everything really does happen for reason. The question is whether you will take advantage of it or not. Understanding this simple fact set me free on the top of my mystical mountain. It let me face the future and the present, filled with optimism and trust.

I stood up, dusted myself off, and let go of what society expected from me, or at least what I thought society did. Sure, there were lots of practicalities that needed to be figured out—money, work, love—but I finally understood the basics of what I wanted out of life. I wanted freedom, I wanted choice. I wanted to do what I loved, and love whatever I was doing. If I stopped liking something, then I would move on, change to something new. Each successive change would keep me on the correct path, just like walking through the difficulties on the pilgrimage.

The path left the high ridge behind and descended into a dark forest behind Temple Forty-Five, the Temple of the Rocky Cave. I felt completely at peace as I hiked the ancient path, winding through thousand-year-old cedar trees, past moss-covered wooden shrines and age-worn stone statues of gods and Buddhas that increased in number and regularity. I had arrived at the *okunoin*, the sacred inner shrine of an already

mystical temple, used for millennia as a place of ascetic practice and clarity. It was here, exactly 44 temples into the 88, that I
had my own moment, one that has guided my life ever since. A
clarity about myself and how the world works would fuel
countless adventures yet to come.

Temple Forty-Five sits below a tall cliff high up in the
mountains. The rock is cut deep with caves where ancient
monks meditated in search of enlightenment, and where
mountain ascetics sought to become gods. I took extra time
praying at each of the halls, to give thanks.

The temple was closing so I followed the stone stairs down
the mountain to the road and a nearby hotel. I wasn't staying at
the hotel but at the covered bus stop next door that was little
more than a roof with no walls separating it from the road.
Towering rock cliffs shot up above the area, shrouded in mist
like an ancient Chinese ink painting. The bus stop was a gathering spot for a variety of *henro*, as five different people ended
up staying the night there, more than I had seen camping out
in one place this whole time.

A married couple from Tokyo were doing the pilgrimage by
bicycle. They ran a *fugu* (the potentially deadly puffer fish)
restaurant in Ikebukuro, Tokyo. They talked of nothing but sex,
fuck buddies, and orgy groups, and that was just over dinner. A
young, quiet bicycle *henro* with a soft face, from Nagoya, named
Moriyama-san, showed up next. Then there was a mother and
daughter team from Sendai, in northern Japan, whom I had
seen walking here and there over the past two days. They were
staying at the hotel and visited the bus stop to say hi. Finally, a
skinny young guy named Kikuchi-san, from Tokushima, the
next prefecture we would soon pass through, showed up. He
sported long, fluffed, dyed blonde hair and a white ball cap
tilted to the side.

After getting naked with the boys in the hotel hot spring
and soaking our weary bodies, we had a group dinner of curry

and rice. I attempted to drink a beer but all it did was make me groggy and tired of listening to the older couple discuss their sex lives in thoughtful detail. So much had changed that day and I needed to sleep.

I laid my head down at 8:00 p.m. under the roof of the bus stop, but couldn't sleep. Instead of thinking about my spiritual awakening, my ears were filled with the escapades of the husband as he held court with Moriyama-san and Kikuchi-san, who were mesmerized at the promise of free sex in Tokyo, the big city.

The husband related the whole range of sexual experiences, from his various girlfriends' sexual needs, to his preference for orgies. "The best are, of course, the ones that happen with no planning. But those don't happen much anymore. I must be old or something. Now we pay to visit rooms. Everyone is ready to fuck, but the lights are dark, and girls are old like me."

He praised his current wife, who slept in a tent two feet away, for not getting mad at him for having sex with other people. It seemed his previous four wives were not as accommodating.

I've met a few other people in Japan like Ikeda-san, who were open to talking about sex. Their audience never say anything and just let them talk. I've always wondered why. Was it impolite to interrupt? Was it that socially acceptable to have sex with high school girls, cheat on your wife, or visit "soap lands," where you pay a stranger to jerk you off?

After all my time in Japan, I have begun seeing it as a large clenched fist. Societal rules capture 90 percent of the population. They ensure that the vast majority of Japanese appear the same, at least superficially, where it matters. Everyone is middle class, everyone has a job or is a homemaker. Everyone is in perpetual motion, always doing something, trying to make things better, to become perfect at something. People keep moving, even if it is not productive and is in fact harmful, to avoid being deemed lazy. The fist is tight and holds just about everyone, forcing them to conform. But there is a price. By squeezing so hard, extremes pop out between the fingers and 5 to 10 percent of the population experiences mental disorders that are expressed in a frightening array of inappropriate sexual behaviors and a tendency for some to withdraw completely. Ikeda-san and his wife were shining examples of this.

As a foreigner who is outside of the social system, I was often a lightning rod for people's confessions. During my first teaching job in Japan, my supervisor related her sexual exploits in graphic detail to me in the teacher's room almost every day. My desk was next to hers and without fail, 11:00 started with something like this:

"Hi Todd. See the gym teacher? I fucked him last night in his car while parked in the rice paddies."

The next day:

"Hi Todd. See the assistant gym teacher?"

"You mean the gym teacher's best friend?" I'd confirm.

"Yes. I fucked him yesterday, here in the teacher's room."

This went on for two full years. When she got back from a vacation to Thailand:

"How was your trip?"

"Great. I met a guy at the bar, and we fucked on the beach that night."

"Did you use a condom?" See, this was phrased in perfect Japanese, asked with a high level of disapproval to convey, with the correct intonation, "I hope you used a condom."

"Of course not! He bought me drinks all night, and it would have been rude to ask." Her tone was just as disapproving of my naivete.

Another time, I was visiting my girlfriend's family in a rural village on the Japan Sea. A drunk, distant uncle grabbed me in the middle of a formal party and yelled, "I'm glad we lost the war. Before, I couldn't have sex with anyone. Everyone was too uptight. Once we lost, I could have sex with anyone I wanted, all over Japan. And believe me, I did."

That was an awkward way to meet the family.

A fisherman all his life, he had somehow seduced a rich geisha from his area. When she passed away, she left him a whole mountain. Instead of retiring on it, he sold the land and used up all the proceeds on more women and even more booze. By the time I met him, in his 80s, he was broke and fishing off the beach each day.

The many kind, reserved, and generous friends I had in Japan often couldn't believe the stories I shared. I wondered if many Japanese people didn't hear these secrets as often. Maybe it was mostly foreigners who were exposed to them since we were outside of the normal social rules. Of course, Ikeda-san didn't have any such inhibitions. That night, poor Moriyama-san, the sweet, innocent university student, and Kikuchi-san were exposed to the full brunt of Ikeda-san's stories and life-style. They listened patiently, quietly.

"I must be hot, as you haven't fallen asleep yet," Ikeda-san yelled over to me on numerous occasions throughout the night. It took one and a half hours before he realized it was his yelling and the lights that were keeping me up.

13

SEX CAFÉ

There is a peculiar and unexpected lonely feeling that accompanies the transition from countryside to city. As I made my way towards the city of Matsuyama, the trees disappeared, traffic increased, and the pavement extended forever, as the *henro* path became nothing more than a road. As the people increased, I felt more isolated rather than less. In the countryside I felt a part of people's lives as they took the time to see me, to speak with me.

Suburban Japan is haunted, filled with the ghosts of traditional homes that have been replaced by cheaper, plastic-like, prefabricated houses. They are crammed together to save space, each one a copy of the next. Narrow roads twist and turn until you're lost in the uniformity and forget that there is any other way to live. Occasionally, you'll see a dilapidated older house, filled with character but abandoned, waiting to be knocked down and replaced with a "modern" home.

In these suburbs, the temples and shrines are islands of vegetation and singularity. Well kept, they offer proof that tradition and a more modern existence can coexist. And yet they are the exception, not the rule. Offering solitude, the thick trees and buzzing cicadas block out the world, the cars, the responsibilities, the sameness. But there were very few of these islands

spread out before me, or in any of the countless suburbs I have
visited across Japan. Everywhere I looked, ugly prefabricated
buildings filled each inch of space, leaving no room for gardens
and barely enough room to park a car.

I walked in and out of uniformed continuity, rushing from
one solitary tree to the next. Not for the first time, I wished
Japan would match the stereotype it is often sold as: smarter
than the rest of the world, able to hold onto its past as it
marches towards the future. I wanted Japan to be a place where
ultra-modern cities and pilgrimages live in harmony. Maybe
these two extremes could live in harmony, but everything else
was being squeezed to death in between, into plastic prefabricated dullness, a middle-class lifestyle.

I had planned to stay the night at Temple Forty-Seven,
Yasaka-ji, the Temple of the Eight Slopes, in a *tsuyadō*, but I
couldn't bring myself to do it. I was tired, but the town made me
feel uneasy. A mix between the countryside and a plastic
factory, it was devoid of any human beings that I could see, and
it left me feeling empty inside. The Japanese have named these
commuting communities "bed towns." I couldn't stay there.
Besides, it was only 2:30 p.m. and I had plenty of walking I
could do. I needed to find a happier place to sleep.

I was about to enter the city of Matsuyama, and that was a
problem. It's a quaint historical city, but a city nonetheless, and
finding a place to camp was all but impossible. As I scoured my
map on the faded blue bench, I heard a familiar voice. The
mother and daughter from Sendai who had visited the bus stop
where I'd spent the previous night were just arriving.

"Where are you staying tonight?" the mother asked.

"That's what I'm trying to figure out now," I said. "Any
thoughts?"

"We are staying the night in Kenko Lando. You should join."

Ah, I knew Kenko Lando, "Healthy Land," well. It was a
modern version of a public bath. I stayed there seven years ago

and now was surprised to hear it was still in business. It lay just beyond Temple Forty-Nine, in Matsuyama, and was cheap. It meant another two and a half hours and five miles of walking, but the reward would be worth it. I would get out of my suburban nightmare.

Sentō are public bathhouses that were once widespread throughout the country. They were the center of village communication, gossip, and relaxation at a time when very few people could afford their own bathtubs at home. They are like the more commonly known *onsen*, except that they are artificially heated, rather than naturally through volcanic activity.

Sentō are dying out and being replaced with *supa sentō* (super *sentō*), such as my destination, Kenko Land. The modern versions are one-stop relaxation stations where, after putting your belongings in a locker, you are given a towel, a *yukata* (robe), and are let loose to forget the world. You are free to enjoy any number of hot, cold, tepid, salty, tea-flavored, rocky, whirling, and bubbling baths that you can tolerate.

There are massage chairs (for a fee), human masseuses at $130 an hour, video games, a movie room, a TV room, a restaurant, and countless vending machines all ready to gobble up your disposable income.

For *henro* and truck drivers, Kenko Land was a steal. For $23 (2,300 yen) you could spend 24 hours inside, using the baths, coin laundry, and supposedly finding a place to sleep wherever you wanted. However, since the lights never turned off, the truck drivers never stopped drinking, the video games kept clinking, whirling, and buzzing, sleeping could be a challenge.

After a hot bath and a dunk in the cold pool, I sat down to another dinner with the sex-crazed Tokyo couple, who were excited to see me and the Sendai ladies. Even Kikuchi found his way back to us by the end of the meal.

No sooner did we finish dinner than the husband lit up a cigarette, adding to the thick haze of smoke floating throughout the common area. For a health-focused bath house, they permitted smoking just about everywhere in an attempt to keep people from leaving. My head was spinning from just one beer and a marathon worth of miles, so I left to find a place to sleep. Kikuchi followed. We headed straight for the TV room, where rows of reclining seats faced 20 television screens that wouldn't turn off until 1:30 a.m. It was only 8:00 p.m., and kids ran around chasing each other. But the lack of lights and presence of headphone jacks to dull the noise provided the best chance for sleep.

It took hours to finally fall asleep. When I woke in the morning, my companions were gone. I'd only ever see one of them again.

TEMPLE FIFTY-ONE, Ishite-ji, the Temple of the Stone Hand, is popular, prosperous, and filled with tourists. Part of its success is due to its location in the middle of Matsuyama, near the famous Dōgo Onsen, a quaint hot spring housed in a Victorian building and the setting for one of Japan's most popular novels, *Botchan*. Natsume Sōseki was the Meiji era's greatest author, at a time when Japan was just beginning to open up to the West between 1868 and 1912. The author himself expresses frustration with the clash between the adoption of superficial, elitist Western culture and the moral values of traditional Japanese society. In *Botchan*, a young teacher who has a problem with authority leaves ultra-modern Tokyo for traditional Matsuyama and is often surprised by unusual customs. Surprisingly, it's a conflict that still exists over 100 years later, as Tokyo and Shikoku feel almost like different countries.

As I approached the temple, throngs of tourists from a nearby bus obscured the entrance from view. Poking out above the crowd was a large statue of Kannon, the *Bodhisattva* of

Compassion, riding a magnificent silver dragon. Of course, Kannon couldn't just ride a dragon, but did so in style, standing on the dragon's back with perfect composure and serenity.

High on the mountain behind the temple, a gigantic statue of Kūkai stood patiently watching over the area. When I looked again, the flock of tourists had gone, to be replaced by a familiar face, or rather a familiar hunched back. Clothes hanging loosely off his wasted frame, silver-streaked hair poking out of the top of his broken hat, Suzuki-san eagerly counted the money in his begging bowl. He was probably mentally calculating how many nights in a hotel the last group had just paid for.

He sensed my approach and quickly shifted back to the model of pilgrim modesty. Eyes downcast, chanting, he suddenly looked hungry and poor. Then he noticed it was me, and a bright grin lit up his face. "Oi! You made it."

"What are you doing here?" I said with amazement. Suzuki-san was a hard walking pilgrim, putting in 45- to 50-mile days, but there was no way he could have caught up, especially after I'd ridden the bike for four days.

"I took a bus, of course." He said it so casually it was as if his previous boastful talk of walking was forgotten. "I skipped a few temples as I've been to them more than three times each. I need to complete this last journey from 51 to 88 to finish off my four-time walking goal and get certified as a guide. I've got the stamps to prove it, and no one will know I didn't walk the whole thing, eh."

Another busload of tourists arrived.

Suzuki-san quickly ignored me and went back to chanting. "I'll see you later," he whispered in between chants.

The steady stream of bus pilgrims pushed me out of the way as they entered the temple, each dutifully leaving coins and as much as 1,000-yen notes in Suzuki-san's bowl.

It was good to see Suzuki-san, but I doubted we'd see each

other again. The *henro* path left the temple along a mountain path and did not pass back through the main gate, and we clearly had different priorities. I yelled my goodbyes over the bowing heads of excited tourists and moved on, leaving Suzuki-san to his quickly filling bowl.

Ishite-ji is famous for another reason. It's the birthplace of Emon Saburō, and the place where he was born again after finding his peace with Kūkai. The temple's prosperity has brought it an eclectic following, and it is just a weird place. It is crammed with a wide variety of statues, including an elegant wrought iron Emon, a roughhewn stone Kūkai, and heavily varnished wooden carvings of the seven lucky Chinese gods. What really caught my attention was a statue of a man shaped like a penis with a condom-like hat sitting on his head. Coral-like holes riddled his body. In fact, he was one of many locally carved gnome-like creatures that represent the diversity of the Buddha's followers.

The walkway to the temple and its magnificent three-tiered pagoda is lined with shops selling every sort of knickknack a tourist could desire, from magic amulets to buckets of incense meant to be burned all at once so one bathes in the smoke. I could find nothing remotely appealing to a walking *henro*.

Despite the hundreds of oddly collected statues and centuries-old buildings designated as national treasures, the temple's prized possession and religious artifact is the very stone that was supposedly placed in the dying Saburō's hand by Kūkai. Saburō's dying wish was to be reborn to a wealthy family in Matsuyama so that he could use his influence to make the temple flourish and help the poor of the area. Shortly after his death, on the other side of the island, a child was born in the village where this temple now stands, clutching the same stone engraved with the words "Emon Saburō reborn."

The stone was proof that Kūkai fulfilled the dying wish of Saburō. It is hard to know if the miracle was the rebirth or that the universe decided to be so clear about it. Either way, the stone looks way too big to fit into an infant's hand. It is egg-shaped and measures about two inches in length. Miracles can only go so far, and I guess there needed to be enough room for the inscription. The baby in the story was, at least, a real person, Kōno Yasukata. If you believe that Emon was reborn, then it's not too much more of a leap to believe a baby could be born with a stone clutched in its hand, and that it took a priest and magical incantations to force the infant's hand open to reveal Kōno's true origin.

Stories take on an amazing life of their own in Japan, and the Saburō story is now accepted as the origin story for the pilgrimage. This is good and bad in many ways, as the story is at once touching and divisive. It lays the foundation for how pilgrims, locals, and temples interact. It clearly gives the message that wealth should be donated and used to enhance temples. But it also elevates the wealthy and powerful over the worker in the fields. It's a message that comes through clearly even today, as Emon's rebirth is the celebrated event, rather than his redemption, which took place at the deserted country-side temple back near the beginning of the pilgrimage.

On the other hand, the message also elevates the simple pilgrim to the status of Kūkai, as any poor pilgrim may be Kūkai in disguise. It also impresses on the pilgrim that Kūkai can be encountered at any moment on the pilgrimage. I certainly was beginning to feel like the universe, God, Kūkai, whatever, or whoever, was helping me, offering me choices that could lead to my redemption and a life of happiness.

It's a story that has taken on physical manifestations on the pilgrimage route and is instilled in the collective belief system of the locals and the visitors making their way around the island. Despite an obvious set of rules on the surface, the pilgrimage allows more flexibility than most religious activities. The pilgrim does not have to be Buddhist and does not have to do anything in particular, other than move around the island. The pilgrimage's greatest attraction is its flexibility, and it welcomes everyone. This acceptance transcends the barriers society has erected. Life is stripped to its bare essentials—food, water, shelter, and companionship. When you are able to see the essentials you become less concerned, or attached, in the Buddhist framework, to all the hooks modern life tries to catch you with.

The image of the pilgrim as being closer to, or even possibly being, Kūkai placed me in a different world, separate from the everyday of everyone around me as I walked. And yet, I was still tied to the physical world and interacted with societal norms as the pilgrim's path emerged into the more populated areas of Shikoku. I was starting to feel uncomfortable in normal society, especially in the city, where the difference between a walking *henro* and a businessman was stark.

As I walked deeper and deeper into Matsuyama and the crowds increased, I felt further and further removed from the people around me. They were on their way to school, picking up their kids, taking lunch breaks, falling in love, heading back to work. I had to walk. I had to worry about a place to stay. I wondered what they thought of me. Was I an oddity that broke up their day? Or a strange wanderer who smelled horrible?

I had been out of touch with the "real" world for over a week, since I last emailed my parents to let them know I was still alive. I knew they would be worried, so I was determined to find an internet café despite my rising desire to flee the city. The center of the city offered my best chance, so I gave myself a treat and jumped on the local street tram. It was uncomfortable for everyone. My co-passengers pretended not to see each other. They pretended that I didn't smell. I did, horribly. I tried to ignore the fact that they were trying to ignore me. The air was thick with tension, or perhaps my stench, and when the doors opened at Ōkaidō station there was a mad rush to get away from me.

I wandered down one of the ubiquitous covered shopping arcades found all over Japan, until I found an internet café on the third floor of a boring gray building. After my last experience with the French maids, I didn't think anything could surprise me.

Once again, Japan stepped up to the challenge. There was nothing particularly interesting about the café. Most of the computer booths were empty, except one with a high school boy in his black uniform, with his girlfriend, who was sitting on his lap. As I walked by, the girl, in a plaid skirt, jumped up and shut the curtain. Her face was shiny silver from makeup around her eyes and on her lips.

A disinterested young woman in jeans and a T-shirt showed me to my booth. I was happy to be ignored and happy to help myself to the free drinks bar. I chugged cold blue slushies down my throat until I felt sick. I finished emailing and was getting ready to leave when it started—soft moaning that started to build in frequency and strength. I checked my computer screen to make sure internet porn hadn't popped up. Then the wall to my cubical started shaking.

The moaning got louder as my next-door neighbors gave in to their raging hormones. You would think sex in public was a no-no in Japan. But with most kids living at home well into their 20s, and less disposable income to spend on love hotels, internet cafés were becoming the love den of choice across the country. For just a few dollars an hour, you got four thin walls, enough privacy for you to pretend others couldn't hear you, all the blue slush you could drink, and internet and video games ready and waiting to keep the cuddling to a minimum afterwards.

I gathered my stuff quickly and tried to leave before the climax. Too late.

I headed across the street for lunch at a wonderfully rundown ramen noodle shop where there were no joint tables, just stools along various counters, fit for one person at a time. The fast food of Japan, ramen came in various flavors and regional specialties. I walked through the automatic sliding doors, ducking my head to get under the traditional *noren* cloth. Four staff putting together bowls behind simmering vats of soup stock yelled in unison, "*Irasshaimase*," without ever looking up. It's a common welcome in most restaurants and stores throughout Japan. But the ramen shops take it particularly seriously, and employees show their dedication to the shop and the customer by yelling at the top of their lungs.

They wore traditional headbands that barely contained their furious sweat. It wasn't the type of place where you worry about hygiene, just the taste of the ramen and the broth it came with. In a salute to the high school kids, probably on round two by now, I decided I needed some spice and ordered kimchi ramen, the perfect blend of Korean fermented cabbage and Chinese noodles. The broth in the oversized bowl ran red with deliciously spicy fermentation, and the foot-long noodles hung from my plastic chopsticks. A ceramic Chinese spoon was used to catch any stray noodles that managed to get away as I slurped them up with large inhalations. Slurp, slurp, slurp. The noise rang from each corner of the small noodle house as customers, hunched over their bowls, mouths pressed close to the rims, sucked in their noodles.

When the noodles were finished, hands gripped the sides of bowls. Just because the noodles were gone, it didn't mean the slurping was finished. Bowls to our mouths, we slurped in the hot broth, pausing only a second to catch our breath between swallows. No one stared at anyone else. We respected each other's space. As I stood up to leave, no one looked. I didn't even have to pay, as I had ordered through a coin vending machine at the beginning. My hat and walking stick drew no particular attention. And when I left, each worker yelled a resounding thank you, "*Arigatō gozaimasu*," without even glancing in my direction. It was wonderful. I felt like I was accepted, a part of normal life again.

When I got back on the tram, I felt more comfortable being different. Hell, if the high school kids were fine sexing it up in the internet café, I could deal with the Matsuyama tram. I arrived back at my original station, careful not to miss any steps along the *henro* path. The train ride made me realize how lucky I was to be able to walk, to have time to move slowly. I felt liberated. I didn't need a train, a bike, or anything else. I now had enough time to walk slowly, meet up with whoever I wanted, and go at my own pace. I had been a slave to completion, to doing things the hardest way. I made peace with my bicycle period and now it was time to keep walking.

I left Matsuyama ready for anything, heading towards the next phase of my journey—the northern edge of Shikoku and the Inland Sea.

14

HERMIT IN SECLUSION

Walking along the northern coast of Shikoku, I took in the majestic Seto Inland Sea. The placid emerald green waters are home to over 3,000 small islands and separate Shikoku from the main island of Honshu. Large sea gulls called above me, circling yelling hawkers who sold their daily catch. I walked along a busy road and approached a "Tako Bell," faded orange and yellow letters on a large neon palm tree displaying its gaudiness proudly. We were south of the border, but this wasn't a Mexican fast food restaurant. "Tako" was a play on words, and the little shop sold *takoyaki*, chopped up octopus inside a ball of fried batter topped with sauce and bonito flakes. I took the bait and grabbed a box of six as I pushed on.

"Hee, hee." The thin young man I had met the night before let out a high-pitched call as he limped around a corner.

I shouldn't have stopped for the octopus. I took a deep breath and tried to remember a time when I was a good person. I was sure that was just yesterday, wasn't it?

"Oi, Todo-san. You caught a little octopus, chan, chan, hee, hee." His singsong voice rose and fell from one impossibly high pitch to another and back again. Head tilted to the side, Nobu was a scrawny 18-year-old. Hunched shoulders and a guarded body language hinted at trouble making friends with people his own age and why he might have felt more comfortable around adults, who should have known better than to get frustrated with him. He poked a long finger into his cheek and rotated it with a smile, while squeaking "Hee, hee," when I didn't answer right away.

I had met him while staying in a small *tsuyadō*. Despite sitting at the edge of a smelly oil refinery, the tiny shrine with the free room attracted a few *henro* for the night. While a night with a roof and a futon was always welcome, last night marked the beginning of an internal battle as I struggled to remain patient with Nobu's over the top, in-your-face antics.

The night didn't start off as the beginning of my moral decline. As I was just about to start eating dinner, a long, thin *henro* with the calm face of an elementary school teacher on vacation showed up. In his early 50s, Sasaki-san was walking the pilgrimage during his summer holidays. There was plenty of room in the *tsuyadō* with its eight *tatami* mats. We chatted about life, consoled each other over our feet, and shared what little food we had for the evening. His manner exuded a calmness that enveloped me and made me want to be a better person, at least until Nobu showed up.

"Again!?" Sasaki-san yelled, breathing out heavily.

"Hee, hee." Nobu cocked his head to the side like a Hello Kitty velociraptor, blinking his eyes in rapid succession.

Sasaki-san's tall frame sank into a weariness I hadn't noticed before. "Nobu-kun, there is still time in the day. You should keep walking. You're young and fit."

I was taken aback at his sudden change in mood. There wasn't any time left in the day. It was nearly dark, and the map didn't show any other places to stay for the next six miles.

"Hee, hee. Sasaki-san, you're so funny."

"I'm not joking. We have stayed at the same place since Temple Thirty-Six! It's been over two weeks, and it's time you were on your own."

I immediately felt bad for Nobu as the teacher tried to get rid of him. It was hard to imagine why the man I had started to like so much could turn into such an asshole with a kid who was just walking and needed help. Life is, of course, filled with all sorts of irony and loves to find a way to kick you in the teeth, especially when you start judging others. I was feeling confident in walking the pilgrimage at my own pace, and thought Sasaki-san was being too mean. What happened next was another challenge the pilgrimage would throw at me, one that I would ultimately fail.

That night I stayed up with Nobu and looked over my map with him. We discussed places to sleep and what the path would look like. Sasaki-san pulled away from us both and barely said another word. In the morning he was gone, slipping away in the middle of the night.

The next day, as I munched on my octopus balls under the sweltering sun, both the Seto Inland Sea and Nobu would become my constant companions. In less than half a day, I saw all too clearly why Sasaki-san had fled. Nobu, to put it nicely, drove me nuts. Unlike other pilgrims who go at their own speed, Nobu moderated his pace to stay with me. If I walked faster, he was there. If I took a one-hour break, so did he.

Nobu and I soon rounded the top left corner of Shikoku together as we turned east along the northern edge of the island, and making it back to Temple One suddenly became all too real. It is a funny thing to feel like your goal is unattainable for so long, and then one day it draws too close and you wish there were more days in between you and the inevitable end of the journey.

As the sun settled into the late afternoon and 3:00 approached, I hadn't seen Nobu for at least an hour, and I thought that I had outpaced him. I wished him the best of luck, knowing I wouldn't have to deal with him any longer, as I climbed the long stairs lined with countless stone Buddhas up to Temple Fifty-Eight, The Temple of the Hermit in Seclusion. My goal for the day was still over six miles away, a public rest area close to the highway and a train station. Despite the prospect of a noisy night, it had a hot spring that called out to my tired body.

Emerging from the shaded forest path, the mountaintop temple initially revealed very little of itself. Heavy forests pushed in from all sides. Small shrines and large, pruned, intricate trees punctuated a courtyard before me. On the far side, a large wooden temple invited me to cross the hot, open yard.

The stamp office and trinket shop were located directly inside of the main temple hall. The clear money-making business of selling magical amulets and souvenirs so close to the worship hall made me feel uncomfortable. Commercialism and detachment did not sit comfortably together. The presence of an upscale temple hotel just a few feet to the right compounded my uneasiness. I chanted, paid money for my stamp and slip, and was halfway back to the path in under 10 minutes, oblivious to just about any other part of the compound. Blinded by what I thought was a glitzy temple, I wanted to move on and be done with it.

As I rushed to the safety of the trees, a short, bald man off to the side, face crinkled in a perpetual childlike smile, dressed in simple white clothes deeply soiled by the earth, caught my eye. He held a shovel and was tending to a young tree.

"Would you like to stay and help me with my work?" he asked.

What? I looked around to see who he was talking to. He shuffled a bit closer. His head only just managed to reach my shoulder. He repeated his question in unwavering Japanese.

I was positive this must be the resident monk. He embodied all the stereotypes of Japanese animation's take on a Buddhist monk. His turtle-like smile split his face in half, swallowed his eyes, and captivated me. I had no idea what "work" meant but I found myself nodding in agreement. After all, I wasn't under any time pressure, and this was a perfect opportunity to enjoy the moment presented to me. It might just throw Nobu off my trail at the same time.

The bald man somehow smiled even deeper. He turned and shuffled away, motioning for me to follow. We headed towards the hotel and met another bald man, who wore elegant wire frame reading glasses and an immaculate light blue work jumpsuit. My guide shuffled to a stop and bowed low. They talked quietly for a few minutes, just softly enough that I couldn't make out a word.

They finished speaking, and the first man turned to me. "I'm Mukai," he said. "Follow me. I'll show you where you can drop your stuff off and sleep tonight."

"Wait," I said, rushing to catch up. I tried to find out what was going on, but Mukai-san just kept walking toward the hotel.

The other bald man went back to his gardening tasks. I barely spared him a thought. I was hot, sweaty, and I couldn't wait to stay in an actual hotel with air-conditioning once again.

As quickly as the thought entered my head, we turned away from the hotel and headed back past the main temple, past the small shrines, and down a small slope. I looked longingly back at the hotel as we stopped near its service entrance at the edge of the temple grounds, at a concrete bunker cut deep into the surrounding mountain.

Mukai-san yanked the heavy door, and metal screeched in protest as a blast of hot, stale air rushed out. The concrete storage room had no windows, and the sliding metal door was the only exit. Boxes filled the corners, and a loud boiler sent pipes carrying hot water back to the hotel, supplying the baths with heat and magnifying the summer air.

Plywood covered bare concrete walls, making the space feel like a coffin set for cremation. The only inviting part was the three *tatami* mats resting on a raised wooden platform against the far wall.

What had I gotten myself into?

As the night wore on and more travelers joined me, I would come to realize this was the temple's *tsuyadō*. It wasn't listed on any sheet that I had, and I never figured out how other walkers found out about it, other than being lured there by smiling Mukai-san.

"Okay, you can sleep here," he said. "Unpack and let's get to work. You'll need a towel."

By "unpack", he meant "drop your bag and let's go," so I hurried to follow him out the door.

Mukai-san shook with excitement to show me what we had in store. Every few steps he turned and smiled, checking to make sure I was still with him. We walked past the hotel to the east and down a large but unused path to a corner of the temple's grounds. We arrived at a collection of handcrafted wooden buildings overlooking the Seto Inland Sea far below. They were each built using a traditional Japanese architectural design with curved tiled roofs and framing using joinery only.

Mukai-san turned, spread out his hands, and beamed in pride. "This is all mine. I'm building these for the temple."

"You're a monk carpenter?" I asked, a bit confused.

He smiled even deeper, accentuated by a blush. "I'm not a monk, just the groundskeeper."

It turned out that Mukai-san was a professional carpenter who specialized in temples and shrines, called *miyadaiku*. Seven years ago, he gave away all of his possessions—his house, car, everything—and moved to the temple. He worked and lived on the temple grounds in a small, shared house, and received nothing in return but room and board.

He showed me around the area, which consisted of a cedar-built traditional house complete with an indoor *irori* (fire pit) and an amazing wooden bath with a window that opened out across the mountains and the sea below. He dashed over to the traditional pottery house and kiln, and finally to a long, partially dug ditch.

The shape of the ditch and the gray tiled roof above it gave few clues as to its final purpose.

"The *obōsan* wants to create a traditional center here to nurture Japanese arts. This is the last building in our set, where we can make traditional Japanese swords."

"The monk wants to make swords?" I asked, sure I hadn't heard correctly.

"Of course not!" Mukai-san exclaimed. "He'll invite sword makers here."

The tour complete, it was time to get to work, so we headed up the hill to grab a jackhammer. Just as we entered the courtyard, a white *henro* appeared out of the forest.

"Tee hee, hee, hee. Todo-san. Toooodoooo-san. I see you. Chan, chan," Nobu called from the tree line.

"Is this your friend?" Mukai-san asked, staring with me at the young man skipping his way towards us.

It was impossible not to be gentle around Mukai-san. I nodded and waved Nobu over for introductions.

"Great," Mukai-san said. "You can stay and help us too. We have a lot of work to get done. Todo-san, please show Nobu-san to the guest room."

"Chan, chan, this is amazing, Todo-san!" Nobu enthused. "Wow, we get to spend even more time together, just when I thought you had become lost, hee, hee."

I couldn't wait to start up the jackhammer to drown out the squeaking pilgrim.

We spent the next few hours laboring under the hot Shikoku sun, breaking rocks, moving dirt, reshaping nature into an artful function. Nobu learned to hold a shovel, I learned a little more patience, and we exalted in exerting our bodies in completely different ways than walking.

By the time evening descended and a cool breeze blew across the mountaintop, I was exhausted. We made our way to our beds, barely noticing the suffocating sleeping arrangements. Nobu curled up next to me, and as the evening wore on, more and more travelers stopped into the boiler room to find respite from the fresh air outside. Before the night was finished at the secluded mountain temple, six others were packed into the room —two pilgrims and a group of college kids trying to save money.

DEEP, rumbling chants rolled out of the cedar temple, pushed by the rhythmic precision of perfectly timed drums, as the Buddhist monk with the elegant glasses led the daily dawn service. Mukai-san sat behind him, head bowed solemnly, pounding the drums. The morning air was crisp and carried the scent of pine and earth from the remote Japanese mountaintop. Prayer beads comprised of 108 plastic balls wrapped around my left hand, each one reminding me of a different impure thought. I knelt, Japanese style, on my knees in the dimly lit temple. My legs had fallen asleep almost right away, distracting me from the moment. An intricately carved thousand-armed statue of Kannon (the *Bodhisattva* of Compassion), the main Buddha of the temple, sat directly in front of me.

One hour later, my prayers were answered. The monk concluded the ceremony and encouraged us to relax our legs. Sighs of restrained relief and pain filled the dim temple as seven Japanese pilgrims to either side of me shifted their legs on aged *tatami* mats.

The Buddhist monk, dressed in flowing purple, orange, and vermilion colored robes, bowed his shaven head and said in impeccably polite Japanese, "Welcome to Senyū-ji, The Temple of the Hermit in Seclusion."

"Where have you traveled from?" he inquired of everyone. The monk quickly mentioned something interesting, important, or beautiful about each person's hometown, putting everyone else at ease. He only nodded when I mentioned I was from the United States of America.

Pleasantries dispensed with, he began. "I hate America," he intoned, letting the force of his words pound the still air.

"If it weren't for America, the world would be at peace. America has ruined all chance for peace in the 21st century," he preached.

I shifted uncomfortably. The other pilgrims had their heads down, shying away from the directness of the monk.

"I don't hate Americans, only your country and what it represents," the monk continued, now looking directly at me.

An awkward silence hung thick in the air.

Wow, glad we cleared that up. I sat through the remaining hour, planning my escape as the monk rambled on about Afghanistan and Iraq. He condemned the wars and painted America as an evil nation with probably a few good citizens, like me.

The worshippers nodded quick acquiescence as the preaching continued. Heads bobbed in agreement. America was not as peaceful as Japan, it was not as refined, and it was filled with selfishness. People didn't know how to treat each other with respect in America.

He moved on to other topics, but I couldn't listen. My head was filling up with counter arguments that I couldn't bring myself to launch.

I had no idea what to do in the face of his unexpected sermon. So, I kept quiet. For the most part I agreed with him about the wars we found ourselves in. I didn't agree with his stereotyping or using black and white examples of good and evil represented by countries. Moving on from the temple and back onto the path was a better option than to debate not only the intricacies of international politics, but where I thought the monk failed in his Buddhist principles.

Mukai-san just sat in the dark corners of the Buddhist temple behind the monk with an expressionless gaze, his child-like glee gone.

Immediately after the sermon finished, I rushed back to the room and packed up my belongings without sticking around to speak to anyone.

I was almost to the steep path when Mukai-san caught me and said simply, "Shall you stay another day? There's lots of work to be done."

I searched the face of the man who had given up everything he had ever known, dedicating himself to the temple and to this seemingly hate-filled monk. He received little in return, not even a vacation day. He woke up every morning to perform the rituals in the temples before the monk arrived for sermons, and then spent the day building and maintaining the grounds. Yet, a sense of utter peace radiated from his almost perpetual smile.

There was no pretense to Mukai-san, and it was hard to do anything but accept who the monk was and leave his words behind in the temple. I found myself nodding my head once again, not sure why I felt so compelled to be around Mukai-san, or what new path I was being sent down. But for now, it wasn't meant to be the pilgrim's path.

I put my bag back in the boiler room and met Nobu and Mukai-san at the work site. By afternoon the sun had burned any lingering resentment away. Curiously, neither of my two companions mentioned the morning rant, and in keeping with true Japanese mysticism, they just pretended it didn't happen, until it no longer did. We were resting in the shade of a large tree when a familiar figure emerged from the woods, baseball cap hanging halfway off his head.

"Kikuchi-san!" I ran over and almost hugged him. He looked startled but hugged me back. Life with Mukai-san was great, but even his calming nature couldn't fully buffer the growing annoyance with Nobu and his constant observations that were almost questions.

"Todo-san, you have blonde hair, hee, hee, chan, chan. I bet all Americans have blonde hair." This was one of his most profound statements.

"You are so silly, Todo-san, chan, chan. You love to hide, don't you? Hee, hee."

I was like a kid separated from my best friend for years. "Kikuchi, Kikuchi, we are staying here at the temple, building a forge. Please stay with us, please, please, pleeeeease."

I grabbed his arm and led him to Mukai-san. A few beaming smiles later, Kikuchi was enlisted. I had been certain Kikuchi would be far ahead of me after spending my days at the temple. It turned out that he had spent a few extra days in Matsuyama, visiting friends.

I now had another friend to help with Nobu.

"Kikuchi-san, hee, hee," Nobu said. "We are going to be great friends, chan, chan, chan."

I left Kikuchi to be devoured by the cuteness, walked back to our ditch, and let the jackhammer move me towards enlightenment. There was only the task at hand that drowned Nobu's bird whistles, making it that much more enjoyable.

As evening descended, we realized we had no food left. Kikuchi was no help, as he wasn't expecting to get sidetracked and had nothing on him. The temple provided breakfast and Mukai-san had shared instant noodles for lunch, but everyone disappeared at dinnertime. We were left to ourselves as the workday ended and darkness started to creep in. We had resigned ourselves to walking down the mountain to a nearby store when the head monk appeared, carrying a platter of rice balls, fried chicken, beef jerky, and *sake*.

"My wife and daughter prepared this," he said. "Mukai, start a fire and let's enjoy the night."

We were thankful for the food after the long day. But it was a bit weird too. If you paid to stay at the temple, you got three square meals of vegetarian temple food. This was in keeping with most Buddhist traditions of not killing animals. But if you were the monk and his family, (yes, most monks at temples in Japan are married with kids), it seemed meat was no problem, alcohol too.

Japanese Buddhism defies many of the Western stereotypes associated with the religion. Many monks marry, have children, drink alcohol, earn money, and eat meat. If you add in the political hate speeches, you begin to see the interesting expressions of Buddhism in Japan. Most Japanese don't identify as belonging to any religion, while at the same time most claim to be affiliated with the traditions of Buddhism or Shintoism rather than any particular sect.

Japan has an amazing flexibility when it comes to religion, and it is often said that one is born Shinto, gets married Christian, and dies Buddhist. The married part is usually in a fake church built as a commercial enterprise, with a foreigner cast in the role of a priest. There is a fluidity of rituals that is woven into people's lives. Most people have a Buddhist shrine to their ancestors in their house, everyone visits a Buddhist temple or shrine at the New Year, and yet very few have ever meditated or read the sutras. If a relative dies, you are not supposed to visit a Shinto shrine for a year, so Buddhism fills this gap and offers funerals.

The head monk poured us all *sake* and passed around the various meat products. Mukai-san politely refused all but the vegetables. The monk's speech never came up, nor did politics. In the haze of broken Buddhist dietary vows, the monk and I came to a silent agreement to simply accept the other.

The next morning, I sat again in front of the head monk. This time his wife was beating on the drum. This time I started to hear his real message.

"Everyone thinks being a monk is easy. But you might never get a temple," he said with a sweep of his arms.

"You could meditate and study at the head temple for years and then, one day, you are turned out. You have no temple, no career, and you have to start over. If your only goal was to get a temple, your life would become meaningless." He paused and looked at each of us in turn.

"It is pointless to pursue something for fame or fortune. Those are all external, and they can be taken away. Instead, find something that you love, that fulfills you. Then, success will come quickly if happiness is the only goal," he concluded, with a deep bow, head to floor.

The pilgrimage offers lessons at times when you least expect or want them. It gives people the opportunity to help others and to really see them. We learn to let go of our preconceived notions and just help each other. How often does a person stop their car and offer a dirty, smelly stranger a ride in the regular world? It happens all the time on Shikoku. Accepting allows us to see each other as humans, rather than simple stereotypes. The monk was now human, and I could see his passion for the temple, and the Japanese arts.

I left the mountain two days later with a light heart, certain I had met the true hermit in seclusion, disguised as the groundskeeper.

15

EVEN MONKEYS
FALL FROM TREES

"Hee, hee, chan, chan. Todo-san," Nobu called while sashaying his way down the steep rock steps to join me at a bubbling spring on the way to Temple Fifty-Nine. Like every other "miracle" on the island, the inscription next to the water gave the credit to Kūkai, this time for tapping the spring with just his staff.

"Where are we staying tonight, tee hee?"

I remembered the haunted eyes of the elementary school teacher who had been worn down by Nobu. The past few days had made life with Nobu tolerable as others shared the burden, but the thought of continuing with him alone made my heart sink. And yet, I couldn't leave him.

As I departed in the morning from the Temple of the Hermit in Seclusion, Nobu was nowhere to be seen. But when I reached the mountain path, there he was, waiting with all his gear. He needed help, and I was feeling like a good person from my time on the mountain with Mukai-san. I thought I could handle it. We would both end up paying the price for my inability to be honest with him.

"Here." I pointed to a blank area on my map.

Nobu blinked and hunched his shoulders even more, trying to find something that wasn't there.

"That is where I'm going to sleep," I said. "There is a small Shinto shrine just before the path leading up the mountain to Temple Sixty. It has a gazebo and a toilet, at least according to the list of places to stay, even if it's not on the map."

Despite loving my map, I'd come to accept that it wasn't perfect and often didn't show all the places to stay. Given the changing nature of free places, it would probably be impossible to keep things up to date anyway. I was now working off four different lists of places to stay that I had come across, including one handwritten by the homeless pilgrim, to help get me through to Temple Eighty-Eight.

"There are other places to stay. Look, here, here, and here." I pointed to a few different options along the way. "You should be on your own more," I added hopefully.

"Great. Hee, hee. Chan, chan. We lost Kikuchi-san. I don't want to lose you." He set off down the path.

Mukai-san had persuaded Kikuchi to spend a few more days helping out around the temple. There was a lot to be done.

"Silly, silly, aren't you coming?" Nobu called over his shoulder.

Sunlight filtered through the vibrant green forest cover, illuminating the outline of two towering stone lanterns on either side of the path. A mix of aged, toppled, cut stone and natural rock blended together at the base of each lantern and marked the exit down to the so-called civilized world below. The sun glared over the valley filled with tiled houses, where scorching asphalt waited for us.

I lost Nobu around lunchtime. He stopped for noodles while I pushed on with a small fermented bean bread I was given along the way. I wanted to get to the path early. While staying with Mukai-san, I had learned from a number of *henro* that the path to Temple Sixty was impassable due to a recent typhoon and resulting landslides. It wouldn't hurt to scout the area and talk to the locals a bit. I was also taking it easy and only planned to walk 17 miles due to a late start from Mukai-san's temple. Somehow, 8:00 in the morning had become a late start.

Verdant rice paddies swept over the valley I crossed, and layered mountains rose in the distance, waiting for me to find a path through. The pilgrimage route was a study in contrasts, weaving through and around the lives of the people on Shikoku, while purposely climbing mountains rather than avoiding them.

As I approached the mountains, the land started to constrict, forcing both homes and paddies into constraining channels running against the steep slopes. Up against the mountains the stalks changed color to a yellowish green, bowed from the weight of the heavy rice almost fully formed at the top. On my left the wind rippled through the old stalks in wave-like fashion. On my right orchards grew around me, tempting me with plump tangerines and plums. But I was already weighted with provisions for the night, not to mention the whole issue of stealing.

Worrying about what I'd find in the mountains, I had already bought extra water and food six miles back, as the map didn't show anything closer to the trailhead. After walking well out of my way to get the heavy provisions, adding considerable weight to my pack, I started passing supermarkets not listed in my book that would have saved me the effort. The first super-market I passed was annoying, the second depressing, the third built obviously just to mess with me. The fourth made me want to cry. When I reached the convenience store located right across from the mountain path, I laughed out loud. It must have spooked a cyclist coming up behind me.

Chring. Chring. Chring.

I heard the sound of the bike's bell and squeaky brakes as the cyclist swerved right into me. Thankfully, all I got was a light tap from the tire.

"I'm so sorry."

"No. I'm sorry."

"No really, I'm sorry."

"No, no. That was me. I'm sorry."

"You must be American. You must speak fluent Japanese. And you are between 20 and 30," the man said in a matter-of-fact way. It is quite common for people to point out the obvious to start off conversations.

"No, no, I'm sorr . . . what?" I looked up from my half bow, surprised but glad he had pulled us out of our black hole of polite apologies.

Hairless. Not totally, of course, but that's the only word that comes to mind when you see some older Japanese men's skin. It was taut, with thick veins, and bulging muscles from hard work stretched the skin even further. It was smooth and rubbery at the same time. I know because he asked me to touch his arm, as if to emphasize something that he never quite shared with me.

At 65, he rocked a white T-shirt with the low neckline falling just above his nipples. The Fashion Channel would have been proud. Paired with a wide-brimmed straw hat with a panama black band, this fashion-forward farmer nodded enthusiastically when I told him he was right on all accounts.

His energy was infectious.

"Yup, yup. Of course I'm right. I know people. And I bet you're headed to Temple Sixty." This was, of course, less impressive, as my pilgrim gear gave me away. "Look, you can stay down here but that would be pretty stupid. You're not stupid . . . are you?" he said.

"The path is open now, and there is a hut halfway up the mountain with water and a toilet. Just stay right at the bridge. Don't cross the bridge. Do you understand? Stay right. Okay? Where do you go? Yes, stay right. Don't cross it. Okay? Do you get it? Don't be stupid. I'll draw a map."

Hmm, maybe he did think I was stupid.

"*Ojiisan*, it's okay. Thank you." He didn't look like he believed me, but he waved goodbye and took off on his bike.

Chring. Chring. He raised his hand as he rode around a corner.

The prospect of staying farther up the mountain was too good to pass up. First, I didn't want to be stupid. Second, it would be cooler, and I'd be closer to the temple. Losing Nobu for the night was just a possible bonus.

I followed slowly up a narrow road that twisted and turned alongside a river that grew increasingly distant the higher I walked.

"Hey!" A small white farming truck overtook me and then slammed on the brakes just ahead. Two *shiba inu* (small Japanese hunting dogs) rode in the back, their tongues lolling.

"*Ohenro*-san. Can I give you a ride up to the hiking path?" a farmer yelled from the window.

Offers to ride in cars were always hard to resist. At the end of the day, with a mountain left to climb, who wouldn't want a ride? It was such a temptation, but I resisted and thanked him. He shrugged his shoulders, and the small engine whined as he drove up the mountain.

Fifteen minutes later another farm truck pulled up, driven by the 65-year-old cyclist who had hit me with his bike. "Hey, you have to turn right at the bridge," he said. "Get in. I've got beers. Plus, you'll never find the path on your own." He lifted the beer he was drinking, as proof. A brave gesture, considering the heavily enforced zero tolerance laws in Japan. Alternatively, it highlighted just how far into the countryside I really was.

"I stay right at the bridge, right?"

"Get in."

"I'll be okay. I'm only walking."

"Get in."

"No, really. I can't. Thanks."

"I've got beers." He looked at me like I was stupid.

It was the perfect set up for an abduction—isolated path, no witnesses. Did he know that he was wearing me down? I wasn't going to survive another offer of both beer and a ride.

"Thank you, but I'm walking the whole way," I said. "Like Kōbō Daishi."

Something clicked. He tossed a beer out the window. It was a tallboy, and ice cold. Just the way Kōbō Daishi would have liked it.

"Don't forget. Stay right." Three beeps later he disappeared around the corner, and I had beer.

Villages are small in Japan. When there is only one road, they are even smaller. After a few more turns I came to a small farm that seemed to be a gathering area to watch the foreign pilgrim pass by. Eight older people, their collective ages approaching 800, including the 65-year-old and the guy with the dogs, lined the road, beers in hand, cheering me on.

"Stay right at the bridge," they yelled in unison.

"He's from America, is between 20 and 30, and speaks Japanese," the 65-year-old said.

"How do you know?" a grandmother yelled.

"I know people," he yelled back.

An older lady in a dirt-stained blue smock shuffled forward, gray hair tied back by a faded blue bonnet. Her back was alarmingly hunched over.

The crowd grew quiet as I paused.

"Here, *osettai*. Please take my placenta." She said the last word in English. Reaching into a homemade purse, she pulled out a small brown vial.

The rules are clear: you have to accept all *osettai*, the gifts given by locals on Shikoku to pilgrims.

"Thank you for your placenta, grandmother." I bowed. There is not much else one can do when receiving placenta.

"Don't forget to turn right at the bridge," the group yelled.

I popped the placenta in my bag and moved on, forgetting about it until the next day.

My home for the evening was better than I could have hoped for. The wooden gazebo would keep me dry, and the toilet was clean enough, with a private sink perfect for a shower. Across the road a mountain spring sprang from pipes extending from a steep rock cliff. A hand-painted sign, red on white like most signs on the pilgrim's path, said the water came from the temple above and was fine to drink. I drank right away and then dropped my beer in the flowing water to cool it down even more.

Of course, colder was not something that I really needed. As the sun disappeared, a mountain chill set in, and I discovered the next gift from the villagers. In a small box along the railings of the gazebo, they had left various blankets for pilgrims.

Beer, shelter, water, placenta, cool air, a shower sink, and blankets—there was nothing else I could possibly want. It was far and away the most perfect home I had found myself sleeping in thus far. Plus, I was alone. I had shaken Nobu. By 8:00 p.m. I was breathing the clear mountain air, and the single beer was about to knock me out.

"Chan, chan. Tee hee, you're so silly Todo-san. You must have forgotten that we were staying at the *jinja* together. I'm lucky I found you! The villagers told me where you were. Chan, chan."

I knew they couldn't be trusted.

"Goodnight, Nobu."

"But where am I going to sleep?"

"Anywhere you like. How about that bench on the other side?"

He chose the bench right next to my pad that I had laid on the ground, his body hovering just above mine. Only my mosquito net separated us, which 10 minutes ago had been a savior. It covered my body fully for the first time, hanging from the wooden cross beams above, rather than off my walking staff propped precariously in my backpack. Now it was a prison, keeping me uncomfortably close to Nobu.

My sweet mountain air was lost soon after, along with the sounds of the forest, as Nobu began humming and lighting mosquito coils. As my frustration grew, I stayed quiet. It wasn't his fault, and he didn't have a mosquito net.

How could I get so annoyed so quickly by someone? I wish I had been honest with him. I wish I had talked to him. I still don't know what I would have said.

"You're a nice kid but leave me alone."

"I just want to walk by myself."

"It's not you, it's me."

But maybe it would have saved us both in the end. Instead, I kept silent, turned on the emotional pressure cooker, and set the timer for my own personal failure.

I PASSED the mountaintop Temple Sixty early in the morning and headed down through dense cedar forests on my way back into the Shikoku beltway of houses and fast trucks. From here the temples group together again, and I'd come into closer contact with people leading lives unrelated to the pilgrim's path, as if to prepare me for the end of the journey and re-entry to normal life.

My feet were tape free, and I hadn't had a painkiller in over a week, although Nobu tempted me every night. I was walking alone, as Nobu had got an early start and left first. I kept my pace slow, hoping he'd leave me this time. The pilgrimage was fun again, and I was ready for anything. Since I was feeling optimistic, it was time to dig into the placenta I'd received the night before.

I pulled out the vial of placenta and was thankful that it had a label on it. It wasn't, in fact, the grandmother's placenta, but a vitamin drink. Japan is obsessed with them. Life in Japan is anything but relaxed, its pressures ranging from social obligations, to long nights drinking with the boss, to making the perfect meal for a child to bring to school for lunch. Everyone is looking for a boost. You can drink 1,000 lemons' worth of vitamin C, or just about any other letter of the alphabet you want. Need energy? Have some vitamin D, along with a ton of caffeine.

Placenta is thought to help rejuvenate the body and has been used for centuries in Japan and China as a skin cream. If it was good enough to rub all over, why not just start drinking it? Besides, at $10 for a 200-milliliter bottle, it had to be good, right? The bottle promised an energy boost from the pure horse placenta.

I downed it in one swig.

It tasted slightly better than I imagined horse placenta would taste.

I turned a corner and almost choked on my placenta as I ran straight into a naked Nobu, relaxing in a river pool.

"Tee hee, hee. Todo-san, come on in."

I politely refused the offer and started walking faster. The placenta was kicking in.

The mountain path brought me to the entrance of a small modern shrine. Nothing about it was attractive, except for its obvious newness. Even that turned me off, as it was made out of concrete. And yet, there was something that made me walk around the back of the concrete box, where I found, hidden in the forest, one of the most beautiful shrines I've been to.

A simple river grotto served as the shrine, where two mythical Buddhist warriors, covered in aged green patina, stood guard over the falling waterfall. The first brass guardian sat framed in flames and dharma wheels, wielding a sword and an impenetrable stare. The other crouched below on an opposite cliff, holding a stick with a lantern of enlightenment balanced on the end. The statues, frozen in time as water pours eternally from the rock face, are set up to practice water purification under the chilly mountain waters.

The concrete inner shrine building was just a precursor to the massive three-story concrete block that is The Temple of Incense Garden. Founded by Prince Shotoku to help his father Emperor Yomei recover from a sickness, the temple might not have worked, as he reigned for a brief two years, from 585 to 587 CE, before dying.

From the outside, most of the history has been erased in an architectural mix of an American convention center, Cold War bunker, and a church, complete with a vaulted ceiling and chairs for worship. Or, as the city of Ehime lovingly writes on its webpage, "Kōon-ji is a modern temple constructed of rein-forced concrete."

While there is nothing wrong with pushing the bounds of architecture, somehow, in comparison to the grotto and the mountaintop sanctuary I had just left behind, it was hard landing back in society. Its size diminished any hope of quiet reflection, or the ability to blend with the neighborhood like so many other temples that serve the inhabitants of the island. Of course, with less traditional houses being constructed, maybe it was adapting to the neighborhood better than a wooden temple.

Sometimes it feels like you can only catch the Japan you hope for out of the corner of your eye. Every time I turned to admire some green bamboo, a sculpted garden tucked purposely into the corner, a cypress-wrapped, weathered shrine, it would slip away, overwhelmed by surrounding concrete, electrical wires, and vending machines. Most of what we love about Japan, in fact, needs to be framed carefully to exclude all the other necessities of modern life. With the mountains at my back, it felt like we were covering the world with concrete, blocking ourselves off from the tide of nature with retaining walls in the shape of apartment blocks.

Or maybe, used to sleeping outside every night, I was reading too much into the large, square, ugly temple. Maybe this was the way Japan had always valued beauty, in controlled bursts, where structured confinement isolated and amplified specific acts of nature's beauty.

There is, of course, plenty of beauty to be had walking the back streets of Japan, and I didn't waste any more of my thoughts on the concrete temple.

FOR TWO DAYS I wound my way through a belt of small towns wedged between mountains on my right and a toll highway filled with traffic on my left. Vigorously lived-in wooden houses mingled with new molded model homes, held together by mom-and-pop shops, stone Buddha Jizō statues, and shrines. The world was becoming compact again as the temples clustered together, and visiting more than one a day was once again the norm.

The days were also starting to pick up pace the closer I approached the end. Where I was once overwhelmed by the enormity of the task at hand, now I tried to comprehend a life not spent walking each day. No longer looking forward to the end, I was looking around, excited about what was happening now, and on the lookout for what the universe would send my way next. I found joy in waiting for the next person to talk to, as everything seemed connected to a larger purpose that only those who were quiet enough could hear.

It also helped that I hadn't seen Nobu for at least a day and a half.

Chring. Chring.

I jumped to the left as the bell drove me out of my head and I came face to bike. The bike teetered for a second before an older woman dressed all in white managed to jump off. Short, she had a rounded nose, and her smile revealed leathery teeth that matched her tough, sunbaked skin.

I stared.

She smiled and then, for some reason, hit me on the arm. "I'm so happy," she said.

I could tell.

"Thank you for walking. It is so hard." She hit my shoulder again.

"I . . ."

"Shhhhhh." She hit me again and narrowed her eyes in disapproval at my outburst. "Walking is very hard. I know."

It would be easier if she stopped hitting me.

"Have you walked before?" I managed to get the question out before she hit me again.

She smiled. "Are you American?"

I nodded.

She flashed her leathery teeth again, gave me another smack, and said, "No. I'm too sick to walk. I was a young girl living in Kumamoto, southern Kyushu, when the Americans started bombing. After the bombs kept falling for three days, my family fled into the mountains. We had no food, no water, no paper to study with. We had nothing to ride on, so we walked 13 miles. It was so tough, but we kept going and lived in the woods." She didn't say any of this with animosity. In fact, she was probably the bubbliest person I'd met on Shikoku.

I didn't know how to respond, so I just introduced myself.

Like so many people I'd met in Japan, she never shared her name, even after I offered my own. She just nodded, smiled, gave me 500 yen (about $5), bowed, and hit me one more time. Like a child, she ran her bike to get up to speed, hopped on, and rode out of my life.

I found a convenience store five minutes down the street and bought a vitamin drink. They didn't have any placenta, so I settled for D.

It had been two amazing days walking on my own when Nobu found me in a small park at the base of a mountain. Night was falling, so I used it as an excuse to skip the small talk and get some shut-eye. The next morning came fast, and after a morning hike, we sat together 1,600 feet up the mountain on the uneven rock steps leading to Temple Sixty-Five. We looked out over the sweeping mountains and above that to a layer of haze from a smoke-spewing factory that hid the Seto Inland Sea far below. It was 7:00 a.m. and as we waited for the temple to open, I listened to Nobu's stream of questions, interspersed with "hee, hee" and "chan, chan."

"Where are we sleeping tonight? Chan, chan." He cocked his head to the side like the warbler sitting above us in the twisted branches of a long-needled Japanese pine.

Nobu's superpower was his ability to misread every social cue out there and keep plodding away anyway. I could only imagine how hard that made his life in Japan, where all of the most important details were left unsaid.

I sighed and pulled out my map to show him a small village temple called Shirafu-ji. It had a *zenkonyado* and was about 15 miles away, just after the highest temple on the pilgrimage. He buzzed contentedly to himself.

Temple Sixty-Five is named Sankaku-ji (literally Triangle Temple) after the triangular altar that Kūkai supposedly used to banish a ghost that was haunting the temple. It is a beautiful temple with a large wooden gate and a giant hanging bell that you ring as you walk through.

But it was hard to notice the temple's details, as I was distracted by having to walk one more day with Nobu. I tried my best to pray my way to peace, but it didn't work. I found myself instead asking for respite, a way to banish him, like Kūkai did the ghost.

As we left the temple, Nobu took the lead and was well down the steps as I passed out of the gate, looking down on him and the road below. Without a map, he was following the *henro* signs religiously. He turned left, following the little white and red sign that pointed the way to the next temple. I opened my mouth to yell down, to tell him he was going the wrong way, that the road was for cars, and that it was six miles longer than the path to the right.

I didn't yell. I let him keep walking and the farther he got, the worse I felt. But I let him keep going. I just stood there and waited until he disappeared, as if not seeing him would make me feel better. Of course, it didn't.

I was supposed to be the adult. I was supposed to have my shit figured out. I was supposed to be a bigger person than the people who bullied him in high school. I had given up on Nobu, and in doing so showed myself just how much more work I needed to do.

I turned right, looking for the path. When you walk all day long, you have plenty of time to think about what you did wrong and the type of person you would rather be.

16

THE BUDDHA'S UNDERWEAR

The skies opened up shortly after ditching Nobu. I would never see him again, but the rain wept with me and would be my constant companion for the next few days. Despite the heat on most days, summer made walking in the rain so much easier. I didn't have to worry about getting cold, and so I didn't wear any kind of rain gear except my hat.

The path cut through misted mountain valleys as I wound deeper into the woods on my way to Temple Sixty-Six, the highest on the pilgrimage. The road was deserted due to the rain as I passed *Bangai* Fourteen, Jōfuku-ji, a small but beautiful temple. Since I had the time, I decided to stop in and pay my respects, as I had stayed there the last time I walked, in a small apartment the head monk kept for walking pilgrims.

As I prayed and chanted the Heart Sutra at the main Buddha hall, something didn't feel right. It felt like someone was watching me, but as I turned around, no one moved. Perhaps the rain was keeping all other visitors away.

Instead, I found myself staring at an enormous penis.

Just out of touching distance from the Buddha behind me were three statues, about three feet high each. The middle one caught my attention. How did I not notice when I first arrived?

Modeled after one of the seven lucky gods, Daikokuten, who supposedly brings wealth and good fortune, the middle statue was draped in a yellow robe. A thin strip of cloth failed to cover his massive erection. Rather than holding his normal magic mallet that brought money, his left hand held his erect penis, while his right hand was pressed against his bald head. His chubby, happy face was lifted to the sky, and his mouth was wide open in unspoken joy.

This was not what I had expected.

I looked around to make sure I was still alone and then moved closer to see what his friends looked like. On the left was a woman, wrapped in layers of modest cloth smocks, one after the other. The bottom layer was red and gold, one layer up was black Buddhist verse on white, then flowers, followed by a red bib, and finally a striped bib of alternating yellow stars with what might have been tomatoes, pulled up to her chin. She presented an image of modesty, except for lips painted bright red and a right knee poking out to show a bit of raw granite.

On the right stood a man and a woman carved from marble. Impeccably detailed *kimono* flowed around them, capturing their elegance. The man's hand rested on her shoulder in a tender gesture as they paid their respects to the Buddha across the way. And yet, she wore a faint smirk, as if the two shared a private joke. A cloth blanket covered them both from the waist down, with a suspicious bulge coming from the man.

I looked around, but the rain all but ensured no one else would visit the temple today. I decided to see what his friends were up to. I lifted the blanket from the couple first, and a red stone penis, overly sized to highlight his virility, jumped out. The woman was still clothed, but her right hand had been secretly stroking him, her smirk a hidden touch of whimsy by the artist.

I felt a little weird peeking under the statues' clothes, but I put aside my feelings, and lifted the smocks of the woman sitting on the far left. And there it was. No underwear, even. The men's penises were detailed, carved down to pulsating veins. The woman, on the other hand, had her legs spread, one knee up and the other laid to the side with a seed-shaped carving painted in red. Wavy lines of red pubic hairs radiated out.

The three statues were actually not all that uncommon in rural Japan, where fertility and children are linked to farming and getting food on the table. Despite their in-your-face anatomy, the blankets and bibs all carried the handwritten hopes of men and women praying for babies. Fertility, and large penises, are just a normal part of life and shouldn't be hidden.

It seemed like a paradox for spiritual salvation based on untethering one's self from desires to be sitting right across from the humorous expression of fertility across the way. But contradictions abound in Japan, and rather than being seen as opposing forces, they are in fact each part of the natural way of things. There is no reason to cover up what is natural—inoffensive in as much as it serves a specific purpose and is contained.

"What are you doing?"

I jumped out of my skin, pulled my head out of the statue's fire bush, and spun around. My heart raced, and embarrassment burned my cheeks. At first all I saw was white, and then I saw skin, and then I looked up.

I stood quickly, trying to figure out what was happening. Standing just a few feet in front of me was a wet, bald, half-naked man. All he wore was a pair of overly large round glasses, and a pair of soaking wet tighty-whities underwear.

"I . . ." No words came out. I tried again. "What . . ."

The man started laughing heavily, his large belly bouncing to the rhythm of deep gasps. He looked just like the middle statue. I looked around, trying to find a clue as to what was going on. I found it, lying under the temple's roof just behind him. Laid out to dry were a monk's black robe, walking staff with elaborate linked rings on top, and a monk's straw hat, larger than mine and rounded rather than conical.

"Oh, you should have seen your face." He giggled as he walked back to the shelter of the main temple.

I followed him, not just because I was curious, but to put a bit of distance between myself and the statues he'd caught me peeping at.

"So, you are a monk?" I asked, pointing to his robes.

He must have heard the skepticism in my voice because it caused another boom of laughter.

"Of course I am," he responded after his laughter subsided. "Monks are people too. You know that we have bodies under our robes, right?"

My cheeks burned again from embarrassment. "I'm sorr—"

He waved his hand and cut me off. "It's fine, it's fine. We look all pretty in our robes and with our bald heads, but we wear underwear just like you. Even the Buddha wore under-wear. We are all just people."

I can honestly say that in all my images of the Buddha, his underwear had never come to mind. I doubted the fact they even had underwear back then. But it had the effect I assumed he wanted, and the Buddha suddenly became a lot more relat-able as a normal human being.

The monk's name was Moriyama-san. He was in his early 30s and was a Shingon monk, practicing the same type of Buddhism started by Kūkai. I had no idea where to even begin with Moriyama-san. But he wasn't the type to keep quiet, and he barely let me talk anyway.

"Look at your friends over there." He waved his hand towards the three statues. "It isn't what most people think they'll find at a Buddhist temple, right?"

That had been my first reaction.

"But what are they? It's no secret that men have penises and women have vaginas, is it?" He didn't wait for an answer. "It's the way things are. Just accept it. That is what Buddhism really is. You need to accept the truth. I can be in just my underwear, a normal person, and a monk. Accept it."

I liked Moriyama-san, and I wanted to hear more. Plus, it is not often you get your own personal, half-naked spiritual advisor. I asked him to walk with me to the next temple, but he couldn't. He was walking the pilgrimage in the opposite direction. He had walked it the normal way three times already, and he wanted to see the path from a different angle. I couldn't ever imagine him seeing the world from anything but a different angle.

I decided to leave first. I started to bow as he came in for a hug. Somehow, we managed a partial hug, a firm handshake, and a poorly executed bow; it was an awkward mess. He was a strange monk indeed.

I REACHED the top of a steep climb along a lonely road and was greeted by a cluster of porn vending machines.

Videos, books, DVDs, and toys!
Open 24 hours a day.
Surprising prices.
Sale on NOW.

It makes sense, of course. The path moves from one prefecture to the next, from the Land of Awakening Faith (i.e. foot pain), to the Land of Discipline (greater foot pain), to the Land of Enlightenment (there are no feet), and finally, to the Land of Entering Nirvana (there are feet, but they don't control me). I was about to enter Nirvana in Kagawa Prefecture. But before entering Nirvana you are tested one last time to see if your enlightenment is false or not. Normally, you are tested at Temple Sixty-Six, the highest of the 88 temples at

2,800 feet, and one of the four *nansho* (perilous places) on the pilgrimage.

The vending machines sat close enough to the temple and they could be my test. How well had I let my base desires go? I was always up for a challenge. I had just looked under the skirts of three statues.

I ducked inside the rusting corrugated-steel-sided shack. After all, who am I to argue with the 14th century Buddhist master Ikkyū, who was convinced that people would never become enlightened if they "love the sacred and hate the secular." He also chose to express his enlightenment in the brothels of Osaka. I dove into the single siding of sin and found that it wasn't the prices that were surprising but such breakout titles as:

Innocent Lolitas. Rough way to start the window-shopping.

Paradise Lost. In this case, Paradise was a group of high school girls in uniform.

There was, of course, some porn with extremely attractive, scantily clad women having sex with fat old guys and loving every non-sensual second of it. Great acting all the way, I'm sure.

I got as far as the DVD and *manga* set of tentacle porn—women being ravaged by demons and octopuses with spiked tentacles on the front covers—before I went back out into the rain to clean myself.

Tentacle erotica burst onto the scene officially in the early 1980s but was based on 18th century prints and the delusion that women like being pounded by large octopus tentacles, a mistake so simple that anyone could have made it. It's easy to relegate this to the fringes of Japanese society, but, in fact, the artist who was the forerunner to it all, Katsushika Hokusai, is renowned worldwide for his *Thirty-Six Views of Mount Fuji.* His most famous block print, a large wave overtaking two boats, with Mt. Fuji in the background, has been seen worldwide, even by people who know very little of Japan.

Now, tentacle porn primarily deals with *hentai* (perverted) *manga* and *anime* of demons or space creatures with multiple appendages ravishing women. It was reinvented as a way to get around penetration censorship, but it has taken on a life of its own. The internet, and wackos, have helped.

Ikkyū also thought that one should sin like a madman until you can't do anything else but let go of everything and find enlightenment. Pedophilia and stylized rape should be way out of bounds for any society, but somehow in Japan this is still accepted. While these deviations don't jump out at the average visitor, they are pervasive across society, and found as frequently on lonely mountain passes as they are on your local 7-Eleven's magazine rack. How is it that Japan allows such deviancies in what by many is considered a conservative society?

The short answer is that Japan simply has a different definition of conservative. For the most part Japan is free of the guilt that is associated with sex in the usual Judeo-Christian morality. This means that people are freer with their sexual attitudes and less guilt-ridden. But at the same time, it usually remains hidden, never really discussed openly.

This tendency to keep personal feelings private is fundamentally a reflection of the Japanese concept of *honne* (real value) and *tatemae* (face value). These values rule most interactions in Japan and separate what is shown in public and what is really going on. It is considered taboo to show your feelings publicly, even kissing. This reluctance to voice any kind of overt commentary on sexuality has probably led to less reflection on what does and doesn't go too far. And so, if something is done in private and doesn't affect the group, then there is no problem. Everyone remains quiet, conservative, hardworking, middle class, and loyal, on the surface.

On the pilgrimage you end up seeing more of what is hidden in everyday life. It allowed me to experience Japan in a way that was not always according to the script of polite society, that prescribed how people interacted and what they said to each other. Meeting people on the *henro* path meant seeing them at their weakest moments, usually struggling to figure something out in their lives.

17

PUBIC HAIR
AND PRAYER BEADS

I t turned out fried curry bread tasted just as good for breakfast in the Land of Nirvana as it did back in the land of base desires. That crispy fried outside with the soft curry inside is just one of the things I wished I could have taken home with me. Maybe it was the overcast morning that was making me nostalgic, or the fact that I was already on Day Twenty-Five and the end was near. With each step I took, the reality that my walking days were coming to an end sank in deeper and deeper. I had spent the past four weeks desperately hoping to finish, but now that I was getting closer, I found myself slowing down and trying to prolong the trip.

By the end of the day, I didn't feel tired at all. The slow pace allowed me to soak in everything, trying to commit it to memory before the end. Slim fish, the size of my forearm, leapt out of the winding river running next to me, feasting on a swarm of bugs. I wound my way through a valley of green rice paddies and lotus fields, broken up only by impossibly white flowers and city buildings in the distance. The flowers and I both grew out of the mud and dirt, but at this point, my white clothes were noticeably less dignified. My smell would be all the more noticeable as I emerged from camping in the country-side into the more civilized areas of Shikoku.

I rounded a bend, and a five-story pagoda poked out of the approaching tree line. Temple Seventy, Motoyama-ji, the Mountain Origin Temple, had no mountain connected to it. Its grandiose name refers to the fact that it used to be the largest temple on Shikoku. Built in the 9th century, by Kūkai of course, it has somehow staved off fires and the wrath of the clan wars that wracked the island in the 15th century.

Now its large buildings and wide-open spaces felt overly formal and were completely deserted. No longer the main temple located in a major city, it is a victim of its own indestructibleness. It had outlasted everyone and sat by as the modern age passed it by. Yet it still has a pull for some people.

The deep, reverberating intonations of a young pilgrim begging at the gate greeted me as I entered the temple grounds. Looking on like a proud father was none other than Suzuki-san, my long lost *henro* who I last saw begging back at Temple Fifty-One. He was lounging under the shade of the pagoda in baggy jeans cinched around his skeletal waist, all remnants of pilgrim's clothes gone, replaced with more stylish summer fashion.

"Oi, it's about time you got here." He jumped up, grabbed my hand, and pulled me in for a bro hug. He still smelled like rotting oil and his mustache seemed wispier.

"What are you doing here and where is your gear?" I asked.

"The kid's got it all. He would have died out here if I didn't find him," he said as he pointed to the young pilgrim begging near the gate.

He was dressed in Suzuki-san's broken hat and dirty pilgrim's vest.

Suzuki-san leaned in close. "Plus, it's a sweet deal. I've been here for the past two days teaching him to beg. I get 50 percent of everything he gets from these tourists."

I dropped my bag and we settled on the stone steps leading to the pagoda.

I stared at Suzuki-san's protégé, who couldn't have been older than 19. He had even taken on Suzuki-san's pathetic, ravenous slump in the hopes of earning more money, although he wasn't nearly as convincing.

"Really?" I said. "You seem to have this whole thing figured out. How about you tell me how you really got here ahead of me?"

Suzuki-san looked at me, confused.

I tried again. "I left before you. You said you were walking again from Temple Fifty-One? There is no way you could have gotten here two days ago."

He looked at me with pity, as if seeing for the first time that I had bought into his story. "Ah, man, I took buses and hitch-hiked here from Temple Fifty-One. This temple has it all— a steady stream of bus pilgrims and a train station close by where we have been sleeping."

I looked back at him. Suzuki-san took it defensively.

"Look, man, I've been at this thing for two years. Two years!" He held up two fingers. "I've been to all the temples. I've walked them three times. This is what experience is for— to build a system to make things sustainable. That kid over there is making things easy."

It only took a few more prods to finally get the whole story out of him (well, maybe the whole story).

Suzuki-san really did walk the first two times. But his money had run out after one and a half years on the path. After a little more prodding, he admitted to taking long breaks at home between the first and second walks. He also admitted that his girlfriend was his banker. She was worried about him and paid for him to stay at hotels every night the first time around. He was halfway through the second time when she wised up and dumped him. Suzuki-san had a thing for hot spring resorts and might have stayed at one too many. He wasn't quite sure.

"It's okay, man. There's no way to keep a girlfriend when you're a *henro*. Now I'm free to do things the way I want, and I got me a new deal." He nodded his head toward the kid, a smug grin escaping through wisps of facial hair. "We will have a few more days before he earns enough to buy his own bowl and he wises up that he doesn't need me taking half his money."

I remembered the Suzuki-san I had met at the beginning of my trip. I thought he was amazing, a real walking *henro*. I couldn't help thinking about the changes I had gone through. The Todd at the beginning would have been disappointed to learn who Suzuki-san really was. Now I could see him for who he really was, without my own prejudices weighing in—just another *henro* looking to make his life a little better. Possibly in an illegal way.

"Hey, where are you staying tonight?" he asked.

"Not here, for sure." I grinned. Despite his flaws it was hard not to smile when Suzuki-san was around, but sleeping was a serious concern. I was heading into the towns again, and it would be difficult to find places to camp out in the coming days. It was already late in the day, and the clouds that had been building looked like they were getting ready to soak us at any moment. A quick scan of my map showed a *minshuku*, like a guesthouse, just a few miles away. I had a little bit of money left and decided to take a night off, something I never would have done just a few weeks ago.

As if on cue, the heavens opened up. Suzuki-san yelled an expletive, jumped up, and started running towards his meal ticket. Over his shoulder he yelled that I should stay at the *zenkonyado* near Temple Seventy-Five if I could. "Just ask at the temple," he yelled, as the rest was lost in the downpour. He waved goodbye and then they were gone, running back towards the train station.

I DIDN'T BOTHER to run, or even get up right away. I was already wet from sweat, and wet is wet. There was no use rushing from overhang to overhang. I had stopped wearing my rain suit long ago and used it now mainly to keep my bag dry by draping it over for added protection.

I attended to all of my normal temple duties, then prepared my bag for the downpour waiting for me. At first, just little streams flowed down my plastic-wrapped hat, but the water volume soon doubled into a raging waterfall falling before my eyes. Head down, I could barely see the cars buzzing by on the now darkened street. But I felt them as they eagerly splashed their way home away from the storm.

After two hours in the rain, I arrived, soaked and shivering, at the small inn, with night fully upon me as I slid open the main door and stepped through the entranceway. Water pooled around my feet. I dropped my bags at the entrance and was greeted by a bent, elderly couple. A row of neatly arranged plastic slippers waited just a step up onto a smooth wooden floor, above the now wet stone beneath me.

"Welcome," the gray-haired man said. Dressed in deep blue robes, he and his wife bowed.

"Is it possible to have food tonight?" I asked, hoping I wouldn't have to go back outside.

"I'm sorry, but we don't serve food here. At this time of night, the closest place that is open is a *yakitori* (grilled skewered chicken) bar down the street." It was only 7:00 p.m.

I looked out the sliding door and saw rain and darkness. My heart sank at the thought of going back out, but I needed to eat. The innkeepers kindly lent me an umbrella, but since I was already soaked, it made no difference.

Donning my conical hat and staff, and with money bag in hand, I set out through the small town that was packed with houses huddled close to a train station. I wound my way through the narrow streets for 10 minutes, until I found the only shop with lights glowing through its frosted windows.

The *yakitori* bar was as typical a Japanese bar as you could ask for. A blue cloth banner with slits for walking through, called *noren*, hung at eye level just in front of a wood and glass sliding door. Sliding the door to the right, I took one step in and reached the bar straight away.

"*Irasshaimase*," the staff shouted in unison without looking up. In front of me was a wall-to-wall bar counter. Seven men sat with their backs to the door, occupying all but the last two stools on the far right.

One of the men turned around and shouted. "Oh! Pilgrim!"

Everyone else turned around.

I took my hat off, and more men yelled, "Oh! A foreigner!" All eyes jumped from me to the man at the end of the bar, who was next to an empty seat. He had a small Japanese keg in front of him and was treating the room to round after round of beer.

This was a working man's bar, not some fancy Tokyo eatery. The thick overhead beams were coated black from the constant charcoal grilling, empty beer bottles filled every corner, and faded posters advertising beer, *sake*, and local businesses covered the walls. The owner and chef was bald and wore a twisted towel around his head in an attempt to keep the sweat off the chicken.

"Move down, move down! Come over here, *ohenro*-san, and sit next to me," the local big shot shouted, waving me over. Dressed in business clothes, in contrast to the factory workers at the other side, he was in his late 50s, and his business seemed to be doing quite well, judging by the number of over-sized glass beer mugs he was handing out.

I was too tired and hungry to argue. I dropped my bag, hat, and staff in the corner. The big man ushered me into the seat next to him and poured us a couple of beers.

"*Kampai*," we yelled to each other, and that cold beer leaped down my throat faster than nature would normally allow. He served up another right away, despite my protests that I was tired. He took the lead and ordered a course of minced chicken breast, livers, hearts, and, of course, cartilage. In Japan every part of the chicken is served and only sometimes interspersed with leek, skewers of onion, or mushrooms. The chicken skewers come with either sauce or just salt, and most parts of Japan have a firm opinion on which is the correct way. Here it was sauce all the way.

We got through the normal range of questions from the big man as our chicken came out on small plates. I was from the US, yes, I spoke Japanese, yes, I liked sushi, and no, I didn't like fermented beans (*nattō*). Grilling the food right in front of us behind the bar, the chef would put a plate of two skewers up on the counter between us once we had finished the previous round. We'd take one at a time, eat it off the stick, and slug back another drink.

I wasn't focused on much beyond juicy chicken and beer, but it seemed my new friend had more than just the normal questions on his mind.

"So, you must have a big dick?" he said.

I choked on half my beer, the other half running out of my nose.

I wiped my face and tried to calm the man down. "No, no, I can assure you it is quite normal." But maybe this was the wrong tactic, as most Japanese wouldn't brag about something. He might have thought I was being polite.

"Come on, it must be big."

I waved him off with a noncommittal negative grunt and sought refuge in examining my chicken. The bar suddenly seemed too small.

Even the chef was looking at me now. "I bet it's huge!" the big shot yelled, holding his hands out wide to convey the full impact to the now raucous crowd, who roared their support.

My protests were drowned out as the bar started up a chant, "Show us your dick! Show us your dick! Show us your dick!" I'm sure someone was pounding the bar to the beat.

The chef chuckled as he cooked our next batch of chicken livers.

I stood up, setting the room off even further.

"Show us your dick! Show us your dick!" they yelled.

But I just put my hands up to calm them down. "Look guys, it's the same as yours. Nothing too big, and there is no way I'm going to show you anything." How was I even having this conversation? But that seemed to do the trick, and the furor in their eyes began to die down. I sat down as everyone retreated back to their beers.

And then, a smart guy next to the big man had an idea. "Wait. You're blonde up there . . ." he began, pointing to my head.

I could see where this was going.

"What color are your pubes down there?" No pointing this time. Instead, he just shifted his whole face towards my crotch.

The crowd went crazy with approval.

Again, perhaps the wrong tactic, but I said, "They're brown."

"WHAT?" The crowd erupted at the absurdity of the blonde foreigner having brown pubic hair.

I tried to calm them down again, but the chanting and banging drowned me out.

"Show us your pubes! Show us your pubes! Show us your pubes!" they chanted over and over.

I was getting drunk, or maybe I was drunk. I must have been drunk if I was still there. I hadn't had more than three or four beers in total over the past month, and walking almost a marathon a day does not build up your tolerance.

Everything was getting hazy. Hopefully they hadn't roofied

my drink! But it was clear they weren't going to quiet down any time soon.

I took another long chug of my oversized beer and decided it couldn't hurt to give them a peek. A little peek. Nothing too revealing, just enough to quiet them down so we could get back to our beers and chicken bits in peace.

I was too young to realize I deserved to be treated better. They should have been old enough to know better. It shouldn't have mattered if we were in Japan or the US. In the end I didn't realize that I deserved to be treated with respect as well. When you first visit Japan, it is beaten into your head that Japan is unique, that you need to be careful to respect the culture and not to offend by mistake. It seems no one was giving the same cultural sensitivity lectures to my barstool comrades.

I pushed back my stool, and every eye narrowed in on me. I pulled down the elastic top of my boxers, just enough to reveal the upper section of my pubic hairs. It was a modest display, given that we could easily all have been naked in the public bath on any other night. But this night was different. The room vibrated with surprise and joy. Seven men climbed over each other to catch a glimpse, sputtering disbelief that it was actually happening, that there really was a difference in color.

Time slowed. From the corner of my left eye, I saw a blur. Moving fast, a man seated two stools away launched himself at me, jumping clear across his companions. His hand darted out and suddenly, as if by magic, he held up three strands of my pubic hair.

"They're brown!" he yelled

Shock rocked the bar as the other patrons swarmed the thief, knees low, eyes and faces lifted in reverence. "Heeeey," they exclaimed in unison. "Wow!"

The fanatic lowered his hand reverently and gave one of the hairs to the big man. He took the other two, turned slowly to his big-bellied friend on his left, and suddenly started tickling his ear with my pubes. "Wuji, wuji, wuji, wuji," he said, as if talking to a baby

I finally realized this was not the place for me. I threw some money on the counter, grabbed my gear, and made for the door.

"Wait, where are you going?" someone cried.

"Show us your dick! Show us your dick! Show us your . . ."

I slammed the sliding door shut and half ran, half stumbled down the road at a drunkard's pace.

They probably have enshrined one of the hairs in the bar, while another might be at the international pubic hair museum back in Uwajima city. And the third? Who knows—another mystery for hopefully not another day.

I had no words to describe what had just happened to me. But I fell asleep that night in my safe, protected inn, muttering a new mantra over and over, "What the fuck? What the fuck?"

18

YAKUZA IN MY BATH, FREETERS IN THE HOUSE

I put as much distance between myself and the *yakitori* bar as I could, rushing through temple after temple until I arrived at the walled compound of Zentsū-ji, Temple Seventy-Five. I was placing my hopes for the night on the half-heard recommendation of Suzuki-san. Somewhere inside I hoped to find directions to a free house to sleep in.

Located in a small city with the same name as the temple, Zentsū-ji takes on an oversized place in the pilgrimage and the life of Kūkai. The largest of all the temples on Shikoku, it marks the town where Kūkai was born. It was the first temple he built when he returned from his training in China. It is a sprawling, beautiful temple with three different gates, a treasure hall, accommodation, and a five-story pagoda that rivals the one back at Temple Seventy.

But with the rush of visitors, bus groups trying to get through at the end of the evening, and the city streets just outside, it was hard to find a moment of peace in all the grandeur. I approached the temple's office to get my scroll signed and ask about a place to stay.

"Do you want to add in a guided tour of Kūkai's birthplace?" the young priest asked as he worked on my calligraphy.

"No, thank you. Do you know of a *zenkonyado* where I can sleep tonight? I . . ."

"It's only an extra 500 yen," he continued, working his upsell without even a glance up at me.

"No thank you. I'm walking, so . . ."

"Oh, then you have to take the mini temple tour. Visit all the 88 temples at one time."

"No thanks. Do you know . . ."

"You can even see where Kūkai buried his dog," he said.

I guess they were catering to all different markets, but his appeal to my love of dead dogs fell flat.

"Look, can you please tell me if there is a free place for walking pilgrims to spend the night?"

He looked up, finally finished with his work and clearly done with me, as I wasn't buying anything more. He fished around his desk for a few moments and produced a key with a large wooden block attached.

"You mean Takemoto's house. You should have said something earlier." He handed me the key and gave me quick directions. He had me register my name before shouting, "Next," to the line that had formed behind me.

As I turned to leave, he made one last go of it. "You should really come back for the naked festival in the spring. It is really something."

I accepted his brochure with a grace that I didn't feel. After walking for so long, looking forward to reaching each temple, it was always hard to adjust expectations. For me, getting my scroll signed was something special. I wanted to talk with the people at the temples and learn about them and the area. But to them I was just another person in the long line that filled up each and every day. They weren't rude (well, most of them, at least) but I just didn't matter to them as much as they did to me.

But if I couldn't get information from a nice talk, I guess I could get it from the brochure. He was right—the naked festival was, at least in their minds, something to behold. Officially, it is called Zentsū-ji Daieyo. Zentsū-ji is, of course, the name of the temple, and *dai* means "great." The *eyo* is where it gets tricky and, according to the temple, means, "to enter spring suffused with light and happiness after overcoming the severe cold of winter." Japanese is great that way. And how do you do this? Why, you get a bunch of half-naked men dressed in *fundoshi* (loincloths) and have them fight it out over a tree branch imbued with magical powers that grant happiness.

It is a curious thing that happiness is something that you have to fight over. Something that only one person can have each year. I guess it was easier than walking the pilgrimage, but the chances of success were much lower.

If you are not sold yet, the brochure has this to say: "This impressive festival is shrouded in mystery and excitement and is well worth viewing."

Takemoto-san's *zenkonyado* was not quite as easy to find as the office priest had let on. After walking up and down the supposed street a couple of times, I was aided by a kind man walking the streets in his underwear. It really was odd how many people I had met who were walking around in their underwear. He couldn't find his clothes, but he pointed me in the right direction.

Old and worn, like most of the traditional houses in the area, it was nonetheless a proper house, with two stories, a simple but full kitchen, and *tatami* rooms with soft futons that could have slept at least eight people comfortably. But I had the whole house to myself.

Takemoto-san no longer lived in the home, trusting the nearby temple attendants to give out and collect the key. But touches of Takemoto-san adorned the house. A hand-drawn map to the local bathhouse, convenience store, and coin-operated laundry down the street helped *henro* visitors get situated. A handwritten message above an ancient rotary phone further asked only that you call and leave a message with where you were from, and not to smoke. "It is bad for your health," was scribbled in brackets, almost as an afterthought.

I was thankful for Suzuki-san's parting words of advice. Armed with Takemoto-san's map, I wound my way through the neighborhood until I found the local bathhouse, or *sentō*. It was old school, made of what seemed to be concrete, although years of steam and grime obscured the walls. Other than hot water, there was nothing remotely similar between this local *sentō* and the Super Sentō Healthy Land I had stayed in a week ago. These grime-covered concrete boxes, once a staple of all neighborhoods in Japan, were dying out as the culture shifted to private baths built into homes.

Sentō have existed in Japan for over 400 years. While first developed for purely hygienic reasons, they quickly took on a social element. They are a place where neighbors, friends, and strangers catch up on the day's events and gossip. They have also maintained a level of equality that is at odds with the strict social structure of Japanese society. They are a space where not only do you strip yourself physically, but also remove all signs of social status and material wealth. It is hard not to feel like equals when someone starts scrubbing your back and then expects the same treatment in return. Perhaps it is this equality that *sentō* try to preserve by banning all tattoos and thus the ranking systems of the *yakuza*, the Japanese mafia.

My concrete box for the evening had two entrances, one for men on the right, and the other for women. Immediately upon entering I took off my shoes and put them in a locker secured by a wooden, rectangular key with grooves. In front of the divided entrances, an older woman, stuck in that magical Japanese condition where she had no clear age other than "older," waited for customers to arrive. She worked both sides of the building, connected by her box, with clear views of each changing room. I paid her 300 yen (about $3) and undressed under her disinterested gaze. My naked body lost in the competition for attention to the TV that blared loudly in front of her. Her white cat, on the other hand, never took its eyes off me.

I put my clothes in yet another locker, this time with a metal key attached to a faded green rubber bracelet I slipped on my wrist, and walked into the male bath area naked. The rectangular room was laid out simply, and no amount of scrubbing would ever make it look new. The water at least looked clean enough. In the center sat a large main bath divided into two sections, one with jets and the other calm. The jets might as well have been boiling water, as they felt like they could take skin off.

There were baths lined up against the far wall. The first two were different shades of green from various added oils, and the third was a cold bath used to close up the pores at the end of a long soak. Along the side walls ran shower stations to clean at before sharing the bath water with others. Two others were already in the baths; one looked to be in his 50s, the other was older, but muscular, and had an air of reliability. Neither paid me any attention.

I had just sat down to shower, when in walked a group of three men.

I took one look at the three bathers and seriously considered leaving. Being naked with strangers can make unknown social situations just that much more awkward, and I had no idea how to deal with naked *yakuza*. *Yakuza* are members of crime organizations in Japan, sort of their own mafia, and they get most of their money through illegal activities and intimidation—not people you'd want in your family bath.

A dragon tattoo ran up the arm and covered the left shoulder of the first man, snuggling its head against his heart. So much for not letting the *yakuza* into the baths. He had a top row of oversized dentures that stuck out of his perpetually open mouth. Jet-black, permed hair curled around his face, accentuating the unnatural teeth. He was it, the "Yakuza," the main talker of the group, and everyone deferred to him. He made straight for the large bath without washing, and jumped right in.

The second guy was the "Businessman." Quiet, in his late 40s or 50s, he had a clean, straight haircut, an easy manner, and a bigger potbelly than most. After a token splash of water on his body, he jumped right into one of the colored baths. Eventually, he moved on to the edge of the big bath, pulled out a straight razor, and proceeded to shave every part of his body with just a thin layer of soap. And I mean everything—his cheeks, forehead, eyebrows, upper and lower arms. He rinsed the razor in the bath, not caring about the Hep C he was probably spreading.

The last guy was the "Sidekick." He had a thick body and a massive, perfectly round potbelly. He was without a doubt mentally challenged. He followed the Businessman around, trying to get in the baths together before being scolded and sent away. Yakuza called him over, squirted shampoo in his hair, and told him to wash. They looked out for him in a demeaning way, showing enough affection to keep him around, but never any respect.

I was now questioning my sanity for staying in the bathhouse, especially after I realized the other two men had vanished. But the jet bath felt soooo good after the long day. I tried to soak peacefully, pretending not to listen to the three oddballs. Eventually though, they all converged in the main bath next to me.

"Oh man, that's hot," Yakuza said.

"Really hot," the Businessman agreed.

"So hot," said the Sidekick, as the group faced each other.

"Yup, really hot," Yakuza confirmed. This went on for another round until everyone was convinced the water was hot. No criminal secrets to hear just yet.

"Hey, who the fuck is that?" Yakuza asked. No one attempted to answer.

I tried to shrink deep into the bath.

"Get him outta here."

The Sidekick leapt into action, jumping over the wall into my side of the bath. The Businessman stood with his straight razor out. Everyone was staring at me, but none harder than the Sidekick. He got closer, and closer. I held my breath; the sound of my heart racing filled my ears. What was he going to do to me? I looked for the exit. He stopped just in front of me, reached down, and started jerking off with a large grin, the jet bubbles suddenly more vigorous.

The other two gangsters laughed hysterically, egging him on.

Yup, that was enough. The water was indeed hot. I jumped out and tried to walk nonchalantly to the exit as if there wasn't a deranged criminal masturbating in my tub. If there is one thing I had learned on the pilgrimage, it is that while it is dangerous to expose your pubes in a bar, it is probably doubly so if you are already naked, the guy next to you is jerking off, and his friend has a straight razor. Unfortunate life lessons all round.

The white cat stared intently as I rushed to get dressed. The old lady never bothered to look up from her TV.

I don't know what was going on with people between Temples Seventy and Seventy-Five, but I couldn't wait to get away.

IN THE MORNING the temples rolled by in quick succession as the houses closed in and the distance between temples shortened. I marched out of Temple Seventy-Seven, drenched to the bone from the torrential downpours that hadn't paused for three days.

I was on a busy main road with no sidewalk and plenty of puddles to be splashed by. Fortunately, the small, white 16th century Marugame Castle was perched on a hill overhead and reminded me that I was having fun, and it was only water. The fact that no one was abusing me was a welcome bonus.

Soaking wet, I didn't want to test the patience of restaurant owners, so I settled on a Lawson convenience store and an over-hang in the parking lot at lunchtime. It was such a treat to find a real Japanese convenience store after stuffing my body with various fish sausages over the past month. I was amazed to find a *gyūdon bentō* box of marinated beef over rice. Add in one *inar-izushi* (fried sweet tofu stuffed with rice and sesame seeds), a Snickers bar, and one liter of Pocari Sweat sports drink, and I knew why this part of Shikoku was associated with Nirvana.

I had just wedged myself between the trash cans and the entrance to stay out of the rain, when a young man on a bike screeched to a halt in front of me.

"Where are you from?" he asked in halting, heavily accented English.

I looked up with a mouth full of rice and beef.

Short and wiry, he had a bowl haircut that fell over shaved sides. He got off his bike and squatted right in front of me. "WHERE ARE YOU FROM?" he yelled in my face. His wretched breath flowed through crooked yellow teeth, behind a sudden smile that never reached his darting eyes.

I looked back patiently and pointed to my full mouth. He didn't seem to care and started to get agitated. He breathed in again for what looked like an even louder question.

"America," I rushed through a full mouth before he breathed on me again.

A quick nod of the head and he moved from a squat into a

sitting position, staying right in front of me, blocking me in. His English exhausted, he launched into a tirade in Japanese. "I'm Haru. Tomorrow's my birthday. But I don't care about that." The information came in rapid-fire bursts. "I'm 25 now, so I'll be 26 tomorrow. But I don't care about that. Man, you are so *lucky* to be doing the pilgrimage." His eyes darted, never resting on anything.

"Happy birthday," I said.

"I TOLD YOU, I don't care about that," he screamed.

"Do you like life?" he asked suddenly, shifting both his tone and level.

"Of course," I said. "Don't you?"

He ignored me. "How old do you want to live to be?"

This was taking an odd turn. "At least 100. What about you?"

"Yeah, yeah. Me too."

But somehow, I didn't believe him. Over and over he asked me the same thing. Was I happy with life, and what was I doing? Each time I said yes and told him I was on an adventure, he grew more agitated.

"Haru, what do you do?" I asked.

"Nothing. I'm a *furītā*." And there it was—his first true answer.

A *furītā*, taken from the made-up word "freeter," is a combination of the English word "free" and the German word "*arbeiter*," which means "worker." It refers to someone who is unemployed by choice and who chooses not to become an office worker like everyone else—or maybe they are unable to become like everyone else.

Over 20 years the number of freeters grew from 500,000 in 1982 to over two million by 2002, and is probably higher today. Someone not keeping busy or working is hardly revered in Japan. The turn of phrase created for kids in their 20s and 30s who live with their parents and don't contribute to the family is "parasite *shinguru*," or "parasite single." Japan can be a harsh place for the nonconformist.

For many of these young men and women, the pressure to conform, finish school, get a job, and get married is causing them to withdraw even further. Known as *hikikomori,* literally "pulling inward, being confined," they are young people who seek extreme degrees of isolation. They refuse to leave their rooms, even to meet their parents, sometimes for decades at a time. They are unable to become what society expects them to be, and so they belong nowhere.

In many cases it is not really their fault. Perhaps they had learning issues and were diverted away from good schools by the school system early on, separated by test scores. Gone are the days when blue collar jobs pay enough to support families, or even exist at all in depressed areas of the country. The pressure to live up to society's expectations, without the means to do so, must be overwhelming.

Haru was starting to show signs of making the leap to *hikikomori*. In our short conversation he ranged from anger towards his parents, to sadness, fear of life, and finally, jealousy that turned to more sadness. He was on his daily trip out of the house that his mother forced him to take. She gave him 500 yen each day, and he came to this convenience store.

The questions kept coming:

What was American TV like?

Did I have money?

What was I doing?

Did I like life?

We kept coming back to these last two questions. It was clear Haru was lost and didn't know how to get out of his current situation.

As I tried to relax and eat my lunch, I tried to encourage him to find something he liked doing.

"Do you have muscles? I do. Feel my biceps," he demanded.

"Yup, those are big biceps," I complemented him.

He beamed like a five-year-old. "Have you ever been in a fight?"

"No," I lied.

"I love fighting. I've been in lots of fights. I'm small and lose a lot, but I like it anyway."

"I hate fighting," I said, hoping to change the subject. "What else do you like to do?"

"Watch TV."

"What about work?"

"I hate work. All I want to do is travel, like you."

"Why don't you do the pilgrimage?" I said. "It would be good for you."

His eyes grew distant, and he stopped talking. Advice was not what he was looking for.

There wasn't much else I could do, so I wished him luck and told him to think about the pilgrimage again.

He grunted and went into the store without saying goodbye. At least he didn't try to fight me.

Would our conversation make a difference? I'll never know. But I hope he found what he was looking for and that it wouldn't be a life of fighting, like the *yakuza* in my bath, or the perverts in the *yakitori* bar. I was sure the pilgrimage could help. It is the one place in Japan where the constraints of everyday life fall away, and you are not bound by what society keeps trying to convince you, you are. It's where you begin to see a pattern to your hardships and your joy, and you begin to realize what is important in life.

You realize that any problem will work itself out if you just keep making forward progress.

19

DRUNKS

"Sorry, we are full." *Beep, beep, beep, beep.* A man hung up before I could respond. It was pouring outside again, and I was under a covered shopping arcade, trying to find a room for the night.

I dialed another inn close to Temple Eighty, Kokubun-ji.

"*Moshi moshi.*"

"Excuse me, I'm a walking pilgrim. Can I reserve a room?"

"Why does your Japanese sound funny?" the innkeeper asked suspiciously.

"Actually, I'm from America, but I speak . . ."

"You need to speak Japanese."

"We are speaking Japanese."

"No, we aren't," she replied in Japanese. *Beep, beep, beep.*

There was only one other place left, the Seto Public Inn, so I gave it a try.

"Yes," said a wispy voice.

I kept it short and sweet to obscure my accent.

"Hmm, we are really full tonight. But I'll find you something."

"Thank yo—"

Beep, beep, beep, beep.

That was as enthusiastic a yes as I was likely to get, and given the downpour outside, there were no better options.

Kokubun-ji sits just on the other side of railroad tracks, shaded in beautiful pine trees. With dusk descending early from the heavy rains, I was thankful to have arrived in one piece after slipping down a mountain path behind the temple. The sculpted green grounds were dotted everywhere with large, decorative rocks and gray carved statues depicting different Buddhas and the seven lucky gods. Turtles made their home in green lily-pad-laden ponds. Shiny temple roofs gathered the rain into gutters that then flowed down long, intricately linked metal chains hanging from each corner.

"Hey! Todd, over here!" someone yelled.

I looked around, confused, until I found three people huddled under an awning, one waving wildly. Kikuchi, ball cap still tilted to the side, sat with two older men. The first was walking only in sandals, his feet too swollen to fit back into his shoes. The other, Yoshikawa-san, was drinking a beer.

They were debating where to stay for the night. I told them I was at the public inn, and Yoshikawa-san jumped at the idea. He called right away and luckily had no problem getting a room.

Kikuchi called the second place. Apparently, his Japanese was just fine, and his room was booked. The last man called the first place, and, magically, they had plenty of room too.

Kikuchi and I promised to catch up in the morning, and the drunken Yoshikawa-san and I headed down the road to find our home for the night.

"Pale, nondescript, and a bit grungy" described both the inn and the 90-year-old caretaker who answered the door.

His wife sat in a chair in the dimly lit common room that looked the same as just about every other public building I've visited in Japan. Brown overstuffed chairs and couches surrounded a TV from the 1990s, upon which a large, tacky clock sat. A thick glass ashtray sat on a heavily lacquered coffee table that stuck to a deeply stained linoleum floor. Finely carved pottery sat protected in a glass case, as if to shield the lively colors from being dulled by the gloom of the inn.

Yoshikawa-san and I greeted the wife together and then yelled hello at the same time when no response was forthcoming. She didn't even blink.

"Sit," the caretaker mumbled.

We sat.

Brown oolong tea came out and was placed next to a box of cigarettes and a lighter on the coffee table. We managed to take one sip before we were ordered again.

"Stand," the caretaker commanded, and started to slowly climb the wooden stairs attached to the common room.

I guessed no tea for us.

My room had walls, a roof, six *tatami* mats, enough to sleep three people, and one of the first TVs ever made in Japan. The screen was the size of a telephone book, the rest of it the size of a small refrigerator, with dials at the bottom to change channels. Two circular bunny ear antennae served to control the level of fuzziness. The only way to turn it on was by inserting 500-yen coins.

I felt lonely in the old room and took a quick bath and then retreated downstairs to the 1994 decor. Unfortunately, the innkeeper had spread the word that guests had arrived, and the entire extended family, eight strong, descended on the living room to watch TV, taking up all the seats before we could.

Yoshikawa-san and I were the only guests in the inn that was supposed to be crowded, and it was hard not to feel unwelcome.

Everyone avoided me as I looked for a place to sit and get off my weary feet.

"There's a floor," the innkeeper remarked. His stoic, paper-thin face never changed.

So I sat in the only space left, near the entrance, on the dirty linoleum floor, waiting for my feet to stop throbbing and for dinner to begin.

Dinner and Yoshikawa-san arrived at the same time, and I gratefully retreated from the family TV room. While Japanese inns are sometimes horribly outdated and cluttered, food is never something that is treated haphazardly, and we were served a feast.

Wave after wave of small dishes was presented to us. A large *aji* fish (horse mackerel) was served lightly grilled, together with a bowl of impossibly fluffy rice, red beans, a small cabbage salad, deep-fried breaded mashed potatoes and meat (*korokke*), pickles, and miso soup. A big bottle of beer rounded off the perfect end to a long day.

Yoshikawa-san was skinny, with a thin mustache and a small tuft of hair shooting out of his chin at an awkward angle. His hairstyle gave the impression of a rat's tail or mullet, yet I could never quite find either. His front teeth stuck out too far but were otherwise perfectly aligned. He was from Tokyo and was walking the pilgrimage in stages. He claimed he didn't work, but he seemed to have plenty of money and threw it around easily. He had started walking three days ago.

"*Kampai*." We clinked our glasses together.

"Drink up! Beer's on me tonight," he offered after downing his glass in one go.

"Thanks, but I haven't been drinking much these days," I replied after taking a small sip. Normally I would have jumped at the chance of a drink. But walking all day and scraping by for any possible nutrition to keep the body going had almost eliminated any desire to drink at the end of the day.

"What the hell are you talking about?" Yoshikawa-san yelled.

The innkeeper came running in and must have assumed something else, because he ran to me, grabbed my chopsticks, and muttered something about foreigners not knowing how to eat fish. Smelling like an expired medicine cabinet, he pushed me aside to scrape fish off the bone, while I suffered politely.

The innkeeper retreated, and Yoshikawa-san didn't miss a beat. "Alcohol is the fuel that is keeping me going. I keep a small bottle of whiskey in my front pocket and sip as I go. It's all you really need. Well, besides beer, wine, and *sake*."

"How far did you make it today?" I asked.

His face was red, indicating that he might already be drunk. "Well, I ended up drinking a lot last night and was hungover and puking for most of the walk today. But I made it seven miles! Which is more than the day before," he said smugly.

"You like drinking?" the innkeeper asked as he came back in. Then he saw me eating and disapproval got the better of him. He pushed me aside again. This time he drowned my fish in soy sauce. If it wasn't dead before, it was now. He shook his head at Yoshikawa, who quickly pulled his plate off the table before the innkeeper could ruin another fish.

"Look here," the elderly man called over his shoulder as he grabbed a book off a shelf. He held it lovingly in his hands. "You have to read this book if you love to drink. My inn is even in the book, right here. I don't know how much you drink, but this guy drank like a fish!" He framed this like a challenge.

The book's pristine condition proved that he had only ever read the page that mentioned drinking at this inn. I loved the title. It was to the point and didn't take the pilgrimage or itself too seriously: *Blue Sky and Ocean: makes the beer taste so good.*

Yoshikawa took it with a sudden gleam in his eye, like a priest reverently examining a sacred text.

"You know," he began, never taking his eyes off the book, "all of us walkers are changed by the pilgrimage, but it's different for everyone. Kūkai teaches you what you need to learn, when you need to learn it."

I didn't need the constant drinking to agree with the sentiment. The first time I walked the pilgrimage, I needed to learn that I was, in fact, a strong person. This time around, I had to learn the same lesson again, but the definition of "strong" had changed. I had to learn how to let go of being the "best" and caring about how others would see me. I was finally learning to be happy with what I wanted in life, rather than trying to be what others expected.

We all face difficulties in life. We all have our doubts about what we should be doing with our lives. The trick is to keep moving forward, while appreciating where we are now.

"You know, the pilgrimage teaches you to have goals. You have to reach a certain point by the end of the day. Every morning you need to set a goal, and your own legs and mind get you there," Yoshikawa reflected.

He confided in me that he had been moving in circles his whole life, with no goals in sight. Yoshikawa needed the structure of the *henro* path and proof that he could stick to goals he had set. The pilgrimage was a different type of circle. It was not an aimless pursuit, but it still dropped you back at the same place you started, just with a different understanding of who you really were.

Yoshikawa ordered his last drinks, a large beer glass full of *sake* and a large glass full of beer, before saying goodnight. He slept in, and I never saw him again.

THE SHIKOKU PILGRIMAGE attracts a wide variety of people—adventure junkies, spiritual wannabes, societal escape artists, truth seekers, alcoholics, religious diehards, tourists, scam artists, the homeless, and freedom seekers. As I found out along the way, many of the people I met fit multiple categories, sometimes in outrageous ways. Shikoku has something for everyone, and the beautiful part of the pilgrimage is the freedom to learn what you need, when you need it. In a world and a society that dictates how to live, the pilgrimage is medicine for the soul, where we are able to see each other more clearly, as well as how we fit (or don't) into the larger movement of society.

I was out the door and on the path by 5:00 a.m. as was customary now. My shoes were completely dry from a trick I had learned the last time I walked. After a long day in the rain, you take out the insoles, wrap them in newspaper, and walk on them until all the moisture is squeezed out. Leave them out to dry completely overnight. At the same time, ball up the rest of the newspaper and pack it into the shoes. By morning most of the moisture will have been soaked up, and your feet will thank you. My feet were certainly stronger now, and while blisters still occupied most of the available real estate, they were manageable.

The walk to the next two temples was along the old paths, bringing back the joy of nature and sense of adventure. Bang for your buck, or yen, Temples Eighty-One and Eighty-Two are hard to beat. After climbing 1,200 feet under the canopy of fresh green, the weary pilgrim is rewarded with 192 more stone steps to climb. Shiromine-ji holds its own as a beautiful mountain temple, with full-bodied pines protecting rough cut stone steps and sweeping eaves. It would be easy to spend an eternity there.

One unfortunate emperor was, at least, lucky enough to be buried there. The mausoleum of Emperor Sutoku is modest, possibly due to his exiled status after 19 years of rule and then his assassination near Temple Seventy-Nine in the year 1164 CE. But beyond the historical Sutoku is the belief that he transformed into Sutoku Tennō, one of the most famous

yōkai to haunt Japan. *Yōkai* are supernatural monsters, spirits, and demons that range from the malevolent to the mischievous.

Not satisfied with being exiled and assassinated (who would be?) this badass emperor changed careers and transformed into an *onryō* (a type of ghost), or some say a greater *tengu* (a supernatural being or a type of Shinto god), and single-handedly rained calamity on all emperors to follow. And he was good at his new job. He is ranked in the top three evil *yōkai*, together with the former imperial courtesan turned mean-spirited fox Tamamo no Mae and the devil god Shuten Dōji.

Yōkai began as myths from isolated tribes living on the Japanese isles. Over the years they were influenced by Shinto and then Buddhist teachings. But they came into their own during the Edo era that began in the 16th century, when artists started to compile the various folklore from across Japan. *Yōkai*, and the idea of the supernatural, invaded all parts of Japan, from the crassest bar tale to the high form *Noh* theaters for the palace elite.

Like most things traditional and popular, they fell from grace during the Meiji era (1868–1912), when Japan embarked on rapid modernization to keep pace with the West. Talk of ghosts and demons was seen as an embarrassment. It took the end of World War II and the advent of *manga* (comics) to reintroduce them to modern Japan. Once again, they spread like unquenchable supernatural wildfires, penetrating just about every part of Japanese society. Ask anyone these days about a haunting nearby, and you'll get multiple stories told with a straight face by people who would normally identify as nonreligious, nonspiritual, and nonmagical. Ghosts are different. They are real.

Luckily, the emperor left me alone, and I was happy to meet up with Kikuchi, who was arriving at Temple Eighty-One as I was leaving. We discussed our sleeping options, or lack thereof, in Takamatsu city. With no place to sleep outside, we agreed to meet at a 24-hour spa land. It was new and not on my map, but Kikuchi was from the area and knew where to find it.

Upbeat, I walked slowly and savored the meandering mountain path that traversed the Goshikidai Plateau with its five colored peaks. I wove through lush forest under the gaze of Jizō statues that hid amongst tree trunks, aided by the ever-present white and red *henro* signs that encouraged the walker onwards. The trail cut across highland grasses, and the sweet fragrance of flowers flirted with my senses, hinting at what lay just out of sight and tempting me off the path.

Three short miles later I passed through a massive wooden gate into Negoro-ji temple. I looked down upon a large, bright green valley filled with temples, altars, and ancient stone carvings, shaded by massive cedar boughs. The main Buddha image is carved from the roots of a large tree in the courtyard. The temple and Kagawa Prefecture (literally "fragrant river") are named after the river thought to flow from the roots of the tree.

As you walk into the temple grounds, you are confronted by a towering statue of an ox devil. The ox head looks more like that of a giant cat, with bulging eyes and horns sticking out from its mouth rather than the top of its head. Standing on two feet, it has wings and a wicked set of four claws on each hand. It depends on whom you ask, but either a young samurai or the resident Buddha, the thousand-armed Kannon, felled the devil beast with an arrow and chopped off its head. The horns are supposedly housed in the temple to this day. What better way to repel evil than with the bones of a felled dead devil?

But all good (and bad) things must come to an end, and it was with a wistful heart that I walked out of the mountains and away from the ghosts, magical beings, and ancient dirt paths, down into the city of Takamatsu, where 400,000 people went about their normal everyday lives. Japan is like this; one moment you are in the countryside and then suddenly, you are not.

At least the transition into Takamatsu was interesting, as I walked through a small town filled with thousands of diminutive *bonsai* trees in even rows, four deep, twisting majestically at waist height on rough wooden benches. I leaned against a concrete wall and pulled out a rice ball snack filled with tuna that a couple had given me as *osettai* at the last temple. Across the road an older man in a gray jumpsuit was trimming a pine *bonsai* that came up to his knees, but which had a trunk as thick as a basketball. Three surgical snips, and he moved on to the next in line.

I got up to leave and politely said, "*Konnichiwa.* There are a lot of *bonsai* here." There is no better way of being polite in Japan than stating the obvious. It is the greatest of conversation starters, giving everyone something safe to talk about.

As a reward for my good behavior, he reached deep into a pocket and pulled out a large canned beer. "*Settai desu,*" he said, handing it to me before turning back to his plants. What was I going to do with a warm beer? And why did he have it in his pocket? But those aren't questions you bother a gift giver with. I put it in my bag, thanked him, and moved on.

The universe's plan fell into place a few blocks later as I walked along a concrete river embankment. A retired man with a small dog tied to his bike slowed down and matched my pace. Our pleasant conversation was a good distraction from the approaching wall of civilization looming at the end of the river. As we prepared to part, I decided to push the limits of our new friendship.

"Do you have a refrigerator?" I asked.

He stared at me. If obvious statements are to be rewarded, off-script questions are likely to earn suspicion.

"Do you have a refrigerator?" I asked again. "You know, the machines that keep things cold. I hear everyone has nice refrigerators in Japan."

"Yes, it's true," he admitted, probably regretting it the moment it left his lips.

"Here, please take this beer." I handed him the warm can. He stopped and looked even more troubled.

I frowned as I realized the position I had just put him in. It is fine to give gifts to pilgrims, but to accept one from a pilgrim was another thing. Now neither of us was happy, which seemed strange when gifts were involved.

A small light wormed its way slowly through his brain until his face brightened. He had found a way out.

"Buy yourself a cold beer," he said, smiling, and handed me 200 yen. To make sure the deal was sealed and no more gifts were on their way, he jumped back on his seat and sped away with a wave and a swiftly fading, "Be careful."

I wound my way through increasingly dense neighborhoods until, before I knew it, I was no longer just passing homes, but dull-looking apartment complexes and railway stations, and walking on a sidewalk, of all things. How long had it been since I had seen a sidewalk? It felt like weeks.

I arrived at the spa by 6:00 p.m. and was in a bath by 6:15. The new spa was massive and packed with tourists, residents, and the odd pilgrim needing a cheap place to sleep. I didn't see any tattoos except my own. For $20 a night, it was a hard deal to beat. By 7:00, Kikuchi had arrived, and we sat together in the outdoor bath overlooking the Inland Sea, as boats swarmed the busy port across the way.

There was no better place to catch up, and we dove deep into our stories from the time since we had parted ways at Temple Fifty-Eight, which might have been a lifetime ago. Kikuchi thought it impossible that I had caught up to him. I, of course, thought I had been walking slowly. It turns out Kikuchi's father picked him up after Temple Fifty-Eight, treated him to a dinner, and dropped him off 15 miles farther up the path.

It's odd that I never knew where he came from until just then. Kikuchi grew up just outside of Takamatsu. Despite talking with him for days at a time, somehow, we never learned much about each other. But we had time that evening, and the approaching end made us both more reflective than usual.

Dressed in matching Hawaiian-style robes provided by the spa, we sat down for dinner. I chose a bowl of thick *udon* noodles, while Kikuchi settled on curry rice.

"I can't eat that stuff," he said, pointing his nose towards my dinner.

"You mean *udon*?" I managed through the hot noodles stuffed into my mouth.

He waved to the noodles I was slurping and the hot broth dripping from my lips. "Yeah, those are a sorry excuse for *udon*."

I wasn't sure what he was getting at. They tasted great.

"I started walking the pilgrimage because I didn't know what I wanted to do in life," he said. "My parents are farmers, and I didn't want to follow them into the fields. Well, I figured it out. I want to own an *udon* shop and bring *Sanuki udon* to the rest of Japan."

Ah, I understood. His problem was that he was an *udon* purest. Takamatsu is famed for its particular style, called *Sanuki udon*, with its square shape and flat edges.

"It doesn't have to be here on Shikoku, though," he said. "I'm thinking about Kyoto."

It seemed I wasn't the only one who had figured out his life on the path.

We talked long into the night. There wasn't much else to do, after all, certainly not sleep. We should have known better from the last spa we stayed at. The lights, noise, blaring TVs, and karaoke streaming from behind sliding doors attracted a steady flow of new visitors looking for fun while we were looking for sleep. How I longed for a simple wooden bench on the side of a mountain.

"Ooh, you're so cute," said a woman passing by. She slumped into a chair next to us without even asking, a large lemon liquor drink in one hand and an unlit cigarette in the other. "I'm Seiko, but you can call me Seiko-chan." The "chan" was supposed to make her seem younger.

She was at least 60 and wore large rose-colored sunglasses that covered half her face. They went perfectly with her dyed red hair. Drunk, her face was flushed. She was sweet, desperate, and intensely lonely.

Kikuchi had the gentlest way of talking to her. He made her feel relaxed and welcome at the same time. Depressed from the life society had squeezed her into, being drunk was a way to cope. Kikuchi treated this stranger with a kindness that I have seen over and over again in Japan. It is a credit to how self-aware most Japanese are to the pressures everyone collectively puts on each other. Seiko-chan was traveling by herself from Osaka. But that was as far as we got, as each time something personal came up, she pulled heavily on her drink and started singing a new song.

She had a beautiful voice but was too drunk to make it through any one song. We ended up being treated to a sample of Japan's greatest hits.

"I love you," she declared suddenly, and grabbed my leg, a bit too high up. "Will you marry me? Will you love me?"

Kikuchi laughed his ass off.

"Do it, Todd. Do it now! Ask her to marry you!" he encouraged me.

A few weeks ago, being caught in someone else's problems when all I wanted to do was sleep would have annoyed me to no end. But now all I felt was enormous sympathy for Seiko-chan, and empathy for everyone and their story in life.

I really did love Japan. With all its quirks, its beauty was accessible yet unfathomably deep. When I left, promising never to come back, my problem wasn't really with Japan. It was my own inability to accept how people are, the places life has pushed them into, and where my life in Japan was trying to push me. I felt like I had finally let that go. I was ready to embrace Japan once again.

We carried on like this for over an hour. I promised to propose in the morning, and Seiko-chan announced she was going to get another drink. We never saw her again. Her songs made my night and kept me smiling until 1:30 a.m., when the lights dimmed, and the sounds faded.

PARTING
WORDS

For a whole month I had heard nothing but warnings from fellow pilgrims about the criminals that inhabit Shikoku, ready to snatch my money while I slept, to ambush me along deserted mountain passes and leave my body to join the throngs of *henro* graves marking the path. According to one such doomsayer, I was now in the most danger. With my scroll almost complete with flowing calligraphy from all the temples, the gangs were ready to steal it and make a quick $2,000 on the religious black market. I'm not sure what buying stolen karma does to one's own karma, but I'm pretty sure it is not good.

Despite all the warnings, the only real criminals I met were in a bath, and the only thieves I met wanted my pubic hairs. But to remind me to stay vigilant, Temple Eighty-Six had a bulletin board of criminals reported on the path. "*Henro* beware," a grainy, faded, photocopied poster proclaimed next to the picture of a smiling man. "This person impersonates *henro* and deceives." He was 48 years old, from Fukuoka city, and was not to be trusted.

After all this time hearing about criminals on the *henro* route, it was odd that the only warning posters were all the way at the end. More concerning than the scam artists was the collection of seven sad posters.

They were a mix of handwritten pleas, graphically designed posters, and personal photos stuck to the side wall in the main temple hall. Each had the same general story about a loved one who had gone missing. One poster read, "Onishi was 57 years old when he was last seen departing from Osaka station to look for a place to be buried on Shikoku. We haven't heard from him since." Another poster spoke of Ms. Kyoko, who started walking on March 3 and disappeared on March 5. The poster ended with a heart-wrenching plea: "Please call me if you see my mom."

Kikuchi and I were almost done with our pilgrimage, and it looked like we were in the clear. Of course, I had had my run-ins with the bike gangs, *yakuza*, swindlers, zealot hair collectors, masturbators, angry monks, and porn vending machines, but nothing quite measured up to the dire warnings I had received early on. While my wallet was lighter, temples were the main culprits, rather than a coordinated syndicate of pilgrim thieves. But the *henro* stones, along with the modern missing persons photos, made it clear that things can and do still happen on the pilgrimage.

I GAVE KIKUCHI SOME CHEESE.

"Man, you foreign *henro* get way more *osettai* than the rest of us. Plus, you get cheese. I haven't gotten any cheese this whole time," he said with a smile and a nudge as we sat under the eaves of Temple Eighty-Seven, thinking through our last steps.

Kikuchi and I had become quite close these past two days, partly a product of sharing the journey together, but also because he was just so likable. I don't think any Japanese who walk the pilgrimage imagine they will end up walking with a foreigner, let alone finishing it with one.

We walked along the flat country roads leading away from Temple Eighty-Seven in silence, each trying to figure out what ending our journey would mean. The houses slowly disappeared as we made our final march towards the mountains in the distance. It was too late in the day to make it to Temple Eighty-Eight before the stamp office closed. Who would want to rush to the last temple anyway?

We decided to end our day on the early side at the "*Henro* Salon," a rest stop and museum sponsored by the *Henro* Association of Kagawa, one of the groups helping to keep the *henro* route marked and relevant in the modern world. Located next to Maeyama Dam, the Salon rested smack-dab in the middle of nowhere, with nothing beyond except the steep climb to the remote Temple Eighty-Eight high above.

Conveniently, there was a *michi no eki* (rest area) just across the street, where we planned to spend the night. If we arrived before 4:00 p.m., when the Salon closed, we could get a commemorative *henro* pin and certificate, free! It was an oddity that regular residents of Shikoku and associations gave things away, while temples only sold things, trading money in exchange for luck and salvation.

The first thing you notice about the Salon when you enter is a massive model of Shikoku, right in the middle. It shows just how mountainous the island is, how precariously each temple clings to its mountain, and the model makes you thankful and a bit sad that you missed the higher, more rugged interior of the island.

Wandering around the Salon, I was reminded just how hard the journey used to be, as historical pictures showed what the paths once looked like and the difficulties (besides sucking truck fumes) *henro* used to face. Just in case you were still feeling self-congratulatory about your own accomplishment, there was a display dedicated to Mohei Nakatsukasa. Born in

1845, Mohei started walking his first pilgrimage at 22 and completed it 280 times, leaving behind 240 stone path markers before his death at the age of 78. He walked so many times that every page in his stamp book was a solid vermillion red from hundreds of overlain stamps. Assuming it took an average of 45 days each time around, he walked for 34 years, or 12,600 days.

We picked up our bags at 4:00 p.m., ready to move across the street for the night as the Salon closed for the day. But just as we were leaving, a middle-aged man poked his head inside and scanned the room. He quickly locked onto us, as we were the only pilgrims there, and motioned for us to follow him outside.

Thick gray hair lay heavy across his head, and thin glasses sat low on his short nose, threatening to fall off at any sudden movement. A brown necktie fell far below his belt.

Oddly, the businessman was standing next to a thin walking pilgrim with a severe limp. We walked over to introduce ourselves and found out that the pilgrim's name was Kimura-san. He had earned his limp by finishing the route in just 28 days. It had taken me 29 days, and I had used a bike for part of it. I could almost feel how bad his feet must have looked.

"Do you want to come home with me?" the businessman asked me suddenly, not even bothering to tell us his name.

"Um, thanks, but I'm with a friend," I replied, nodding my head towards Kikuchi.

"Don't worry, bring him too."

Hmm. When to keep your guard up and when to let people in? It is a difficult call to trust strange men who hang around remote service areas trying to pick up exhausted, dirty, young pilgrims.

"I'm taking Kimura here to the bus station in Takamatsu. We can drop him off and then you can stay the night at my home with my family."

Deal. Kikuchi and I shrugged, and we piled our smelling bodies into his car. A home sounded like heaven.

On the ride to the station we learned his name was Matsuoka-san, and he was a Rotary Club member and architect by profession. It also seemed that he really was a pilgrim junkie and spent a lot of his free time waiting around the Salon trying to pick up walkers.

It was a surreal experience—first, riding in a car; second, retracing my steps in a 45-minute drive that had taken me two days to complete.

After dropping Kimura-san off, we proceeded to Matsuoka-san's sixth floor apartment in the heart of Takamatsu city. Neither his wife nor mother seemed overly surprised that he had brought home two stray *henro*. With practiced ease they helped set us up in a spare *tatami* mat room with two futons and an already-running air-conditioner.

Matsuoka-san took us out to dinner at a local *izakaya* (like a Japanese version of a tapas bar), leaving his wife and mother to relax at home without having to entertain. We sat at our own low table on *tatami* mats, away from the bar counter and potential pubic hair thieves.

Over dinner of *miso* grilled fish, we learned more about Matsuoka-san and his passion for the pilgrimage.

"The Rotary Club sponsors the placing of signs for pilgrims, benches, rest areas, and even the pins and certificates at the *Henro* Salon. But it's not easy, and not everyone agrees with what we do."

We pressed him for details, and it turned out that even a pilgrimage is not free from politics. My first thought was that there must be competition between the temples, but, in fact, the head priests of each temple make up only one group. Some of the other groups include the Rotary Club, the Cooperative Society to Preserve the *Henro* Trail, which puts out the guide map most everyone uses, as well as the separate prefectural governments.

"You see, everyone has different symbols and signs they want to put up," Matsuoka-san said. "And the prefectures don't want people placing stickers and signs on municipal property."

This was a shock to hear, as the only thing that keeps a pilgrim on the path is the number of signs and stickers placed along the route. Of course, I was only getting one side of what seemed to be a complicated political story.

"So, we started putting up signs that said *"dōgyō ninin"* (two walk together). But the prefectural boards came back and said that was too religious."

That seemed like a funny stance to me, as the pilgrimage was based on a religion and is fueled by the idea that Kūkai walks with you. It is hard to miss the fact that you are visiting 88 Buddhist temples. Maybe they were just worried about using government property for any *one* specific religious activity.

"Okay, so here is the other thing. We also want to make the pilgrimage into a UNESCO World Heritage Site, just like the Camino de Santiago in Spain."

This was not the first time I'd heard the 88 temple pilgrimage compared to Spain's famous Christian pilgrimage. It was common to meet walkers on Shikoku who had already walked the pilgrimage in Spain, or wanted to do so. Once you get the pilgrimage bug, the type of religion ceases to matter. The practices of putting one foot in front of the other and slipping outside of normal society and its distractions take precedence.

From an economic standpoint, it sounded great. More people would mean more money to maintain the route and support local businesses. But something made me feel uncomfortable about the idea. I couldn't quite figure it out.

"All we need is to standardize the pilgrimage first, under

one group, before we can apply. We need to be more like the Camino de Santiago and have a set way of doing everything. This kind of exists but it needs to be more regulated," he said.

There it was. They wanted to standardize what was never meant to be standard. Sure, there are common approaches to being a *henro*, from the clothes, to visiting temples and receiving stamps, to the vows one is supposed to take. But from there, everything is left up to the person. Historically, you started at the temple closest to where you arrived on Shikoku. These days you can walk, ride a bike, drive, take trains, a bus, or a combination, and you are still a *henro*. Given the fact that bus *henro* outnumber walkers by about 150 to 1 each year, some could argue the pilgrimage should be a motorized one, if anything.

A few years ago, I might have agreed with the idea that walkers were the best, the strongest, the purest form of pilgrims. But now that seemed like an easy and arrogant answer. The 88 Temple Pilgrimage not only accommodates everyone but finds a way to teach each person what they need at that time in their life. Not everyone is meant to walk 750 miles. And that is okay.

It seemed fitting to hear about the human side of the religious experience on our last night as I began the transition back into society. It was a good reminder that there are hidden sides to everything, and like the Buddha, who, as I learned, wears underwear too, nothing is ever only pure or impure. The problem comes when we insist on only seeing one side or the other. Everything spiritual exists in the everyday, sometimes messed up, world we live in.

The evening with Matsuoka-san passed easily, and he enjoyed showing us all his research, from old photos to newspaper clippings about the pilgrimage. He capped off the night with a solo *shamisen* (a traditional guitar-like instrument) performance. But by 8:00 p.m., the two beers and deep conversation finally did me in, and I retreated to my bed for a 5:00 a.m. wake up.

Matsuoka-san was, after all, a generous soul, giving up his house and time to a couple of dirty pilgrims. His wife and mother must have been saints. He shared his dream, passion, and compassion with us. I hoped he kept the flexibility of how a pilgrim experience Shikoku in mind as they pursued UNESCO status.[1] The generosity of the people of Shikoku was the real engine of the pilgrimage, and any system should acknowledge the role they play. The pilgrimage cannot be reduced to religious places and artifacts alone.

WE WAVED goodbye to Matsuoka-san the next morning, after being dropped off at the *michi no eki* across from the Salon, and shouldered our packs to set off on our final mountain climb. We plunged into the thick nearby forest and towards the object of our obsession for the last month, Temple Eighty-Eight, Ōkubo-ji.

It was only six miles to the last temple. After walking 744 miles, the last push felt like nothing. And yet, in some ways it was the hardest part of the journey. I didn't want the pilgrimage to end. For 30 days I had separated myself from society and had only one simple job: to put one foot in front of the other, over and over again. I now felt uncomfortable in regular conversations that centered on the latest TV show or news update, and I worried what would happen to me when I re-entered society. Would I lose my newfound perspective on life? Would I become a slave to other people's expectations again?

We hiked past a carved stone memorial dedicated to *henro* who had walked in a desperate attempt to cure a myriad of incurable illnesses. Most were never cured, while a select few were miraculously saved, if you believe the hundreds of crutches deposited at temples around the island. We passed a few solitary, empty houses. Heavy, rice-burdened stalks hinted that at least someone still inhabited the area, if only to collect the rice.

The trail seemed to apologize for all the long days we had spent breathing in car fumes on hot paved roads, as suddenly it fit every romantic image a pilgrimage in Japan can conjure up. We climbed through a tunnel of thick green bamboo that clicked as the wind pushed the towering stalks together, and walked past a hidden Shinto shrine, deserted but for the lion-dogs protecting it from a world filled with evil spirits. We continued up log staircases and razor-thin paths hugging the mountain, and over a narrow bridge traversing a gorge where a swift river churned below.

A family of boars, a mother with four babies, burst across our path. In the trees above, monkeys screeched and jumped from branch to branch. Birds chirped their summer songs as we crunched our way through the forest.

The path came to a sudden end as a deep fog settled in. Rocky cliffs rose around us, lost in the mist swirling overhead. We came to a rock face that presented the clear implication it was to be climbed. Our staffs, for once, were a hindrance rather than trusted companions as we scrambled up, foot over hand. An iron chain bolted into the rock guided our way, helping us to avoid any last-minute tragedies.

Finally, we crested the ridge leading down to Temple Eighty-Eight and entered a world swallowed in a blanket of white swirling fog, overseen by sharp cliffs and curious stone Jizō, peering out of their forest cover as silent witnesses to the end of our journey.

This was it—the last path down. Excitement and hesitation mixed together in the pit of my stomach until I couldn't tell them apart. I felt like I was going to cry, and then Kikuchi snapped me out of my own head.

"What pose are you going to use?" Kikuchi called over his shoulder.

"Huh? What are you talking about?"

"Your final picture at Temple Eighty-Eight. What pose are you going to strike? I'm going with a Charlie's Angels gun pose."

I burst out laughing, liking Kikuchi even more. We took the gnarled path down to the temple valley together, the fog playing tricks on our eyes as the hardships, triumphs, and friends along the way materialized and disappeared back into the mists. How many of the people we had met would walk this same path, or had already done so the day before?

Nobu was out there, "chan, chan-ing" his way here, probably attached to some *henro* or another. Suzuki-san was most likely getting rich off his growing cult of pilgrim beggars, waiting until he had enough money to arrive in a taxi and end his two years in style.

The Tokyo Boyz must have come and gone ages ago. They were probably back in Tokyo, already mesmerizing their friends with tales of the crazy foreigner who took on Shikoku's mountains with only a *mamachari*. Kanako-chan would be back in her parents' home, a free spirit struggling with convention and counting the days until she finished high school.

We all had made it to the end in our own way, and for all of us the pilgrimage would never really be over.

Like the path that leads to it, Temple Eighty-Eight does not disappoint. Boxed in by towering cliffs, mountains, and rocky bluffs, the temple itself is relatively modest, allowing the power of nature to impact the soul of the traveler. There isn't any music playing or cheers to congratulate the pilgrim on completion, simply the silence of contemplation as one comes to grips with the enormity of the task just finished, that had started with a simple step.

Kikuchi and I took our time praying and giving thanks

before we headed to the stamp office. Along the way we passed hundreds of walking staffs, left by pilgrims, as is the custom, to signify the end of their journey with Kūkai. The tradition was based on Kūkai's own actions, as he enshrined his own stick here after completing his trip to China.

"Shall we get a taxi back to Tokushima city?" Kikuchi asked. We hadn't even finished getting our stamps, and he was already done, mobile phone in hand.

"Actually, I'm going to walk back to Temple One today," I said.

"What are you talking about? We are done. This is it. No more staff, no more bags, no more dirty underwear. No more wearing the same shirt day after day."

I smiled back and shrugged. This was a heated debate on the pilgrimage. Some thought you ended at Eighty-Eight, others thought you needed to return to the temple where you started, in order to complete the circle. For me it was about finishing everything, and that included walking back to Temple One, where it all began. It was also how I had done it the last time. Plus, after walking 750 miles, an extra 23 miles seemed like a nice cool down. If I was really being honest with myself, I would have known that I wasn't quite ready to give it all up.

"What are you two talking about?" the monk writing Kikuchi's calligraphy yelled out. "This is the end. Nowhere else, just this."

I shrugged politely. "Thank you for the advice. But, for me, I need to walk all the way around."

"You're an idiot," the monk said. "This is an 88-temple pilgrimage, not an 89-temple one. The only place you need to go next is Mt. Kōya, back on the main island, to report back to Kūkai."

"So that would still make it 89 temples, right?" I couldn't help myself, but I said it with a smile. And he had called me an idiot.

"You're an idiot!" he repeated.

And that was the last talk I had with a monk on Shikoku.

IT WAS 11:00 a.m. when I finally left Temple Eighty-Eight, after spending over one and a half hours enjoying almost being done. I said my goodbyes to Kikuchi and promised to keep in touch, but knowing how *henro* are, I didn't think we would. I followed the road ahead, which trailed a winding river contained by steep forested slopes on either side, as I found my way out of the mountains.

Kikuchi drove by in a black taxi, yelled good luck, called me an idiot, laughed hysterically, and disappeared around a bend with his hand raised out the window.

And then it was just me. I did what came naturally after a full month of practice: I put one foot in front of the other and kept walking.

I thought back to my first pilgrimage, seven years ago. That time, the man who stuck with me through the whole walk, Matsushida-san, decided that we should do a frantic push over the course of 24 hours to walk 54 miles. By the end, the two of us collapsed in a train station not far from Temple Three, at 2:30 in the morning. We slept off our exhaustion in the four hours until the first train arrived and then walked the final few miles to Temple One, finally taking a train back to Tokushima station.

I don't know if it was exhaustion from walking the last day, or exhaustion from walking with me, but Matsushida-san and I never said a word to each other as we parted. We passed through the ticketing gates, he looked at me, took off his hat and white *henro* robe, and disappeared into the oncoming mass of rush hour commuters. It's not everyone who gets a mystically crotchety Japanese teacher who disappears at the end of a spiritual journey.

While not as tough as the last time, it still took me until 8:30 p.m. to finally reach Temple One, and yet it felt like it went too fast. My feet were throbbing, but my mind was clear. I was done. The temple was closed for the night, and there was no way to get a stamp, but that didn't matter to me. I had made it. As I took my last few steps to the massive wooden gate, a shadow shifted ever so slightly, trying to remain hidden.

A figure jumped up and out, right at me. I instinctively pulled my staff up to protect myself, only, I had left it back at the last temple.

"You made it!!" Kikuchi exclaimed. He ran over and wrapped me in a massive hug, not caring how sweaty and tired I was, or that Japanese don't usually hug.

"What the hell are you doing here?" I yelled through a heart pounding from adrenaline.

"I've been waiting. Waiting for a while, actually. What took you so long?" We smiled together.

I gave him my backpack and he showed me to his car. A car!

"You're still a pilgrim and I'm officially done," he said. "Go ahead, smell me. You stink. That's how you can tell. I'm taking you out to dinner as *osettai*."

I tried to protest but gave in quickly, as I couldn't think of a better way to finish.

We spent the next few hours reliving our time and telling each other what happened before we first met at the base of Temple Forty-Five, more than two weeks before. There was no talk of the future, what we would do, or where we would go. It was all about the past, a past that would come back to us day after day as we integrated back into "real" life. The past would always be a reminder of the freedom we experienced and who we really are.

1. In 2010 the Shikoku Henro World Heritage Inscription Council was formed. As of publishing of this book (July 2020), their website lists most of the groups working to preserve the pilgrimage as members. If you are looking for a toilet, they also have a great map! See https://88sekaisan.org/en/

ONE FINAL STEP

Thirty-one days after starting out from Temple One, I approached the resting place of Kūkai in Mt. Kōya, deep in the Kii Mountains. Thanks to the precision of Japanese transportation, it was only 3:00 p.m. and I had already crossed the Kii Strait in a ferry to Wakayama city, hopped on a train to the central Kii Mountains, and hiked up to Mt. Kōya, avoiding the cable car that was packed with tourists. Old habits die hard.

When you visit the *okunoin* after completing the 88 temples, you are meant to report to Kūkai. At the end of your journey, the temple provides that extra emotional punch to help you forget the days of struggle and pain, as the setting is breathtaking. Deep in an ancient forest, dominated by giant cedar trees that disappear into the mists both up and out, the main path cuts across countless side paths that disappear in the swirling mists, centuries-old cedars, and stone-cut faces.

Bright green moss flows around deep brown bark and over thousands of stone graves, *torii* gates, and Buddha statues. Bright red bibs and hats cover Jizō statues and help to keep the worshiper grounded in reality, away from the mists that call to wayward pilgrims to leave the path. This is one of Japan's oldest and most exclusive cemeteries.

I approached the mausoleum, dressed in full pilgrim attire. Tourists gaped openly at the foreign *henro* dressed in road-worn gray, wearing a thick beard, and smelling, I hoped, a bit better than normal. A light rain fell, but the summer heat followed me up the mountain. It was fitting that the rain, initially the source of my torment and worry, was now a gentle partner keeping me company.

No one tells you what format your report to Kūkai is meant to take. Should I include the number of days, how I walked, where I failed, what I overcame or whom I met? I settled on a heartfelt thank you and a sharing of myself, laid bare, like I probably always was, for everyone to see, except me.

I have been plagued by self-doubt my whole life:

I thought I was shy;

I thought I was unadventurous;

I thought I was weak;

I thought I didn't know what I wanted.

It turns out that we are usually the exact opposite of what we fear we are. In my case, it took stripping away the expecta-tions of others to finally see the person I had always been. Shikoku taught me that everything good in my life comes from moving on, especially when things go sideways.

My actions had always reflected who I really was and put me into all sorts of situations that challenged me and fulfilled me. It took a month of walking for my mind to catch up and accept that I always was who I was.

Or, as one of the monks told me, "We can only be where we are."

Breathe. Keep moving. Let go of where you came from. Don't worry about where you will be. Enjoy where you are.

I turned around, took off my now gray shirt, and with one easy step, I was free from worrying about what others thought I might be.

With one little step, no different than the first that had plunged me into a hidden world, all the way around Shikoku, I found myself back at the beginning. A changed man in a world filled with opportunities.

AFTERWORD

My hope is that the reader gets to know Japan better through the stories of the different people I met on my adventure.

I hope that you decide to visit Shikoku and experience the pilgrimage yourself.

A lot has changed on the pilgrimage since 2005, when the events in this book took place, and even more since I first walked in 1998. At the time, there were only Japanese guidebooks. Now, foreign pilgrims can buy English maps and join Facebook groups to get real-time advice on where to stay. But essentially, the pilgrimage is the same, the challenges people face are the same, and the wonderful people of Shikoku are the same.

I wrote this book over the past 10 years, while living in or visiting more than 45 countries. I have thought about the pilgrimage and Shikoku just about every day since then. Everything that happened there was the catalyst for my present life.

Shikoku was meant to cap off my time living abroad so that I could return and become a "normal" American. Instead, it allowed me to accept who I have always been, and it gave me the impetus to embark on new adventures across the world. A world in which normal is whatever I decide it is. Armed with a new outlook on life, I started down a new path just after graduate school, as a highly debt-ridden conflict expert and international aid worker.

But that is a story for another time.

To find out more about the next adventure visit:

www.toddwassel.com/sittingincircles

Did you enjoy *Walking in Circles*? Can I ask your help to review it on Goodreads.com or the store where you bought the book?
Even just a few words will help others decide if it is right for them.

ACKNOWLEDGEMENTS

With any book there is a long list of friends, family, and professionals who help make the final product. With a debut book, you can double the timeline, the number of people who encouraged along the way, and give everyone an extra badge for acting as a counselor.

First, I'd like to thank my Mom and Dad, who have been brave enough to let me be myself from early on. I'm grateful to my grandmother, who gave me an early inheritance of $2,000, money she didn't have, to walk the pilgrimage way back in 1998. That initial investment has changed the course of my life.

I am especially grateful to the people of Shikoku, who have such a unique culture of giving and showing support to complete strangers. Every one of you has made a lasting impression. Thank you to the temple staff, the stamp office calligraphy writers, and the monks who give their precious time and energy to a never-ending flow of pilgrims.

This book was written in one way or another over the course of 15 years, and in at least 10 different countries. Thank you to the countless friends and colleagues who were assaulted with the idea of this book over the years. Your patient ears kept me going to the finish line.

As with any first book, this one was filled with self-doubt, dead ends, crashed computers, and lost data. Thank you to my group of friends who took the time to read drafts and provide feedback and reassurances that it was in fact a book. I'm grateful to Alex Dolan, Gordon Peak, David Billa, Adam Olenn, Mark Notaras, Alva Lim, and John Uchikura. Your feedback has certainly made this a better book.

Thank you to Amy Chavez, who provided advice on publishing and editors, and Daniel Cabezas, who was the inspiration for my website design. Thank you to Jennifer Skutelsky and Anna Mehta, who edited, proofread, and helped me get out of my own way.

A big thanks is reserved for Michael Wachs, who designed the cover and map, as well as schooling me in marketing and connecting with readers. He has also been my travel buddy for 20 plus years. He has never failed in joining me in some far-flung corner of the world, or just for a quick trip to buy beer. He doesn't seem to have the capacity to say no.

Finally, a deep debt of gratitude for my wife, Kaoru, and two kids, Kaito and Sana. They have not only held down the fort while I've been off dreaming, but have had to hear the same stories, over and over again.

LIST OF THE
EIGHTY-EIGHT TEMPLES

1. Ryōzen-ji (霊山寺) Naruto, Tokushima
2. Gokuraku-ji (極楽寺) Naruto, Tokushima
3. Konsen-ji (金泉寺) Itano, Tokushima
4. Dainichi-ji (大日寺) Itano, Tokushima
5. Jizō-ji (地蔵寺) Itano, Tokushima
6. Anraku-ji (安楽寺) Kamiita, Tokushima
7. Jūraku-ji (十楽寺) Awa, Tokushima
8. Kumatani-ji (熊谷寺) Awa, Tokushima
9. Hōrin-ji (法輪寺) Awa, Tokushima
10. Kirihata-ji (切幡寺) Awa, Tokushima
11. Fujii-dera (藤井寺) Yoshinogawa, Tokushima
12. Shōzan-ji (焼山寺) Kamiyama, Tokushima
13. Dainichi-ji (大日寺) Tokushima, Tokushima
14. Jōraku-ji (常楽寺) Tokushima, Tokushima
15. Kokubun-ji (国分寺) Tokushima, Tokushima
16. Kannon-ji (観音寺) Tokushima, Tokushima
17. Ido-ji (井戸寺) Tokushima, Tokushima
18. Onzan-ji (恩山寺) Komatsushima, Tokushima
19. Tatsue-ji (立江寺) Komatsushima, Tokushima
20. Kakurin-ji (鶴林寺) Katsuura, Tokushima
21. Tairyū-ji (太竜寺) Anan, Tokushima
22. Byōdō-ji (平等寺) Anan, Tokushima
23. Yakuō-ji (薬王寺) Minami, Tokushima
24. Hotsumisaki-ji (最御崎寺) Muroto, Kōchi

25. Shinshō-ji (津照寺) Muroto, Kōchi
26. Kongōchō-ji (金剛頂寺) Muroto, Kōchi
27. Kōnomine-ji (神峰寺) Yasuda Kōchi
28. Dainichi-ji (大日寺) Kōnan, Kōchi
29. Kokubun-ji (国分寺) Nankoku, Kōchi
30. Zenraku-ji (善楽寺) Kōchi, Kōchi
31. Chikurin-ji (竹林寺) Kōchi. Kōchi
32. Zenjibu-ji (禅師峰寺) Nankoku, Kōchi
33. Sekkei-ji (雪蹊寺) Kōchi, Kōchi
34. Tanema-ji (種間寺) Haruno , Kōchi
35. Kiyotaki-ji (清滝寺) Tosa, Kōchi
36. Shōryū-ji (青竜寺) Tosa, Kōchi
37. Iwamoto-ji (岩本寺) Shimanto, Kōchi
38. Kongōfuku-ji (金剛福寺) Tosashimizu, Kōchi
39. Enkō-ji (延光寺) Sukumo, Kōchi
40. Kanjizai-ji (観自在寺) Ainan, Ehime
41. Ryūkō-ji (竜光寺) Uwajima, Ehime
42. Butsumoku-ji (佛木寺) Uwajima, Ehime
43. Meiseki-ji (明石寺) Seiyo, Ehime
44. Daihō-ji (大宝寺) Kumakōgen, Ehime
45. Iwaya-ji (岩屋寺) Kumakōgen, Ehime
46. Jōruri-ji (浄瑠璃寺) Matsuyama , Ehime
47. Yasaka-ji (八坂寺) Matsuyama , Ehime
48. Sairin-ji (西林寺) Matsuyama , Ehime
49. Jōdo-ji (浄土寺) Matsuyama , Ehime
50. Hanta-ji (繁多寺) Matsuyama , Ehime
51. Ishite-ji (石手寺) Matsuyama , Ehime
52. Taizan-ji (太山寺) Matsuyama , Ehime
53. Enmyō-ji (円明寺) Matsuyama , Ehime
54. Enmei-ji (延命寺) Imabari, Ehime
55. Nankōbō (南光坊) Imabari, Ehime
56. Taisan-ji (泰山寺) Imabari, Ehime
57. Eifuku-ji (栄福寺) Imabari, Ehime
58. Senyū-ji (仙遊寺) Imabari, Ehime

59. Kokubun-ji (国分寺) Imabari, Ehime
60. Yokomine-ji (横峰寺) Saijō, Ehime
61. Kōon-ji (香園寺) Saijō, Ehime
62. Hōju-ji (宝寿寺) Saijō, Ehime
63. Kichijō-ji (吉祥寺) Saijō, Ehime
64. Maegami-ji (前神寺) Saijō, Ehime
65. Sankaku-ji (三角寺) Shikokuchūō, Ehime
66. Unpen-ji (雲辺寺) Miyoshi, Tokushima
67. Daikō-ji (大興寺) Mitoyo, Kagawa
68. Jinnein (神恵院) Kanonji, Kagawa
69. Kannon-ji (観音寺) Kanonji, Kagawa
70. Motoyama-ji (本山寺) Mitoyo, Kagawa
71. Iyadani-ji (弥谷寺) Mitoyo, Kagawa
72. Mandara-ji (曼荼羅寺) Zentsūji, Kagawa
73. Shusshaka-ji (出釈迦寺) Zentsūji, Kagawa
74. Kōyama-ji (甲山寺) Zentsūji, Kagawa
75. Zentsū-ji (善通寺) Zentsūji, Kagawa
76. Konzō-ji (金倉寺) Zentsūji, Kagawa
77. Dōryū-ji (道隆寺) Tadotsu, Kagawa
78. Gōshō-ji (郷照寺) Utazu, Kagawa
79. Tennō-ji (天皇寺) Sakaide, Kagawa
80. Kokubun-ji (国分寺) Takamatsu, Kagawa
81. Shiromine-ji (白峯寺) Sakaide, Kagawa
82. Negoro-ji (根香寺) Takamatsu, Kagawa
83. Ichinomiya-ji (一宮寺) Takamatsu, Kagawa
84. Yashima-ji (屋島寺) Takamatsu, Kagawa
85. Yakuri-ji (八栗寺) Takamatsu, Kagawa
86. Shido-ji (志度寺) Sanuki, Kagawa
87. Nagao-ji (長尾寺) Sanuki, Kagawa
88. Ōkubo-ji (大窪寺) Sanuki, Kagawa

Printed in Great Britain
by Amazon